LENS
LLEGE

138941

Sept 2018

LIBRARY

The Business
of Personal Training

The Business of Personal Training

Mark A. Nutting

CSCS,*D, NSCA-CPT,*D, ACSM-HFD, ACSM-CEP, RCPT*E

HUMAN KINETICS

Library of Congress Cataloging-in-Publication Data

Names: Nutting, Mark A., 1957- author.
Title: The business of personal training / Mark A. Nutting, CSCS,*D,
  NSCA-CPT,*D, ACSM-HFD, ACSM-CEP, RCPT*E, Jiva Fitness, Easton, PA.
Description: First edition. | Champaign, Illinois : Human Kinetics, [2019] |
  Includes bibliographical references and index.
Identifiers: LCCN 2017030349 (print) | LCCN 2017032111 (ebook) | ISBN
  ISBN 9781492517221 (print) | 9781492562191 (e-book)
Subjects: LCSH: Personal trainers. | Physical fitness--Vocational guidance. |
  Physical fitness centers--Management--Handbooks, manuals, etc.
Classification: LCC GV428.7 .N87 2019 (print) | LCC GV428.7 (ebook) | DDC
  613.7--dc23
LC record available at https://lccn.loc.gov/2017030349

ISBN: 978-1-4925-1722-1 (print)

Copyright © 2019 by Mark A. Nutting

All rights reserved. Except for use in a review, the reproduction or utilization of this work in any form or by any electronic, mechanical, or other means, now known or hereafter invented, including xerography, photocopying, and recording, and in any information storage and retrieval system, is forbidden without the written permission of the publisher.

Note: This publication is written and published to provide accurate and authoritative information relevant to the subject matter presented. It is published and sold with the understanding that the author and publisher are not engaged in rendering legal, medical, or other professional services by reason of their authorship or publication of this work. If legal, financial, or other expert assistance is required, the services of a competent professional person should be sought.

Notice: Permission to reproduce the following material is granted to instructors and agencies who have purchased *The Business of Personal Training*: pp. 220-230 and 232-248. The reproduction of other parts of this book is expressly forbidden by the above copyright notice. Persons or agencies who have not purchased *The Business of Personal Training* may not reproduce any material.

The web addresses cited in this text were current as of September 2017, unless otherwise noted.

Acquisitions Editor: Roger W. Earle
Senior Developmental Editor: Christine M. Drews
Managing Editor: Kirsten E. Keller
Copyeditor: Tom Tiller
Indexer: Karla Walsh
Permissions Manager: Dalene Reeder
Senior Graphic Designer: Nancy Rasmus
Cover Designer: Keri Evans
Cover Design Associate: Susan Rothermel Allen
Photograph (cover): CIHP/Neil Bernstein
Photographs (interior): © Human Kinetics, unless otherwise noted
Photo Asset Manager: Laura Fitch
Photo Production Manager: Jason Allen
Senior Art Manager: Kelly Hendren
Illustrations: © Human Kinetics, unless otherwise noted
Printer: Walsworth

Human Kinetics books are available at special discounts for bulk purchase. Special editions or book excerpts can also be created to specification. For details, contact the Special Sales Manager at Human Kinetics.

Printed in the United States of America   10 9 8 7 6 5 4 3 2 1

The paper in this book was manufactured using responsible forestry methods.

Human Kinetics
P.O. Box 5076
Champaign, IL 61825-5076
Website: www.HumanKinetics.com

In the United States, email info@hkusa.com or call 800-747-4457.
In Canada, email info@hkcanada.com.
In the United Kingdom/Europe, email hk@hkeurope.com.

For information about Human Kinetics' coverage in other areas of the world,
please visit our website: **www.HumanKinetics.com**

E6658

ST. HELENS
COLLEGE

613.7
NUT

138941

Sept 2019

LIBRARY

Contents

Part I
Understanding the Roles and Responsibilities of Personal Trainers

Part II
Learning and Applying Business Skills

Throughout *The Business of Personal Training*, you will notice references to a web resource. This online content is available to you for free upon purchase of a new print book or an e-book. All you need to do is register with the Human Kinetics website to access the online content. The following steps explain how to register.

The web resource offers electronic versions of the business plan templates and the personal trainer–client forms included in appendixes A and B. The web resource makes it easy for you to customize these materials.

Follow these steps to access the web resource:

1. Visit www.HumanKinetics.com/TheBusinessOfPersonalTraining.

2. Click the first edition link next to the corresponding first edition book cover.

3. Click the Sign In link on the left or top of the page. If you do not have an account with Human Kinetics, you will be prompted to create one.

4. After you register, if the online product does not appear in the Ancillary Items box on the left of the page, click the Enter Pass Code option in that box. Enter the following pass code exactly as it is printed here, including capitalization and all hyphens: **NUTTING-9R27-WR**

5. Click the Submit button to unlock your online product.

6. After you have entered your pass code the first time, you will never have to enter it again to access this online product. Once unlocked, a link to your product will permanently appear in the menu on the left. All you need to do to access your online content on subsequent visits is sign in to www.HumanKinetics.com/TheBusinessOfPersonalTraining and follow the link!

Click the Need Help? button on the book's website if you need assistance along the way.

Preface

I have been a personal trainer for nearly 40 years and have been educating other personal trainers for almost as long. Early in my career, I taught exercise science and basic biomechanics; later, I moved on to more practical strength and conditioning topics. In the past 10 years, I have focused on learning and teaching the business skills that we, as personal trainers, need to know. Knowing such skills and being able to apply them can make or break our careers. Thus *The Business of Personal Training* is a culmination of everything I have learned about business, both in my career and in the hundred-plus books and the hundreds of articles, webinars, and conference presentations I have digested.

This is a book for personal trainers—for every personal trainer—and that includes a lot of people. In fact, according to a 2015 report from the Bureau of Labor Statistics on the occupation of fitness trainers and instructors (www.bls.gov/ooh/personal-care-and-service), there are more than 279,000 personal trainers in the United States. They have a wide variety of backgrounds, education, and training, and they perform their duties in a diverse range of settings. Some are employees in settings such as health clubs, medically oriented gyms, and fitness studios. Others work for themselves as independent contractors in someone else's facility, in people's homes or offices, in public parks, and even online. Still others own their own facilities. One thing is shared by all these personal trainers in all their capacities: They need to understand and be able to apply business skills in order to establish and advance their careers.

This book provides you with a well-rounded grounding in the business skills you need in order to build your business. It also gives you a map for progressing your career. Perhaps, for example, you are currently working for a club but envision owning your own studio. Understanding the next logical step will help you prepare to take it!

The Business of Personal Training is divided into two main parts. Part I helps you understand the various roles open to you, what to expect in each one, and how to choose from among them. Part II teaches you the business skills that you need and helps you understand how to apply them in order to grow your business.

While I believe this is one of the most comprehensive books of its kind for our industry, you must continue to educate yourself after reading it. Like exercise and nutritional science, business practices continue to evolve, and if we stop learning we may find ourselves falling behind the competition. To help you continue your education, appendix C provides a list of online references that will help you learn about specific areas of business in greater depth and thus continue to stay ahead of the game.

This book is accompanied by a web resource, which provides you with electronic versions of the business plan templates and the personal trainer–client forms included in appendixes A and B, respectively. Thus the web resource makes it easy for you to customize these materials to fit your situation.

I have loved (and still love) my career as a personal trainer. If I could change anything about it, I would have obtained key business information early on. Having a book like this would have saved me time and effort and set me up for early success. My hope is that *The Business of Personal Training* provides you with that advantage and helps you reach your goals in this very rewarding profession.

eBook
available at
HumanKinetics.com

Acknowledgments

First and foremost, I thank my wife, Heather Stirner Nutting. She is my partner in life and work (we have almost always worked side by side), and her support and patience during my writing of this book have been amazing. *I'm the lucky one.* Thank you, my love.

Thank you to my two sons, Ian and Jackson, who have also been amazingly supportive and patient. You both make me very proud to be your father. I love you.

To Roger Earle, thank you for being my friend, for believing in me, and for persuading Human Kinetics that I was the right person to write this book. I am forever grateful.

Christine Drews, while I have yet to meet you face to face, your support through the editing of this book has been wonderful. Your gentle coaching through my various writing struggles kept me engaged and positive.

Thank you to Human Kinetics for bringing me on to write this *and* for allowing me to write it in first person. I could never have written it as a third-person text.

Finally, thank you to all my industry friends. Without the stimulating discussions and debates with like-minded people through these many years, I think my brain would have shriveled and died long ago.

Part I

Understanding the Roles and Responsibilities of Personal Trainers

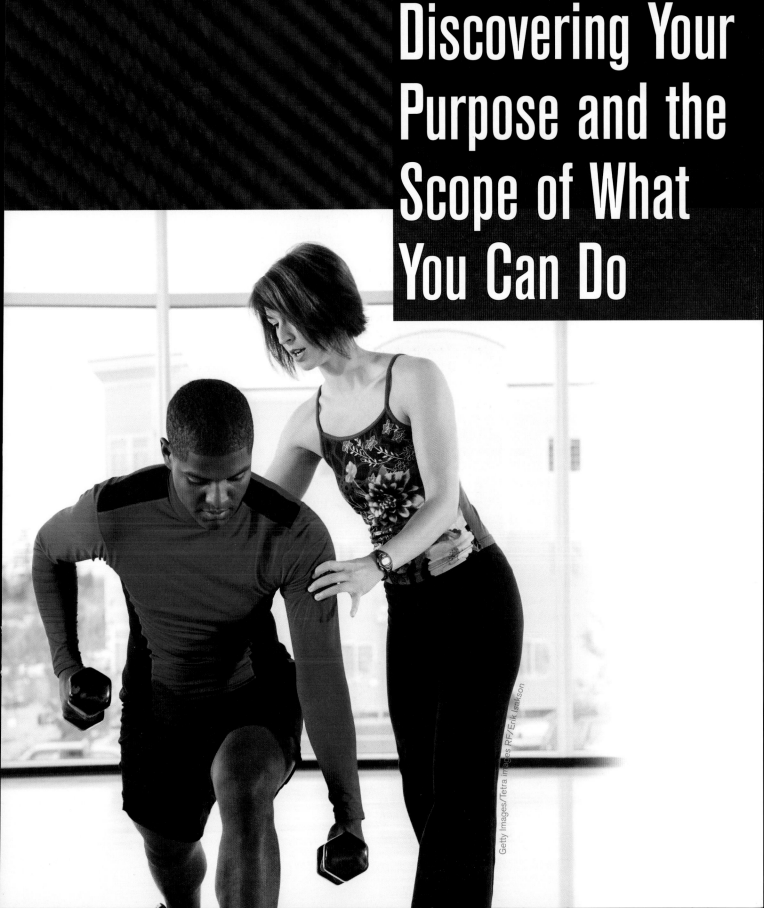

Discovering Your Purpose and the Scope of What You Can Do

Getty Images/Tetra images RF/Erik Isakson

What is being a personal trainer all about? This chapter gives you a tour of the various aspects of this profession. Specifically, we'll explore why you would want to be a personal trainer, what a personal trainer does, and what we should and should not do as defined by our own professional training. Welcome to the world of the personal trainer!

Your Choice to Become a Personal Trainer

The factors that prompt you to become a personal trainer will exert a big influence on how successful you are and how long you remain in this profession. As with any business, it takes time to build a personal training business, and you need to be committed to your reason for being a personal trainer in order to stay the course, survive the challenges, and ultimately thrive in the industry.

So, why *do* you want to become a personal trainer? Your answer will drive all that you do—all of the choices that you make going forward. Therefore, you must define it clearly.

Is it for the money? If so, you could make more money, and faster, at another job. In one recent report (Schroeder, 2015), the average hourly wage for personal trainers was pegged at $30.50; however, the average number of hours worked per week was only 18, making the average annual income $28,548. In 2016, the U.S. Department of Labor reported the median annual pay for fitness trainers and instructors as $38,160 (Bureau of Labor Statistics, 2016). This income change, while getting better, still highlights that personal training is not a "get rich" profession.

What about job outlook? The personal training profession is expected to grow by 13 percent between 2012 and 2022, which is about average for all industries (Bureau of Labor Statistics, 2016). Therefore, although this projection bodes well for the industry, it is probably not a key motivator for going into the profession.

Or do you want to be a personal trainer because you like working out and want to work in a gym setting? That's nice, but it won't sustain you in this industry. You may also choose to become a personal trainer because you want a flexible, part-time job that allows you to pursue another career—and hey, it beats waiting tables! Again, that's okay, but it isn't enough to help you thrive as a personal trainer.

To the contrary, in order to succeed in this field, you need a deep desire to help others improve their lives through physical activity and proper nutrition. Watching the people you help become healthier, fitter, and more physically capable of doing what they want to do in life—these should be your real reasons for entering this profession. Not only will this motivation help sustain you, but also others will recognize your desire to help, which will draw potential clients to you. Of course, being a personal trainer can also provide you with a flexible, part-time career in which you make a good hourly wage in an atmosphere that you love, but that shouldn't be the reason that you become a personal trainer. Fortunately, as the saying goes, we can do well by doing good.

In *Art of the Start 2.0* (2015, p. 12), Guy Kawasaki includes "Make Meaning" as one of his "great ideas for starting things." I experienced this potential when I started my career, in the Human Performance Center at the University of Maine, back in the late 1970s and early 1980s. Along with working in the lab, I taught a cardiac-rehab class, and one client in particular stands out in my memory. After getting her doctor's clearance to exercise following a heart attack, 79-year-old

> " **People don't buy what you do, they buy why you do it.** "
>
> Simon Sinek,
> *Start With Why*
> (2011, p. 41).

Mary started taking my class. She continued to attend class like clockwork during the three years that I worked at the center.

After the first year, she asked if I thought if it would be helpful for her to buy a stationary bike and get more exercise at home. Of course, I was thrilled that she wanted to exercise more, and she continued to get stronger and more able to do her activities of daily living. Another year passed, and she asked if I thought it would be okay for her to take swimming lessons. She had never learned but now felt that she could take it on. This was the point when I realized how important this work is—how much positive influence an instructor or personal trainer can have on someone's life. I had found my calling.

Personal Trainer Roles

Gone are the days when personal trainers simply showed people how to use the machine circuit and counted repetitions (a good thing for me, since I could never count reps to save my life!). Personal trainers now wear many hats.

- **Information gatherers:** Through the use of health histories, lifestyle questionnaires, goal listings, and readiness-to-change questionnaires, personal trainers collect the information that is essential to helping clients proceed safely and effectively toward their desired goals.

- **Coaches and motivational interviewers:** Key techniques used by coaches and motivational interviewers will be valuable throughout your relationship with your client, beginning with the initial meeting. For instance, you can use open-ended questions to help clients clarify their goals, discover more about their challenges, and generate solutions for meeting those challenges. When clients help formulate solutions, they are more likely to stick to their programs; in this way, we serve as facilitators in their efforts to change their lives.

- **Educators:** Although helping clients generate their own answers can play a powerful role in their efforts to change, there are also many times when we need to teach clients about fitness, exercise, nutrition, and behavioral change. Members of the general population are often uneducated—or, worse, incorrectly educated—about the science behind health and fitness. In such cases, we need to provide research-based information, which means that we carry a responsibility to keep up with current research.

- **Program designers:** This role involves practicing the art of exercise prescription. Based on the information collected in the initial client meeting, the personal trainer creates a plan that specifies frequency, intensity, time, and type (FITT) of exercise to help the individual attain his or her goals.

- **Movement educators:** When teaching a client how to perform the exercises that will form his or her prescribed fitness program, a personal trainer uses the "tell, show, do" method of instruction. *Tell* the client what each exercise is and what it's for. *Show* the client how to do the exercise by demonstrating it. Then have the client *do* the exercise while you provide guidance and correction as needed.

- **Cheerleaders:** A personal trainer also supports clients and encourages them to achieve more than they thought possible. Any individual will face many challenges on the journey to becoming healthier. Therefore, your clients need to know that they have someone in their corner cheering them on who will not judge them but *will* support and guide them in their efforts to improve their health and fitness.

Integrating these roles makes the personal trainer an invaluable asset for individuals who want to change their levels of health and fitness.

Scope of Your Training

You must define your scope of practice for the simple reason that there are limits to what we can do with our clients. These limits—what we should and should not do—are defined by our training, by the law, and by our ethical responsibilities. Even if these limits may seem obvious to many of us, they still need to be clearly defined. You should not train your clients in techniques, routines, or programs for which you have not been educated. Such education may take the form of college degrees, certifications, certificate programs, workshops, conferences, and the reading of articles in peer-reviewed journals. Ultimately, what you do with your clients must be grounded in research-based techniques or accepted standards of practice.

College Degrees

The fitness industry is conducting an ongoing debate about whether a college degree should be mandatory for a personal trainer. Those in favor can point to definite benefits of attaining a degree in exercise science. First, of course, the detailed curriculum gives you a great base of professional information to start with. In addition, nonmajor courses can help you become a more well-rounded individual—something you may not get if you are learning exercise science on your own. Such general knowledge can give you something in common with your clients; for instance, I've been known to talk with my clients about subjects as diverse as art, theater, business, music, and psychology.

Holding a degree in exercise science also gives you a perceived "proof" that you have learned enough to go out into the world and become a personal trainer. In fact, this perception may be more than a superficial appearance. One group of researchers (Malek, Nalbone, Berger, & Coburn, 2002) used a specific questionnaire—the Fitness Instructors Knowledge Assessment (FIKA)—to determine personal trainers' knowledge in core topics such as nutrition, health screening, and testing protocols. As the authors anticipated, participants who held a degree in exercise science fared significantly better than did those who did not hold such a degree.

That said, there are also downsides to getting a degree—or, to be more accurate, downsides to anticipating that a degree fully prepares you for becoming a personal trainer. Granted, some certifying organizations, and some health clubs, require personal trainers to hold a degree in a "health-related field," either as a prerequisite to sit for an exam or as a condition for employment. However, not all degrees are created equal. For example, degrees in community health and in sports management do not prepare someone to be a personal trainer. In addition, although exercise science provides the most carry-over into a personal training career, even that type of degree program may lack key elements, such as hands-on experience and business skills, both of which are critical to your career success.

Another downside of relying on a degree is that, unlike a certification, it requires no continuing education. I've known several personal trainers who never sought additional education because they thought the degree was good enough; as a result, their knowledge was effectively stuck in time at the point when they achieved their degree. For that reason, I often recommend attaining certifications beyond a degree.

Certifications

Certifications assess one's knowledge, skills, and abilities (KSAs). Many certifications are available to individuals who are thinking about becoming a personal trainer. Some are quite specialized and offer unique information to enhance your career.

Some clubs offer their own in-house certifications; in fact, I used to write the in-house certification programs for one of the largest health club chains in the United States. Typically, however, certifications are administered by a third party. These certifications provide a great way to prove to yourself, to employers, and to potential clients that you have achieved at least a basic level of competence and can begin safely training individuals.

Many certifications involve self-paced independent study and therefore require you to apply both self-discipline and organizational skills in order to learn the material. Those skills, of course, can help you in all areas of life. Other "certifications" are tied to a weekend workshop followed immediately by an assessment. While called "certifications," these workshops are actually assessment-based certificate programs.

In order to maintain most certifications, you must participate in ongoing learning evidenced by continuing education credits or units (CECs or CEUs) in order to stay current. This is one of the differences mentioned earlier between certification and an academic degree. Maintaining a certification may be well worth the effort, given that personal trainers who possess advanced certifications say that they earn more because of it (American Council on Exercise, 2013).

I view certifications as an additional opportunity to acquire knowledge—therefore, the more the merrier. Certifications that are third-party accredited offer a better certification program and are more universally accepted by employers as a requirement for hiring. However, there are quite a few accrediting bodies that exist, so which agency should you be looking for? Many organizations that offer personal training certifications stand behind the National Commission for Certifying Agencies (NCCA) because of its more stringent criteria. Of the nearly 300 fitness-related certifications available, only 18 offered are by NCCA-accredited programs. These programs are offered, for example, by the American College of Sports Medicine (ACSM), the American Council on Exercise (ACE), the National Strength and Conditioning Association (NSCA), and the National Academy of Sports Medicine (NASM). Make sure that you hold at least one accredited certification. Remember, accreditation not only assures a better certification program but also makes the certification more widely accepted by potential employers.

Certificate Programs

Certificate programs are usually administered as part of an educational program, wherein assessment is handled by the educational body itself (this is also the case for a few of the "certifications" or assessment-based certificate programs addressed in the preceding section). These programs are less likely than other certifications to cover a broad scope of content; instead, they home in on specific areas, such as nutrition or a particular training implement (say, kettlebells).

Here again, more education is a good thing. It gives you more tools in your toolbox as a personal trainer, which allows you to program more effectively for your clients' individual needs. However, some certificate programs do not require continuing education. This is a problem because, for some people, if they aren't required to keep learning, they won't. That reduces the value of those certificate programs, both in their challenge in keeping you up to date and in validating your expertise to others. In addition, some do not offer an assessment to test proficiency; as a result, what they provide is more a certificate of attendance than proof of knowledge.

Additional Training

Other kinds of training include working as an intern, listening to podcasts, and attending conferences, clinics, webinars, and workshops. Many of these options provide continuing education credits that you can apply to your certifications. Live trainings also offer great opportunities to network and discuss best practices with other fitness professionals. When considering your options, choose sessions that both pique your interest and enhance your career.

These kinds of training can be expensive—particularly conferences, which require you to take time off (thus losing income) and to pay for registration, travel, accommodations, and food. If cost poses a concern, then better options for you might include webinars or podcasts. In addition, conference presentations are sometimes poorly done, both in the quality of information delivered and in how it is delivered. They can also be enormously rewarding. Given these hit-or-miss possibilities, do your research before you commit to attending a conference; specifically, seek out reviews both of the conference as a whole and of the featured speakers.

Further Reading

Books and articles (in journals and magazines) give you a great way to learn on your own schedule. I listen to a couple of audiobooks per month and read various journals and articles. Nowadays, access to e-books and the Internet makes it even easier to get an ever-increasing amount of information. Just make sure that your sources are reputable before you start applying information in your interactions with clients. Your best bets for accurate information include peer-reviewed journals, as well as articles and books that cite peer-reviewed journals.

Scope of the Law

The law forms the legal embodiment of the necessary precautions we take in order to keep our clients safe. Offenses in this area can involve either doing things that we shouldn't do or *not* doing things that we should do. These fall into the category of negligence, which can be understood in terms of four key elements that are sometimes referred to as the four Ds.

1. Duty: a responsibility to another person, such as a client
2. Dereliction of duty: a breaking or neglecting of a duty, such as failing to inspect equipment for safety before putting a client on it
3. Direct cause: the action, or lack of action, that causes an event
4. Damages: damage, injury, or both resulting from the causal event

One infamous court case involved a personal trainer working for Crunch Fitness in New York City in 1998. The personal trainer recommended that a particular client use certain supplements, one of which contained ephedra—a stimulant that, at the time, was often used for weight loss. The client, however, was taking medication for hypertension and should not have taken any supplement containing ephedra. As a result of taking the recommended supplement, she suffered a brain hemorrhage and died.

In this case, the personal trainer had a duty to his client to train her *within his skill level*, and he neglected that duty by recommending supplements. The use of the supplement containing ephedra was determined to be the direct cause of the damage, which of course was the client's death. Thus this case met the four Ds of negligence and now serves as an example to all personal trainers and club owners that it is crucial to stay within one's scope of practice. You must always follow proven protocols and take all precautions necessary to keep your clients safe.

Another legal pitfall involves overstepping your professional boundaries—that is, stepping over the line into other regulated professions. For example, doctors, nurses, physical therapists, athletic trainers, and registered dietitians are all licensed professionals. Each of these licenses is associated with a regimented scope of practice, and personal trainers cannot practice in these professions.

Table 1.1 **Personal Trainers' Scope of Practice**

Personal trainers do *not*	Personal trainers *do*
Diagnose	• Receive exercise or health guidelines from a physician, physical therapist, registered dietitian • Follow national consensus guidelines for exercise prescription for medical disorders • Screen for exercise limitations • Identify potential risk factors through screening • Refer clients to a medical practitioner if necessary
Prescribe	• Design exercise programs • Refer clients to a medical practitioner for questions about medication
Prescribe diets or recommend specific supplements	• Provide general information on healthy eating, according to the USDA ChooseMyPlate.gov or HHS Dietary Guidelines for Americans, 2015 • Refer clients to a dietitian or nutritionist for a specific diet plan
Treat injury or disease	• Refer clients to a medical practitioner for treatment • Use exercise to help clients improve overall health • Help clients follow a physician's/therapist's advice
Monitor progress for medically referred clients	• Document progress • Report progress to the medical practitioner • Follow the physician's/therapist's/dietitian's recommendation
Rehabilitate	• Design an exercise program once a client has been released from rehabilitation
Counsel	• Coach • Provide general information • Refer clients to a qualified counselor or therapist
Work with patients	• Work with clients

Permission to reproduce this table has been given by the copyright holder, IDEA Health & Fitness Association, www.ideafit.com. Reproduction without permission is strictly prohibited. All rights reserved.

Acceptable and unacceptable actions for personal trainers are differentiated in table 1.1. The tasks labeled here as unacceptable are reserved for qualified, licensed health and medical professionals.

Ethical Responsibilities

In general terms, ethics involves the study or practice of moral principles and right and wrong actions. For our purposes here, it concerns what personal trainers should or should not do in regard to our defined scope of practice. Most fitness organizations recognize the importance of ethical considerations and therefore develop their own code of ethics. Here are some of the most common elements of these codes (and, I must admit, the ones about which I feel most strongly).

❶ When making judgments, keep the client's best interest in mind. When you are in doubt, this rule will guide you when nothing else can. It means, for instance, that I

Part of working with clients is understanding your scope of practice.

Getty-Images/Vectered61

don't recommend a product because I get a commission or play into a client's desire to lose weight more rapidly than is safe. As a personal trainer, it is your responsibility to keep clients safe and deliver only what will help them improve their health and fitness.

❷ **Treat all clients with equal respect.** All of your clients have a story about what led them to where they are and who they are. Appreciate each client's journey and respect the fact that he or she has come to you (or your facility) for help in making positive changes.

❸ **Look and act like the professional you want to be.** People hold various ideas about professionalism. Some people wouldn't mind if you trained them while wearing an untucked tank top and a side-turned snapback cap. Some might even like it. Many, however, would view it as unprofessional. The way you look affects the impression you make. You will come across as more professional if you wear a neat, clean uniform; keep yourself well groomed; and stay free of smells—both bad and good, because "good" is subjective and any perfume or cologne will be a turnoff to someone who is sensitive, particularly someone with allergies. You should also act professional by being punctual, greeting clients pleasantly, making eye contact, speaking clearly, and keeping your language clean and on topic.

❹ **Acquire and maintain the training and education necessary to offer your clients the best possible guidance.** The more training and education you receive, the better you can help your clients, because you have more tools at your disposal. This adaptability allows you to avoid what is known as "the law of the instrument," or, more simply, Maslow's hammer—that is, overreliance on one tool or one approach. As Maslow stated, "It is tempting, if the only tool you have is a hammer, to treat everything as if it were a nail" (1966, pp. 15-16). Continued training and education give you more tools.

❺ **Maintain a professional relationship.** It used to be said that personal trainers should not give out personal information because they should keep things strictly professional. What is viewed as professional, however, has changed. We live in a world where sales, marketing, and just doing business are all about relationships—and a relationship is not a one-way street. Thus, we need to share some of ourselves with our clients because that is how they relate to us, connect with us, and, yes, come to like us:

"You have kids in the Boy Scouts? Me too." "You went to the University of Maine? So did I. What years were you there?" Such points in common allow us to elicit more commitment from clients. As a result, they become less likely to miss appointments and more likely to continue working with us. In short, they don't want to disappoint us.

Even so, some things are still *not* appropriate—specifically, those that are sexual in nature (both for moral reasons and to avoid sexual harassment lawsuits) or political or religious. On a more mundane level, how you feel today is also not an appropriate point of discussion. No matter what is going on in your life, as soon as you arrive at work it is show time. In fact, your demeanor directly affects your client: If you're happy and positive, then you can help a client feel better. If, in contrast, you bring negativity to the session, then your client will feel worse—and that is not what he or she is paying to get from you.

Another key aspect of professionalism involves the question of when, or if, you should physically touch your clients. Some schools of thought hold that you should ask permission each time you wish to touch a client. In my view, this repeated asking isn't necessary and may even be off-putting. Instead, explain once that you will, from time to time, touch the client in order to help him or her find the correct position or know where a given exercise should be felt. Make clear that if any touching ever makes the client feel uncomfortable, he or she should let you know immediately. Thus the real question here is not whether you touch the client but how you do so. Along these lines, I recommend that you never use the flat palm of your hand, which can feel very personal. Instead, always use the tips of your fingers or the edge of your hand. This approach, accompanied by a professional attitude, will help your clients feel comfortable when you use touch to guide them.

❻ Provide and maintain a safe environment for participation. If you use a facility or piece of equipment that is not well maintained, you put your client at risk of injury. Of course, risking your client's safety does not serve his or her best interest; nor does it serve yours, and it may open you up to a lawsuit.

❼ Treat all client information as confidential. As personal trainers, we are not medical professionals, but we do have access to some of our clients' medical information. Clients need to feel assured that what they share with us will go no further. Never share personal information about a client with any other party unless you have the client's written permission to do so.

Determining and Defining Your Role and Type of Personal Trainer

At this point, you've learned to define your *why* and your *what*—that is, why you want to be a personal trainer and what training you will need in order to achieve that goal. You have also learned about the scope of practice and the legal and ethical boundaries that you need to respect. Now, how are you going to fulfill your vision, and with whom?

According to the International Health, Racquet & Sportsclub Association (2014), some eight million people use a personal trainer in the United States. Among health club members, nearly 14 percent use a personal trainer, and most users of personal training are between the ages of 18 and 44. These statistics, however, do not tell the whole story of where personal trainers work and what types of clients they work with. In fact, one of the great things about personal training is that you can do it in various settings and with various degrees of control and responsibility. The range of roles that you may take on in your personal training career are discussed in more detail in the following chapters.

Working for Others

While you may envision running your own business, working as an employee offers many benefits. You can do so in a variety of settings—including medically oriented gyms, corporate fitness facilities, not-for-profit organizations (such as the YMCA), personal training studios, and commercial gyms and health clubs— all of which provide unique learning opportunities that can help you develop your career. Working as an employee is a popular option among personal trainers. Specifically, a recent report on trends in the fitness industry (Schroeder, 2015) indicated that 62 percent of personal trainers who work in clubs are club employees, whereas 28 percent are independent contractors.

Working as an Independent Contractor

Owning your business as an independent contractor allows you to minimize start-up costs and can give you a simple way to take your business into your own hands. You can do so while training clients in a variety of settings: at a facility that allows independent contractors, in your home, at a client's home or office, in an outdoor space, or even online.

Personal trainers' roles and responsibilities can vary by the type of facility they choose to work in.

Opening Your Own Gym or Studio

Many people think that having their own space is the ultimate goal in working for themselves. Doing so, however, greatly increases your management responsibility; therefore, if you are not ready or willing to take on that challenge, then this may not be the path for you. If, on the other hand, you are ready to shoulder this additional responsibility, then having your own space where your clients come to train puts you in control of the look and feel that you want them to experience as they walk through your door. You also make the decisions on factors such as equipment, hours of operation, and whom you work with. It's all yours—including, of course, both the successes and the failures.

Looking Ahead

As you read the next three chapters, carefully consider the benefits and challenges of each of these approaches—working for someone else, working as an independent contractor, and opening your own gym or studio—and assess which approach best matches your skills, aptitudes, and interests. In addition, note the specific training needed for each approach and consider how you might get that training. For example, if you want to open your own gym or studio, you would benefit from training in small business practices. If, instead, you want to work at a medically oriented gym (MOG), you might need to do an internship at one.

Consider also what population you most want to work with. For example, you could choose to work with athletes, kids, older persons, postrehab individuals, or clients interested in weight loss. You don't need to choose a group when you first start out. In fact, it would benefit you to work with several types of individuals—you might find yourself surprised at which demographic you connect with the most! Of course, the sooner you identify the right fit for you, the sooner you will be able to target that market. For example, if you're working with older adults, who generally have less experience (and may be less comfortable) with online technology, then using online video workouts as a business model might not be your best bet.

More to Come

We've discussed why you might want to become a personal trainer, what roles a personal trainer plays, and what a personal trainer should and should not do in regard to the scope of the profession. We've also spurred your thinking about what type of environment you might like to work in, whether as someone else's employee or as a business owner yourself. The remaining chapters in part I discuss in detail what is involved in working in various scenarios to help you decide which business option best suits you at this point in your career and understand the preparations required in order to succeed.

Specifically, chapter 2 addresses what it's like to work for a fitness facility, as well as the need to build and run your own business while working under the umbrella of your employer's company. Chapter 3 discusses how to work as an independent contractor for another company; how to work for yourself by training clients online or in settings such as their homes; and how to coach via phone, video call, or e-mail. And chapter 4 helps you understand the various aspects of opening your own brick-and-mortar facility. This process requires you to understand the different hats you must wear as an owner-operator, understand your target market, and determine the type of facility and location that best suit your market.

Chapter 2

Choosing to Be a Personal Trainer for a Fitness Facility

Getty Images/Hero Images

There are many reasons that you might choose to work for a fitness facility. For one thing, it may offer the best-case scenario for building your career. For example, I have worked at various clubs in various capacities—sometimes in conjunction with having my own personal training business—for most of my professional life. To help you evaluate this option, this chapter covers the types of facilities in which you might work, the benefits and challenges of working as an employee, what to look for during the hiring process, and how to build your business within a business.

Types of Fitness Facilities

Fitness facilities in which a personal trainer can work as an employee may take the form of a medically oriented gym, a corporate fitness facility, a not-for-profit or community facility, a college or university gym, a personal training studio, or a commercial gym or health club. Let's take a closer look at each type.

Medically Oriented Gym

A medically oriented gym (MOG) is often set up as an outpatient training facility operated in conjunction with a medical practice, such as a hospital, physical therapy office, or post-bariatric-surgery center. MOGs vary in terms of facility size, programs, and equipment. Some focus on free weights, pulleys, tubing, and upper- and lower-body ergometers; others look like a smaller version of a regular gym. These facilities are unified by the fact that their personal trainers work closely with the client's physician or physical therapist to create a program related directly to the client's medical needs.

Corporate Fitness Facility

Back in the early 1990s in New York City, I managed a corporate fitness facility that consisted of a very small weight room and a very small open area for body weight exercises that, back then, were called *calisthenics*. At that time, it was unusual for a business to offer health and fitness options for its employees. Things have come a long way! Nowadays, corporate fitness and wellness facilities are increasingly used as a way to achieve measureable health outcomes and returns on investment. In one meta-analysis, Baicker, Cutler, and Song (2010) found that every dollar spent on disease prevention and wellness programs reduced medical costs by $3.27 and absenteeism costs by $2.73. Given these benefits, many businesses now offer staff members some kind of workout facility, and a few large corporations provide full-scale health clubs. At these facilities, personal trainers can find positions involving work such as teaching group classes, working one-on-one with staff members, and managing wellness programs.

Not-for-Profit or Community Fitness Facility

Potential employers for personal trainers in this category include YMCAs, Jewish Community Centers, Boys & Girls Clubs of America, senior centers, and local recreation departments. Most of these groups offer a combination of health and fitness programs, as well as social engagement. Because they must raise much of their operating money from donations, not-for-profits are not typically known for high-end equipment or high pay. However, the service nature of their missions may offer a source of greater satisfaction for some personal trainers.

For example, the YMCA of the Triangle (2017) pursues the mission of putting "Christian principles into practice through programs that build healthy spirit, mind, and body for all." In another example, the Easton Park and Recreation Department (2017) defines its mission as follows: "to enhance the quality of life for Easton residents by utilizing all resources under our control including public parks, public buildings, and public facilities to foster beneficial use of personal and family time for recreation and leisure." The department seeks to fulfill this mission by providing and promoting "a wide variety of quality recreation services that meet residents' needs and interests at a reasonable cost."

College or University Gym

I got my first job in both gym management and personal training at a gym in a dormitory complex at the University of Maine. It was a work-study position that paid minimum wage and was intended to help me pay my way through school while learning about the health and fitness industry. Whether such facilities are dormitory specific or serve the whole school, they are typically designed to accommodate students, faculty, and other employees; some also open their doors to members of the local community. These facilities are usually limited to weight rooms, cardio equipment, and perhaps group exercise; other fitness activities, such as swimming and racquetball, are typically handled by other departments on campus.

Personal training employees at university gyms are usually work-study students or interns. Personal trainers who do not attend the school may be hired as well, but that is not the norm. If you are attending school, however, this type of facility may offer you a great opportunity to get your feet wet as a personal trainer.

Personal Training Studio

As you might expect, personal training studios usually offer only personal training, though some also provide more recently developed offerings such as small-group training and "boot camp" classes. Most studios consist of smaller spaces and provide less equipment than do full-service commercial gyms because they don't have the membership base to cover the higher overhead costs associated with larger square footage and more equipment. Although a studio may seem like the ideal setting for a personal trainer, it can be one of the most challenging setups for obtaining new clients because it brings in very few people not already involved in personal training. Therefore, if you want to work in this setting, you must be ready and able to market yourself in order to attract clients from the community.

Commercial Gym or Health Club

Commercial gyms and health clubs are the most common types of fitness settings, and they come in all shapes and sizes. Some commercial clubs include only fitness equipment; many also offer group fitness options; and some offer basketball, racquetball, tennis, or swimming. The variety is endless. With memberships often reaching the hundreds or even the thousands, these facilities provide you with the greatest captive audience and thus the highest potential for gaining clients. Large commercial clubs are also more likely to offer the greatest variety of equipment and programs to help your clients succeed.

These settings also present some challenges for a personal trainer, as I found out while working in clubs of this type for many years. For example, you may have to compete for clients with other personal trainers, as well as group fitness programs. Some clubs also pressure employees to sell certain products, such as nutritional supplements. In addition, at busier health clubs, especially during prime time, the training floor can get crowded, and personal trainers need to be able to adapt on the go when they can't access the equipment they want.

Acting Under the Organizational Umbrella

What is it like to work for someone else in the fitness field? This approach comes with definite benefits and challenges, and the following discussion will help you decide whether it is a viable option for you.

Benefits

Do not underestimate the positive aspects of working for others. I've spent most of my career in the employ of various clubs, performance centers, and fitness facilities. These settings helped me hone many of my skills and develop many long-term friendships.

Access

Working for a company or organization gives you access to a wide variety of equipment to use with your clients. You also have access to the club membership as a potential client base; moreover, it tends to be a diverse population that offers you a chance to work with a range of clients, from youths to seniors and from athletes to individuals who are obese. This varied experience can help you decide what niche you want to focus on as your career develops. There is also huge growth potential to help more members through your services. In 2013, only 14 percent of club members in the United States took advantage of personal training services, and some of them did so for only a single session (International Health, Racquet & Sportsclub Association [IHRSA], 2014). *That, of course, leaves 86 percent who have yet to try personal training!*

Liability Insurance

As a personal trainer, you need professional liability insurance. It protects against professional negligence lawsuits that could financially ruin you, the fitness facility, or both. When you work for a fitness facility, personal training is usually covered by the facility's liability insurance. Even so, it is prudent to carry your own liability insurance as a precaution in case the club's insurance is inadequate. Fortunately, such insurance is readily available through various certifying bodies and is not very expensive, typically costing between $175 and $375 per year. Consider this expense an investment in your business.

Education and Professional Development

At a minimum, you will learn how your chosen club creates programs for its clients and how its leaders run their business. You may or may not agree with their format or philosophy, but I've always been able to find some value in seeing how clubs structure their offerings. What you learn can help you move forward in your career. In addition, many clubs provide in-service education programs for their personal trainers, teach organizational skills, give career guidance, and offer professional development money to aid in your continuing education. These offerings in themselves may be a reason to work for a club.

Teamwork

Being part of a personal training team also creates an opportunity for other learning experiences, such as job shadowing, peer discussions, and mentoring. Some of my favorite moments in my career involve the camaraderie of debating, problem-solving, and joking around with my co-workers.

Payroll and Bookkeeping

Since you are an employee, the club will take care of payroll and bookkeeping related to the work you do for the business. This service gives you a huge benefit because doing it yourself—that is, calculating and withholding income taxes, paying Social Security and Medicare taxes, and paying unemployment tax—can be complex and time consuming.

Scheduling Help

Of course, you can schedule clients on your own. However, when you work at a facility, the service desk person or receptionist can check your availability and book clients for you. This person can also take payment for those sessions.

Business and Promotional Materials

Routine things such as office supplies can eat into your time and profit. Most clubs supply these items, as well as promotional materials, such as business cards, flyers, an e-mail address, and a web listing.

Uniforms

Most clubs require a uniform (for instance, a standard staff-member shirt) and will supply it to you at no cost. A uniform enables instant recognition of your status, and I'm a firm believer that personal trainers should stand out on the training floor, particularly when they are working with clients. Imagine having 10 personal trainers working with clients on the floor. This "sea" of personal trainers and clients leads onlookers to feel that they are missing out; in other words, it's a great promotional tool.

On-the-Job Training

Clubs frequently assign new personal trainers to work on the fitness floor as a free resource to provide members with general fitness guidance and to help them select appropriate exercises and use good technique. This type of work gives you a great opportunity to build your interpersonal skills, practice demonstrating

> " Having spent time in my early personal training days working 'floor hours,' these hours can now be viewed as invaluable. It taught me different ways to engage different personality types and pushed me to become better rounded as a personal trainer. This time also afforded me the opportunity to master the art of communication and build relationships with members. People buy things from other people whom they like and trust. I gained many new personal training clients as a result of simply conversing consistently about fitness- and nonfitness-related topics. "
>
> Robert DeVito,
> founder and president at
> Innovation Fitness Solutions,
> Butler, New Jersey

exercises and correcting flaws in technique, and make connections with members who could very well become your clients.

Career Growth

Most personal trainers who work in a club have the opportunity to move up in the personal training ranks by building their client base, acquiring additional education, and gaining seniority. If you so desire, you may also be able to move into management.

Health Insurance

A few clubs offer full medical insurance, but most provide partial coverage; more specifically, according to a recent report, 71 percent of clubs provided medical insurance for their hourly employees (such as personal trainers), paying an average of 63 percent of the premium (International Health, Racquet & Sportsclub Association, 2015). This insurance support can make a substantial addition to your compensation package, especially in the current health care climate. Be sure to inquire about this when applying for a personal training position.

Paid Vacation

A 2013 survey of professionals certified by the American Council on Exercise found that 64 percent of full-time personal trainers received paid vacation time. The same report also found that only 6 percent of part-time personal trainers reported receiving paid vacation. So, since the majority of personal trainers are part-time, only a small fraction receive paid time off. The most typical scenario is that if you don't train, you don't get paid. This could be a point of negotiation for you during the hiring process.

Challenges

If life were all sunshine and roses, it would be dull. And, as you might expect, working for a fitness facility or organization is not without challenges.

Working for a commercial gym or health club comes with its own sets of benefits and challenges.

Getty Images/Hero Images

Noncompete Agreements

Clubs must live with the fear that a personal trainer in their employ will build a clientele, then open a studio around the corner and take those clients to the new business. As a result, many clubs require personal trainers to sign a noncompete agreement, often referred to simply as a noncompete. Such an agreement typically restricts the personal trainer from training current clients at a new location; training anyone within a certain distance from the club; or using any information, procedures, or forms developed by the club.

Although a noncompete agreement mainly addresses what happens if a personal trainer leaves the club, it may also affect the personal trainer while he or she still works for the club. If you work for a club whose membership base is too small for you to make a living, then you may need to seek out additional work at other clubs or studios to make ends meet. This challenge arises quite often for group fitness instructors, and it can also happen to a personal trainer. Therefore, this possibility is another point to negotiate with the club during the hiring process. Although noncompetes are often hard to enforce, as an employer cannot prevent you from making a living, the mere fact of being taken to court can be financially crippling.

Policies and Procedures

Policies and procedures are necessary, and they are not bad in and of themselves. They can be a source of tension, however, when you disagree with them but still must abide by them. When you disagree with a policy or procedure, you can (and should) voice your concern to the powers that be in order to see if it can be changed, modified, or done away with. That outcome may well be possible in a single-location facility run by an active owner. On the other hand, in larger organizations, such as multiclub chains or franchises, it can be difficult to change a policy or procedure. As an example, let's consider the booking of personal training sessions. Ongoing improvements in booking software mean that there are always better programs available, but, rather than simply switching to a newer software package, you have to wait until the chain or franchise changes it for all of its locations. Having worked in a large multiclub chain, I've experienced the reality that justifying and then implementing a software change for all locations can be a long, slow process.

Set Fee Structure and Payment

A fitness facility typically sets a standard fee for your service, as well as the percentage of that fee that you receive. A club offers personal training and employs personal trainers in order to make a profit, and it compensates personal trainers at a percentage that allows it to make what its owners feel is their fair share. This is the club's incentive for offering the benefits that it provides to personal trainers. For your part, of course, you have to decide whether the percentage offered by a club is fair and sufficient. In some cases, you may believe that you could charge more for your services than the club is currently charging, thus giving both you and the club a chance to make more. If so, then you should have that conversation with your supervisor.

> " The club offered so much for free that it was difficult to market and sell your services. To overcome that, I needed to offer a more specialized service. "
>
> Scott Larkin,
> ATC, CSCS, NSCA-CPT,
> studio manager for
> Orangetheory Fitness,
> Auburn, Alabama

Working Hours and Shifts

Some clubs are very strict about requiring you to work certain shifts or particular hours. They may also require that you serve floor hours, which entails walking around the training floor to help members as needed, give free equipment orientations, clean and organize equipment, or perform other duties that you may feel are not what you want to be doing. Of course, keep in mind that the opportunities to interact with members can lead to acquiring new clients, so it may be worth the tradeoff of having to do other tasks.

Style of Training

Some facilities follow set ways of working with clients. For instance, they may dictate that you perform certain assessments and, based on the results, train clients with a specific progression of exercises. I know of a number of places that use this approach; in fact, I recently spoke with a club owner who has the head personal trainer write the programs for all clients. I also know that a number of personal trainers have left because this system didn't give them a chance to use their own skills to solve their clients' problems.

Mandatory Meetings

Meetings are almost always mandatory. Sometimes they are also necessary, educational, and motivational. At other times, they are mere drudgery; I've been to many meetings that simply rehashed known information. Mandatory meetings may also require you to be at the club at hours that eat into your personal time or your potential training time.

Requirement to Upsell Clients

Occasionally, I come across clubs that require personal trainers to sell certain quotas of various items, such as nutritional supplements. For many personal trainers, this requirement directly violates their desire to serve their clients' best interests above all else.

Reports

Reports can provide useful information. For example, it is important to measure and report key performance indicators (KPIs), such as how many initial meetings you had with potential clients and what percentage of those individuals committed to a personal training program. At the same time, data gathering can be taken too far. KPIs, for instance, should not include all performance indicators but only those that make the biggest difference in building the business. However, some managers and owners like to have everything recorded, which unnecessarily diverts the personal trainer's time and focus away from serving clients.

Some health clubs will require personal trainers to work on the training floor as they build their clientele.

Getty Images/iStockphoto/air

Inability to Choose Whom You Work With

In most cases, your colleagues are chosen without your input, and you may experience stress and aggravation when working with someone whom you find challenging to get along with. You may also have no choice about which clients you serve. Having "fired" clients before, I can tell you that not every relationship between a personal trainer and a client is a match made in heaven. Sometimes you need to be able to pass a client on to another personal trainer who may be a better fit. Thus you would be wise to find out a facility's policy on declining or referring clients before you start offering personal training sessions there.

Uniforms

I realize that this item is also included in the benefits listing. However, if a uniform doesn't make you feel clean, sleek, and professional—or if it doesn't match your personal style—you may dread wearing it.

Thinking It Through

Some of these challenges may be make-or-break factors, whereas others may seem trivial to you. Many of them seem trivial to most people, but some are likely to be a big deal to you. I've simply listed as many pros and cons as I can think of in order to help you make an informed choice about whether working in someone else's fitness facility is the right choice for you.

Getting Hired

You can use the information discussed in the preceding sections—about the benefits and challenges of working for a facility—when you interview for a position at your chosen club. Make sure to ask about any items that concern you. Remember that you are also interviewing your potential employers to see if they offer a good fit for you. Do not take a position at a club that holds beliefs different from yours. If you do, you will butt heads from the beginning, and nobody wins in that scenario.

The Hiring Process

To maximize your chances of getting the job you want, be proactive and approach potential employers. You don't need to wait for a help-wanted ad to appear in an online job market. Instead, stop by the club, drop off a resume, find out who is in charge of hiring personal trainers, and ask for that person's contact information. Then follow up with a polite, formal e-mail introducing yourself and requesting an opportunity to interview for a personal training position.

If you land an interview, follow these tips:

- Be punctual. Nothing sets a bad tone like being late for an interview.
- Dress up but stay casual—that is, no suits required, but you should wear clean, tasteful, pressed clothes.
- Treat all staff members with respect and courtesy. You'd be surprised at how many times the staff members at the service desk are asked what they think of a job candidate.
- Greet the interviewer warmly, with a firm handshake, and make eye contact.
- Be alert, sit tall, speak clearly, and continue to make eye contact.
- Be prepared to ask questions about the organization and about details of the personal training position.

- At the close of the meeting, thank the interviewer and state that you look forward to hearing from him or her in the near future.

What Facilities Look for in a Hire

For the majority of my career, I have held positions in which my responsibilities have included hiring and managing personal trainers. One thing this work has taught me is that a resume can tell you only part of the story; in fact, some of my least successful hires looked great on paper. Everything from personality to self-discipline comes into play when it comes to building a client base. Figures 2.1 and 2.2 present survey results from two organizations that show what qualifications are most valued in prospective

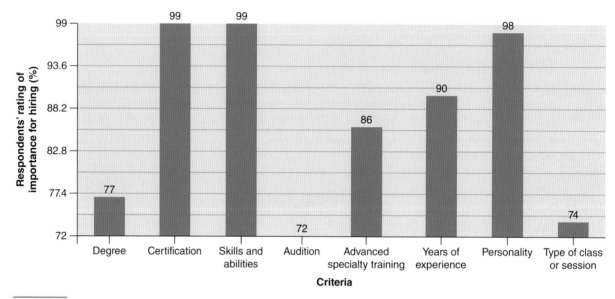

Figure 2.1 Criteria used for hiring personal trainers.

Data from IDEA 2015.

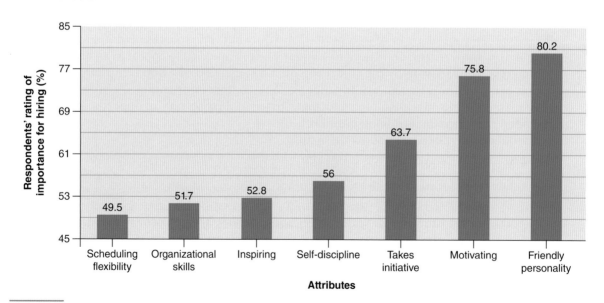

Figure 2.2 Desired attributes other than training and certification for fitness professionals.

Reprinted, by permission, from IHRSA, 2012, *The future is bright, U.S. health club employment outlook*, ©2012 IHRSA International Health, Racquet & Sportsclub Association.

personal training hires by fitness managers and directors. Figure 2.1 focuses primarily on prerequisites.

Beyond your degree or certification, other factors are also important to many clubs. A ranking of these factors is presented in the *U.S. Health Club Employment Outlook* report (International Health, Racquet & Sportsclub Association, 2012) based on the percentage of clubs seeking each attribute.

As you can see, the most sought-after trait is a friendly personality. If you are not open and friendly, then clients will not want to spend time with you even if you're very skilled. (In truth, if you aren't a friendly person, you may be in the wrong profession.) If you combine this quality with some of the others sought by employers—such as being an enthusiastic, motivated go-getter—then you can create a career for yourself at a club.

Building Your Business Within a Business

When you work for a club, the club will typically do certain things to help you obtain and schedule clients. For instance, it will likely train you in using its client management system to handle tasks such as booking sessions, taking payments, redeeming client sessions, and submitting payroll. Alternatively, as noted earlier, some of these tasks may be handled by other staff members.

Some facilities offer free orientations or training sessions to new members, and you may or may not get paid for this work. That's okay. Every time someone is placed in front of you, it gives you an opportunity to get that person involved in personal training. In fact, when new members join—that is, at the point of sale (POS)—clubs commonly try to sell them either personal training or another specific program because they are more likely to succeed (and to remain members) if they work with a fitness professional. However, the POS is also where most employers end their efforts to help you gain clients.

Therefore, even with the assistance provided by your employer, you must still serve as the main driver to build your business. If this task seems daunting, remember that only a small percentage of club members use personal training services, which means that a large number of potential clients are roaming the fitness floor. They are the ones who were not ready to sign up for personal training at the POS because they thought they could do it on their own or because they didn't see enough value in it at the time. Now, however, they may be getting bored, failing to see desired results, or even getting injured. As a result, they may be open to the prospect of receiving help in reaching their goals.

Given this knowledge, you might be tempted to sit back and figure that they know you're available and will come to you when they're ready (that's what I did when I was young and didn't know any better!). In reality, people are not as forthright as you might think. Some are intimidated by personal trainers, or feel too shy to approach you, or don't want to bother you, or don't even know how or what to ask about their situation.

For these reasons, you need to approach members to see how they're doing. More specifically, there are two main ways to gain new clients on the fitness floor: walking the floor and working out on the floor. Both options should be implemented during the time slot for which you wish to gain clients—if they're in the club when you're available to work with them, then your schedules will likely mesh.

Walking the Floor in Uniform

Walking the floor in uniform allows you to establish your presence as a personal trainer regardless of whether you are working floor hours for the club or putting in unpaid, self-promotion time. During this time, introduce yourself and meet the people on the floor. When approaching people who are performing exercises correctly, compliment them on their form and effort. Do this only if it's true—you want to be genuine rather than come across as an insincere salesperson. You might ask such individuals where they learned a particular exercise, then ask about their goals for health and fitness and whether they feel that they are achieving them. If they are, congratulate them and let them know that if they have any questions, you are happy to be of service. If they are not achieving their goals, ask what they think might be holding them back. Listen to their response, then let them know that you'd love to help and that you could schedule a half hour to sit down for an in-depth conversation, after which you could offer more personalized suggestions.

When approaching individuals who seem to be exhibiting poor form, start on a positive note by recognizing their effort. Then ask what they are trying to accomplish with the exercise and, if appropriate, either offer a correction to make the exercise more effective or offer a different exercise entirely. (In some cases, what they are trying to accomplish justifies the form they are using.) From this point on, proceed as you would with individuals who are performing exercises correctly. Specifically, ask about their goals and how they are doing with them. If they're reaching their goals, cheer them; if not, offer to sit down with them to discuss possible changes in their program.

> "When I was first starting my personal training company in 1994, I was interviewing personal trainers as potential employees. One guy had two bachelor's degrees (physical education and exercise physiology) and also the CSCS certification. When he walked into my office, I immediately knew he was *not* going to get the job. The first things I noticed were the sloppy shirt, half unbuttoned, and dirty sweatpants and dress shoes as well as the way he carried his body! He never made eye contact with me. Even when introducing himself to me and shaking my hand, he was looking everywhere but at me. I could barely hear his voice he was so soft spoken, and he stood and moved like a 95-year-old man. I gave him a written test to check his knowledge and he passed with a 100 percent score. But because of his poor communication skills and his slovenly appearance, I could not hire him. In order to be successful in our field, you must be able to communicate effectively and in a way that makes your client *want* to spend time with you."
>
> Gina Lombardi,
> NSCA-CPT,*D;
> president of Coach Lombardi LLC,
> Encino, California

When helping members on the floor, there are two reasons to limit the time you spend with each member. First, if you're locked in conversation with one person, you may be perceived as inaccessible to others. You can come back to that member after walking around, putting equipment back in place, and interacting with other members. Second, spending extended, exclusive time with a personal trainer is why people purchase personal training. If instead you give it all away in informal interactions, then you may reduce the perceived need among members to spend money in order to hire you.

Working Out on the Training Floor

Performing your own workouts in the club creates a casual opportunity for members to approach you, and you should capitalize on it. Granted, conducting conversations on the floor may affect your workout, but you must weigh that cost against the benefit of increasing your chances to gain new clients. These conversations can proceed in the same way described for times when you walk the floor in uniform. In order to make conversations possible, avoid wearing headphones, which sends the message that you are unavailable. The members of your club are your greatest source for potential new clients. Don't let the opportunity pass you by.

Getting Compensated for Your Work

When working for a club, the pay scale varies with demographics and other factors—for example, urban versus rural and high-rent versus low-rent. Such differences can dramatically affect how much is charged for a personal training session and therefore how much you get paid. Your pay can also be affected by the types of products you're delivering. For instance, does the session last 30 minutes or 60 minutes? Is it an individual session, or does it include two clients, or even three (or more) in a small-group format?

Even the size of the facility can make a difference. For instance, personal trainers in the United States who work in a facility of 2,000 square feet (185 square meters) or smaller make an average of about $35 per hour, whereas those who work in a facility of 5,000 square feet (465 square meters) or more average about $26 per hour (Association of Fitness Studios, 2015). Among these variables, there is one near-constant: In almost all circumstances, the more personal training sessions you provide, the higher your income will be.

Service Hours

The hourly wage for service hours—that is, nontraining hours, such as time spent working the training floor and attending staff meetings—averages $12.25 in the United States (IDEA, 2015). Some clubs require floor hours of all personal trainers. Others use floor hours to give newly hired personal trainers some income while they try to fill their hours with paid training sessions.

Personal Training Sessions

Overall, the average hourly wage for personal training sessions in the United States is $30.50, but facilities pay personal trainers in various ways, including by the hour and by the number of participants. Nearly two-thirds (62 percent) of clubs pay personal trainers by the session. Of those, 50 percent pay the personal trainer a percentage (on average, 60 percent) of the client's fee, and 12 percent pay a set fee—that is, a certain dollar amount for each 60-minute session delivered (IDEA, 2015). In my own experience, I tend to see rates in the range of 40 percent to 50 percent, though one facility went as high as 85 percent.

With rare exceptions, I absolutely recommend starting your personal training career by working for a fitness facility. Although working for someone else comes with both positive and negative aspects, the same is true of almost every working situation. The learning opportunities offered by working for a fitness facility will help you understand the personal training business and enable you to work with diverse types of clients, thus helping you discover your preferred clientele.

More to Come

The next two chapters address personal trainers who aspire to work for themselves. The later chapters, included in part II of the book, are also geared predominantly to those wishing to start their own business, but much of the information presented there also applies to personal trainers who work as club employees. I've been a personal trainer for more than 35 years, but I did not concern myself with learning business skills until the past 10 years. That was undoubtedly the biggest mistake of my career. Back then, though, who knew?

For you, developing business knowledge will help you not only gain more clients but also understand why your employers make the decisions they do. That understanding makes you a better employee; in addition, you may be able to offer business insights that management may not have thought of. Finally, the information that follows may even inspire you to own and operate your own facility someday.

Chapter 3

Choosing to Be a Self-Employed Personal Trainer

Getty Images/Blend Images/Shutterstock

Chapters 3 and 4 describe the roles and responsibilities of being a self-employed personal trainer. Self-employment means being your own boss, and it can take many forms, which include being an independent contractor or an independent personal trainer (not specifically hired by the club to train members) while training clients in someone else's facility, training clients in their homes and offices, and training via remote communication. It can also involve being a personal trainer in a facility that you own and operate. To separate these various possibilities, this chapter addresses owning and running a personal training business when you do *not* own the physical location in which you provide your services. Chapter 4, on the other hand, describes how to be a personal trainer while running a business that you own and operate in a physical location that you manage and control.

Did You Know?

In 2009, according to the Bureau of Labor Statistics,
- about 11 percent of U.S. workers were self-employed,
- about 4 percent were self-employed and incorporated, and
- about 7 percent were self-employed and not incorporated (Hipple, 2010).

Independent Contractor Versus Employee

When you work in a club, it is crucial for you to know your employment status. Specifically, are you an independent contractor or an employee? The answer affects where you stand in terms of your rights and responsibilities with regard to your clients, the facility, and the government bodies (such as the IRS) to which all earners and businesses must report.

You are an independent contractor if the following conditions apply.

- You are hired for a job, but the hiring party has no control over how you do that job—for example, if you train clients in a gym, and the gym has no say in how you train them, what hours you work, or what you wear.
- You must pay your own income tax withholding, Social Security and Medicare taxes, and unemployment tax; in addition, if you work in (not for) a club, the club is not going to do your bookkeeping.
- You must provide your own business services, such as making business cards, obtaining contact phone numbers and e-mail addresses, and booking sessions with clients.
- You receive no employee benefits, such as vacation pay, sick leave, and bonuses.

In short, you are an independent contractor if you are hired to provide a particular service but left on your own to build, promote, sell, manage, and deliver it.

IRS Definition of Independent Contractor

Sometimes, it is difficult to define the line between being an employee and being an independent contractor. In making this determination in the United States, all earners and businesses must follow the regulations of the Internal Revenue Service (IRS). According to the IRS (2016), "The general rule is that an individual is an independent contractor if the payer has the right to control or direct only the result of the work and not what will be done and how it will be done. The earnings of a person who is working as an independent contractor are subject to Self-Employment Tax."

In determining the degree of control and independence, the IRS (2017) considers the following three categories of evidence.

Behavioral: Does the company control or have the right to control what the worker does and how the worker does his or her job?

Financial: Are the business aspects of the worker's job controlled by the payer? (These include things like how the worker is paid, whether expenses are reimbursed, and who provides tools and supplies.)

Type of relationship: Are there written contracts or employee-type benefits (i.e., pension plan, insurance, vacation pay)? Will the relationship continue, and is the work performed a key aspect of the business?

The key is "to look at the entire relationship, to consider the degree or extent of the right to direct and control, and, finally, to document each of the factors used in coming up with the determination" (Internal Revenue Service, 2017).

Making the Decision to Be a Self-Employed Personal Trainer

Being self-employed puts all of the control—and all of the responsibility—in your hands. The details of these realities are addressed in upcoming chapters. For now, consider the responsibilities presented in the following list to help you determine whether self-employment is the direction in which you want to go. In order to be self-employed (in any way, shape, or form), you need to do the following:

❶ **Create your business structure.** Specifically, decide whether your business will be a legal entity in the form of a sole proprietorship, partnership, or corporation.

❷ **Carry your own liability insurance.** Working as a personal trainer without liability insurance would risk the financial future of your business and possibly even your personal financial future.

❸ **Determine your services.** What kinds of services will you offer? Possibilities include, for example, 30- or 60-minute sessions in various formats, such as one on one, small group, and boot camp.

❹ **Determine your pricing and how you will receive payment.** This decision addresses everything from how many sessions you sell in a package to whether you will receive payments via monthly billing and whether you will offer the option of paying online.

❺ **Learn to market and sell your services.** Where are your target clients, and what forms of marketing will get the best responses from them? Possibilities include direct mail, social media, and attendance at local meetings (such as Chamber of Commerce and Rotary Club), to name just a few.

❻ **Create or obtain business forms (such as client waivers and medical history forms).** Creating a sustainable system of operations requires you to have the right forms to do your business and keep records. Sample forms are provided in this book's appendix and in the web resource (www.HumanKinetics.com/ TheBusinessOfPersonalTraining), but you may need to create some forms that are more specific to your business.

❼ **Hire other professionals when appropriate.** Examples include bookkeepers and legal representation. I, for one, don't like to do bookkeeping, and I don't trust myself to do it right; therefore, I hire a bookkeeper. Know when you should hire others for specific tasks.

❽ **Create a plan to grow your business.** Whether you need to obtain funding or additional knowledge, map out a plan to get it done so that you don't miss or forget important details.

As you contemplate getting out from under the umbrella of another business and taking the reins yourself, you need to consider the types of venues in which you could work and the approaches you could use. In a survey conducted by IDEA Health & Fitness Association (Schroeder, 2015), the fitness professional respondents are an indication of the many types of venues in which fitness professionals work, as well as the prevalence of each. The majority of fitness professionals are found in health clubs and fitness centers (see table 3.1), but this statistic doesn't necessarily mean that you should work in that type of setting. You might decide, for instance, that your passion involves training your clients outdoors, and that could be the niche in which you dominate the market.

Table 3.1   **Possible Work Venues for Personal Trainers**

Type of facility that IDEA survey respondents work in	Prevalence (%)
Multipurpose health club	16
Fitness-only health club	15
Corporate fitness center	13
YMCA, YWCA, or JCC*	10
Personal training gym	9
Clients' homes	8
Pilates or yoga studio	5
Group exercise studio	5
Personal trainer's home	4
College or university	4
Park or recreation center	3
No facility, off-site classes	3
Hospital fitness center	3
Outdoor setting (personal training)	1
Virtual training or instruction	1

*Jewish Community Center

Permission to reproduce this table has been given by the copyright holder, IDEA Health & Fitness Association, www.ideafit.com. Reproduction without permission is strictly prohibited. All rights reserved.

A Fatal Assumption

In *The E-Myth Revisited* (2001), Michael Gerber cites some sobering statistics about the failure rate among small businesses. Some 40 percent fail within a year, and 80 percent fail within five years. Of those that remain, 80 percent fail within the next five years. What accounts for the high rate of failure?

In Gerber's (2001, p. 13) view, many people make the "fatal assumption" that because they understand the technical aspects of a certain line of work, "they are immediately and eminently qualified to run a business that does that kind of work. And it's simply not true!" In terms of our focus here, personal trainers who succeed at personal training and then decide that they are ready to start their own business often do not realize the commitment required to run a business beyond simply being a personal trainer. Almost inevitably, they fail because they have not worked on the business itself.

Training a Client at a Facility

You can work as a self-employed personal trainer either by being hired by the facility as an independent contractor or, as some gyms allow, working separate from the gym and paying a set fee per client or per day, week, or month. Either way you build your business by training clients who are members of a facility or by training nonmember clients whom you bring to the facility. Although most health clubs have moved their personal trainers to employee status, 28 percent still engage personal trainers as independent contractors (Schroeder, 2015). Therefore, your first step in working as a self-employed personal trainer in this model is to find gyms, clubs, and studios that may be looking for independent contractors or allow independent personal trainers. Search online for local facilities and call them to find out their policies regarding personal training by a nonemployee.

Next, visit any facility that would allow you to work independently. See if it offers the space and equipment that you would need. If so, ask the management what financial arrangement they require. Clubs that allow independent contractors or independent personal trainers often use specific contracts for those roles. Here are some points to clarify:

- Would they charge you a set fee (hourly or monthly), or would they base the fee on how many clients you train?
- Would they require you to be a member in order to train clients there?
- Would they collect fees from clients and then pay you for your service, or would you collect fees and then pay the club its share?
- Is there a membership base that you could tap into in order to build your business, or would you have to bring in your own clients?
- Would your clients need to be members of the club? If they were not members, would they need to pay a guest fee, or would that be considered part of what you were charged?
- Would you be able to advertise within the facility?

Benefits

I worked for years as an independent personal trainer who trained clients at various gyms in Boston and New York City. As I found out, this arrangement offers some distinct advantages.

- You have access to a variety of equipment, which allows you to keep your overhead low because you do not have to purchase your own equipment.
- You may have access to the membership as a potential source of clients. Even without recruiting, I gained many clients from among the membership because they had an opportunity to observe me working with other clients.
- You can use this single location as your home base rather than having to travel from one client to the next.
- You may find opportunities to network with other independent personal trainers, which allows you to discuss best practices for building your business.

Challenges

Facilities vary greatly in how they deal with independent personal trainers. Challenges may involve issues related to clientele, equipment, and payment.

- The challenges may start with how much the facility's management wants to charge you for using its space. I provided personal training at one club in New York City that initially allowed me to train others simply by paying for a membership. Then, as the industry changed, they charged a monthly fee above the membership fee. While this was more than I had been paying, it didn't seem unreasonable. Soon, however, the club wanted to charge me 40 percent of my fee for personal training. That was about the same percentage charged for providing personal training as an employee of the club, but without any of the benefits. At that point, I and the rest of the independent personal trainers took our clients to another facility.

- At some clubs, you may not be allowed to provide personal training to members. This typically occurs in clubs that have personal trainers on staff and don't want an independent personal trainer eating into their potential business. Of course, this restriction dramatically decreases the value of working as an independent personal trainer at a facility. Therefore, if you are not allowed to train members at a facility that otherwise looks like the best option for your business, then you will need to plan an aggressive external networking and marketing campaign to locate potential clients.

- At some facilities, the client pays the facility, which then pays you. In such cases, any discrepancy in the bookkeeping can create conflict between you and your host club. As you can imagine, this sort of conflict creates an uncomfortable situation. To minimize your risk, be diligent about keeping your records so that you will know if the club does not compensate you correctly.

> " If there was ever a concern or issue, it was easily handled by reviewing records, statements, deposits, and so on. The facility owner knew that I am meticulous and detail oriented and keep impeccable records that I show each pay period. Mainly, open communication solved any slight issue quickly. "
>
> Ryan Carver,
> BS, CSCS; fitness coach,
> Leverage Fitness Solutions,
> Salt Lake City, Utah

- Depending on the size of the facility, you may find that certain times are too busy for you to access the equipment that you want to use with your client. In this circumstance, you must either avoid that time slot or get creative by using less popular equipment. For instance, I've created whole workouts based on body weight and tubing that were very effective, and I could always find enough space to perform them no matter how popular the time slot.

Training a Client in a Home or Office

Some clients greatly value receiving personal training at home or at the office because it saves them time that would otherwise be spent in traveling to and from the health club. Their appreciation of this benefit makes them more likely to use the services of a personal trainer.

Benefits

I have held many positions in my personal training career, including that of independent personal trainer at various gyms. Through it all, one ongoing part of my business has

Training clients in their homes or offices can offer benefits to you and your client.

Getty Images/Blend Images/Shestock

been to train clients in their homes, offices, or apartment-complex gyms. Training in a client's space can be a great option for the following reasons:

- You don't have to make arrangements with anyone other than your clients. Do your schedules match? If the answer is yes, then book it.
- Getting paid is simple and easy—cash, check, or credit card. To accept credit cards, you can use a card reader that attaches directly to your smartphone or tablet; for example, this service is offered by Square, Intuit GoPayment, and PayPal.
- Some apartment or condominium buildings contain their own gyms, and some clients have their own home gyms. These options may offer a good choice in terms of both equipment and relative privacy as typically only residents are allowed to use them.

Challenges

The challenges of providing personal training in a client's home or office relate to space, equipment, and travel time.

- If you don't have access to a private or semiprivate gym, then you may need to get creative by working in some very different spaces. For instance, I used to train one celebrity client at her home, which included a large, comfortable space. I have also trained people in spaces where I would need to move the coffee table in order to have enough room to work out. Of course, the available space dictates the kinds of exercises that you will be able to use with the client.
- If your clients have no access to fitness equipment, then you may need to purchase some to carry from appointment to appointment. In this case, you certainly won't be able to use a lot of traditional equipment. Alternatively, you could require your clients to purchase their own equipment as part of your terms for working with them. Here are some equipment choices that offer versatility, portability, and compactness for use in smaller spaces:

> › Resistance bands
> › Yoga mats
> › Suspension trainers or devices
> › Jump ropes
> › Small medicine balls
> › Selectorized dumbbells (not portable but compact and versatile and therefore a possibility for clients to buy for their homes)

- Another challenge is travel time. Whereas a single location would allow you to do, say, four 30-minute sessions in two hours, traveling to a client might occupy 30 minutes each way in order to conduct a single 30-minute session. That's an hour and a half of your time. With this impingement in mind, you must decide how far you're willing to travel for a client and how much to charge for travel time so that your compensation is comparable to that of working in a single place. Clients do know that they will pay more for the convenience of having you meet them at a place of their choosing. In working out these details, recognize and plan for the possibility that your travel time will vary depending on traffic, bus, or subway delays.

> "One of the big challenges with training clients in their homes was the distractions of home life (kids, pets, phone calls, etc.). I just had to do my best to manage the emotions and personalities that would come into play in their home space."
>
> Joe Drake,
> MS, NSCA-CPT; co-owner,
> Gravity & Oxygen Fitness,
> Boca Raton, Florida

Even when you work in a client-selected space, it remains your duty to ensure that the space and equipment used are safe for your client. This responsibility includes moving loose rugs, safeguarding breakable items, and keeping animals and small children at a safe distance. Consider everything that might happen and adjust the space accordingly.

Training Clients Using an Online Platform

Online personal training may be in the process of going mainstream. That's the view of Pete McCall (MS, CSCS, ACE CPT, and ACE expert) at http://petemccallfitness.com/, who has been reporting annual fitness trends for ACE since 2013:

I think that online training will be a major disruptor in the fitness industry. Trainers will be selling their programming via online platforms and won't even need to work in a physical gym to be able to help clients. We, in the United States and abroad, are a society that wants options, and paying a personal trainer a nominal sum of $10 to $15 for a 30- or 60-day workout via an online platform is a cost-effective way to experience the benefits of fitness coaching (P. McCall, personal communication, January 26, 2017).

Some fitness professionals may not support the idea of online personal training because they prefer to be in the room with the client. However, video technology has improved to the point where this approach can be both safe and effective. In the online format, you handle the personal training process just as you would as if you were in the same space. Specifically, you still do the following:

- Get a physician's signed approval.
- Go through a medical history and lifestyle questionnaire.
- Choose tracking assessments (in this case, based on their suitability for being performed by the client on his or her own).
- Review and discuss the results of assessments.
- Help the client clarify his or her goals.
- Recommend a course of action.
- Choose the equipment to use (based on what the client can access).
- Create a feasible and appropriate exercise program.
- Implement (via e-mail and online video sessions).

The ways in which sessions are run may vary widely, but the safest, most effective sessions do not differ greatly from in-person training. (Of course, an online personal training package may use additional tools, such as text reminders, activity trackers, and nutritional journal applications.) The computer or smart device cameras should be set up so that you can see your client's full body (and be able to give feedback as the client moves). The client should also be able to see your full body so that you can give visual demonstrations.

Here are some examples of online tools that can be used for video sessions:

- Skype (www.skype.com/en/)
- FaceTime (www.apple.com/macos/what-is/)
- Google Hangouts (https://hangouts.google.com)

You might also want to use a tripod or other positioning tool with your video devices. Doing so can help you ensure that the camera is set up in the best way to show you and your client.

Benefits

Technological advances will continue to provide new and better ways of delivering personal training services. We need to be open and ready to participate in these new options that offer benefits for both clients and personal trainers. Here are some of the benefits of training clients online with current technology.

- Since you are not in the same physical space as the client, you don't need to have equipment available unless you choose to do so for demonstration purposes. You do, of course, need to know what equipment the client can access before you design the program.
- No travel time is required.
- You can train anyone anywhere. Even when you, your client, or both of you are on the road, you can still train as long as you both have video access.
- Benefits for your clients include easy access, travel time saved, and freedom from needing a gym membership. Clients also gain the ability to work with the most qualified personal trainer, not just the best one available locally.

Challenges

Of course, no single approach to online personal training works perfectly for all clients or for all personal trainers. It's a relatively new practice, and challenges can arise for both parties. Here are a few:

- Some people get spatially confused by using video (or mirrors, for that matter). If this is the case, you might ask the client to face a quarter of a turn to the right or left of the screen so that he or she is not confused by the video but you still get an appropriate view for assessing the client's movements.

- As when working face to face, your client needs to have a safe place in which to work out. Of course, you can't check the space yourself when you don't have physical access to it, but you can remind your client to choose a safe space and to show you that it is safe.

- Online personal training doesn't give you the opportunity to use tactile cues to help a client find or get into correct body position. Therefore, if you aren't as strong at verbal cueing, you may have a difficult time with this kind of personal training. One way to get better at giving verbal cues is to practice with friends or family members by having them turn away from you as you describe movements and corrections for them to make.

- Applicable laws differ across states. What is legal in, say, Maine, may be illegal in Florida. Thus you need to do your research to make sure that whatever you do (for example, explaining how to read a food label) and whatever legal forms you use (such as contracts and waivers) are appropriate for the location in which your client lives.

- Sometimes the Internet connection will be unreliable or too weak to maintain a clear video image. The primary factor is often the type of connection (Wi-Fi, cellular data, or hardwired). It may be that the signal strength of the location (either yours or the client's) will determine when (low usage times) or where (better reception locations) the session is scheduled.

> " Assuming that Internet connectivity is good enough for both parties, the biggest challenge with video conferencing from a personal trainer's point of view is protecting time. It's easy to get carried away and try to do too much over video when the reality is that most clients don't need much coaching. The solution is to prepare thoughtfully. Have a predetermined amount of time for the videoconference with a client and plan the session in advance. What exercises will you teach? Will you be assessing the client over video? What else will you be doing? For each part, break it down into the smallest details you can and have a checklist ready before you start. This saves you from getting off track. "
>
> Jonathan Goodman, founder of the Personal Trainer Development Center (www.theptdc.com) and leader in systematized, online personal training

Coaching a Client by Phone, E-mail, or Text

Given that you cannot see your client when you interact by phone, e-mail, or text message, you also cannot see whether he or she is using proper form. How, then, can you exercise good faith in assigning exercises and taking your client through progressions?

My own ethical response is that you can't. However, if you recalibrate your idea of what you're doing, then you may have another viable business option. For instance, you could recommend that the client seek out a personal trainer at a facility nearby for the exercise portion of a wellness or fitness program while you act as the behavioral coach via phone, e-mail, or text. Behavioral coaching involves acting as a facilitator and helping your clients stay accountable for making fitness and lifestyle choices that allow them to reach their goals.

Behavioral coaching requires different skills than those used for typical personal training. To be most effective as a behavioral coach, seek out specialized training through one of the following sources:

- American Council on Exercise (www.acefitness.org/fitness-certifications/health-coach-certification)
- International Association of Coaching (https://www.certifiedcoach.org)
- International Coach Federation (www.coachfederation.org/)
- Wellcoaches (http://wellcoachesschool.com)

No matter what area you focus on—health, fitness, wellness, or lifestyle coaching—behavioral coaching can be done either face to face or via phone, e-mail, or text. In all of these approaches, it depends on initiating open, honest dialog; asking open-ended questions and using active listening techniques; clarifying or reframing their questions or statements; cooperatively setting goals and creating an action plan; and establishing client accountability.

Behavioral coaching skills can enhance your ability to help your clients succeed.

Getty Images/iStockphoto/Wavebreakmedia

Benefits

When I got certified through Wellcoaches about 14 years ago, it changed my viewpoint on the entire personal training industry. Acquiring behavioral coaching skills has influenced how I work with all clients, whether face to face or from a distance. I listen more, talk less, guide my clients to create their own weekly goals (for activities both in and out of the gym), and keep them accountable.

Behavioral coaching by phone, e-mail, or text offers many of the same benefits as online personal training, such as requiring no travel and allowing you to work with anyone anywhere. It also provides some additional benefits:

- Some individuals find it easier to be fully open—to disclose more—when not looking at the behavioral coach, which makes these options better for them than in-person coaching.
- The behavioral coaching technique of letting the client help design the action plan (a client-centered approach) increases the chance that he or she will adhere to the plan and thus get better results.
- You can wear your pajamas and nobody cares. Seriously, you don't have to wear anything in particular, because nobody will see you.
- The benefits to your clients include ease of access, lack of travel time, and the opportunity to work with the coach of their choice.

Challenges

I recommend getting a behavioral coaching certification because this work involves some definite challenges that can be minimized with proper training. Here are some challenges you might experience:

- If you can't see the client move, you can't create an appropriate exercise program (at least in my opinion) or spot or correct the client. Therefore,

> "The bottom line in coaching, as per the International Coach Federation, is to just ask questions. 'Clean coaching' is trusting the client knows the answers. As a result, we do not have to give advice. If personal trainers can just allow themselves to be curious, they will be on the way to providing more powerful behavioral coaching."
>
> Marjorie Geiser, MBA, RD, BCC; president, MEG Enterprises, Inc., Strawberry, Arizona (www.meg-enterprises.com)

to ensure that the client gets the right fitness program and performs it correctly, you need to rely on her or him to obtain appropriate instruction from a certified personal trainer located nearby.

- Behavioral coaching can be foreign to many personal trainers, especially when conducted by phone. Thus you may feel awkward at first. If so, hone your skills by practicing with friends and family members.

- Interactions conducted over distance will lack many nuances. When I work with a personal training client face to face, I can tell a lot about how he or she is doing by watching body language and facial expressions. Of course, you can't see your client over the phone or in e-mails and texts. In addition, when using e-mails and texts, you also miss the immediate feedback about mood and emotions that can be provided on a phone call by how the other person sounds or even by pauses. Thus you may miss out on or misinterpret communications. Despite these limitations, some personal trainers and behavioral coaches use e-mail or text exclusively, but I think they work better as a way to check in with clients within a phone-based program. The key to making up for not hearing or seeing your client's feelings is to ask open-ended questions that require more than a yes-or-no answer. This approach gives you a way to delve deeper when you notice that there might be something between the lines of written text.

More than any other method of training, behavioral coaching by phone, e-mail, or text requires that we handle ourselves differently. We can't rely on just exercise as the answer. Instead, we focus on behavior modification, which in some cases can make an even bigger difference in people's lives.

In the realm of personal training and fitness, behavioral coaching is often referred to as lifestyle fitness coaching. To learn more about it, see the *Coaching Psychology Manual* (Wellcoaches, 2015) or the *ACE Health Coach Manual* (ACE, 2013).

More to Come

If you decide that you're ready and able to become a self-employed personal trainer, you can choose from a wide variety of ways to build a business that helps individuals become healthier and more fit. You may find yourself using one or more of these approaches at any particular moment. For my part, I've always had at least a couple of variations of personal training going.

Perhaps you feel best when training clients in a club as an independent contractor. If that type of location is not available to you—or if you just prefer another option—then perhaps you'd like to do personal training in people's homes; provide online personal training; or work as a behavioral coach via phone, e-mail, or text. You can also offer all of these options or mix and match them to create your own best solution for your clients. For example, you might train a client at home when he or she is in town and provide online personal training or behavioral coaching by phone when the client is away.

Ready to go a step further? Chapter 4 addresses what it takes to work for yourself as a personal trainer *and* facility owner.

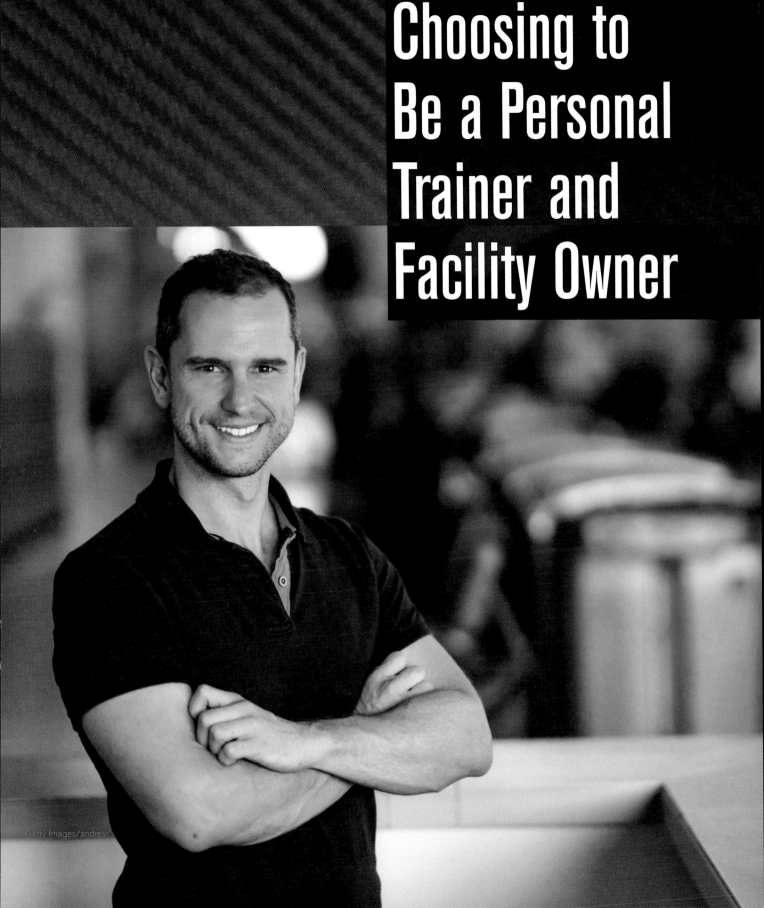

Choosing to Be a Personal Trainer and Facility Owner

Getty Images/andresr

Deciding to open a facility to pursue your career in personal training is a huge step. You must not only meet the responsibilities of an independent contractor or self-employed personal trainer (as discussed in chapter 3) but also address other critical factors that make the undertaking much more challenging.

The Challenge of Your Roles

Woohoo! You are now a personal trainer in a facility that you own. Now what? Well, nothing changes as far as your personal training goes. And yes, you have the freedom to choose your hours, your uniform, your equipment, and how you create programs for your clients. You also still need to work to build your business in the same way as if you were working for someone else. Now, however, you report to you. So, who is that "you"? That would be the personal training manager. When you own the facility, you are a personal trainer and a manager—and a salesperson and a marketing director and a housekeeper and . . . well, you get the idea. You are all of these things; therefore, you must be able to manage your time in order to give each role, each responsibility, its due. Let's take a closer look at the roles of personal trainer, manager, and owner.

Personal Trainer

This is where most of us start. You are a personal trainer, and you want to continue to be a personal trainer in your own facility. You know this. You've got the personal trainer thing down, and you yearn for the freedom to set your own schedule and design your clients' programs as you wish. Indeed, there is huge satisfaction in knowing that with every program you write, every client you help, you are also building your company's brand.

You may start out as the only personal trainer in your business, yet you must generate enough income to pay your business expenses. Do you know what all of your expenses would be? This is one reason to write a business plan. For example, if you decide to pay yourself 50 percent of the fee for a session (the average is 40 percent to 60 percent), how much would you have to charge, and how many sessions would you need to deliver per week in order to pay yourself and still be able to cover your other business expenses?

Let's imagine that business is good and that your schedule has you working full-time—that is, providing 40 hours of personal training sessions per week. (I know very few personal trainers who work this many hours, but we'll go with it to try to maximize your income on paper.) Now, let's do some quick math. If you charge $50 per hour and work 40 hours per week, that's $2,000 per week. Sounds good, right? On average, there are 4.33 weeks in a month, so your gross (total) monthly income is $8,660. Splitting it 50-50 means that you and the business each get $4,330.

Now let's consider your business expenses, which include rent, insurance, utilities, heating and air conditioning, and telecommunications, just to name a few. Can you cover all of these expenses with that monthly $4,330 allocated to the business? Maybe so, and that makes this all sound very plausible, but here's the kicker: Long before you're even ready to take your first client, you need to renovate your space and furnish it with equipment in order to make it into a fitness facility. So, what are your start-up expenses? If you take out a loan for these expenses, then you need to add the loan repayment to your ongoing monthly expenses. You also have to allow time to build your clientele up to your optimal level. Given that doing so could take six months to a year, what kind of debt will you incur before you reach your target client load?

The point of this exercise is not to discourage you but to make sure that you understand the accountability and skills you need—beyond those required for working as a personal trainer—in order to make your ownership venture successful. Specifically, you need skills in areas such as business planning, budgeting, and bookkeeping, as well as time to work on these tasks over and above the time you spend in providing personal training. When are you going to work on the business itself? In *The E-Myth Revisited* (2001), Michael Gerber argues that many businesses fail because the person starting the business wants to do his or her work—in our case, personal training—with more freedom but forgets that he or she will also have to work on the business itself.

Manager

As a manager, you must decide how your business operates. At some point, you may need to hire more personal trainers, either to make the business profitable or to meet your vision of helping more people. At that time, you will need to hire the right people (people who share your vision), train them to work within your structure, and manage them as they grow their own businesses under your facility's umbrella. You may also need to hire other staff, such as service-desk or cleaning personnel.

When you have employees, you as the manager need to meet with them regularly to ensure that they clearly understand their jobs, that they have everything they need in order to do their jobs, and that they are doing those jobs to your satisfaction. To that end, you need to document all systems that you develop in order to ensure clarity and enable you to teach others how you want things done. This documentation may address a wide range of functions, such as how your personal trainers assess and create programs for clients and how often staff members clean the facility to keep it attractive. If you care about how it's done, then you need to document it.

Another question to consider as manager is whether there are other streams of income that you could explore. Common retail options for additional income include food, drinks, supplements, apparel, and even some kinds of equipment. In addition, could you rent your space to

> " Probably the best advice that I can give to a personal trainer who decides to own his or her own facility is to do your homework before you jump into ownership. To me, this means three things: One, get your finances in order. Realize it can take many months to turn a profit after you open. Two, get appropriate advice. Using professionals like commercial real estate brokers, attorneys, and accountants can save you from making a bad business decision that can doom your chances of success before you even start. Three, investigate your competitors. You must know what others are charging for services similar to what you'll be providing. There's nothing wrong with charging at the upper end of the spectrum, but if you overestimate what you can charge, you'll quickly have an empty facility and mounting debt. "
>
> Chad Landers,
> BS, CSCS, IOC diploma in
> sports nutrition; owner,
> Push Private Fitness,
> North Hollywood, California

others during off hours? For instance, if you have classroom space, you could rent it out for meetings, parties, or classes that don't compete with your offerings. One caveat: Check your insurance to ensure that you are covered for such arrangements; alternatively, make sure that your renters carry their own insurance.

Your role as manager will probably also include marketing, at least at first. Specifically, you need to define your market, find out where your desired clientele gets information, and use those avenues to target potential clients. Examples might include social media, newspapers, and community events.

Owner, CEO, COO, and CFO

This is what you wanted—to own your own business. If you were a larger corporation, your role would combine those of chief executive officer (CEO), chief operations officer (COO), and chief financial officer (CFO). Therefore, even before you get to the personal training and the day-to-day management tasks, your job as CEO is to be the visionary of your business and set its mission and long-term goals. In this regard, it's not unlike how you work with your clients in that you start long-term and work your way back: What do you want your business to look like in 10 years? Meanwhile, as COO, you determine the day-to-day operations to support the business brand and culture, which of course were set by the CEO (yeah, you). In addition, as CFO, you make financial decisions to keep the business viable. By accepting these roles and responsibilities, you serve as master of the ship that is your business.

Skills You Need

As you can see, you will need to develop a variety of skills to run your business. Specifically, you'll need to create a business plan and determine a business structure, hire and manage staff, determine your services and pricing so that you can become profitable, understand finances (including profit and loss and cash flow), learn the art of selling and marketing, and learn how to grow your business. All of these topics are covered in the following chapters.

Beyond what you learn in this book, you can develop some of these skills by attending classes at a community college or business school. You can also take free, high-quality business courses online; for examples, see Nisen (2013). In addition, you can attend industry conferences that offer business-related sessions and, of course, find many relevant books. See appendix C for business resources.

Which Type of Facility Will Serve Your Market Best?

As you contemplate opening a facility, you must answer the question posed in chapter 1: Why do you want to become a personal trainer? In other words, what clientele do you want your business to serve? What need or problem are you going to solve by opening your business? To help you consider possibilities, think about the types of facilities discussed in chapter 2. Which type do you see yourself owning and running? Or do you have a completely different idea for your place?

Your decision about whom to help and what need to fill carries implications for the type of facility you need to establish. Each facility type comes with its own opportunities and challenges in terms of finding and renovating space to meet the need. The following subsections provide general descriptions of some of the types of facilities owned by personal trainers.

Personal trainers who plan to open their own facility must first determine their target market.

Big-Box Gyms

Big-box clubs typically fall into two categories: multipurpose and fitness. The target market here is, well, everyone. And these clubs do offer something for everyone—that's the point. They are often dropped into the middle of a densely populated area in hopes of providing the answer to everyone's fitness needs. Although that may sound good in concept, trying to be everything to everyone involves very high overhead costs for equipment, building lease, utilities, and maintenance. These costs require much greater financial investment and carry increased financial risk for you and your potential investors.

Multipurpose Clubs

Multipurpose clubs offer weights (machines and free weights), cardio equipment, an exercise studio, and some kind of sport element (e.g., swimming pool or basketball or racquetball court). I know of one multipurpose club that includes a full water park! Always keep in mind the investment aspect. The more elements you add to your club, the more expensive it's going to be to buy or lease the property, build out the facility (that is, finish the raw space), and maintain it. In fact, the initial investment for a large multipurpose club can easily be in the millions. Beyond that, it is very difficult to provide ballpark figures for what everything will cost. For instance, the price of a climbing wall can vary dramatically depending on its height, width, material, and shape. The same is true for pools, courts, and other setups. Price also depends on your geographic location. What costs $50,000 in Maine may cost $500,000 in New York City.

One way to estimate the cost of the physical build-out of your facility hinges on its square footage. As described by Bruce Carter (2014) of Optimal Design Systems, "Generally, low-priced clubs cost . . . $30 to $50 per square foot. Larger-box club chains and franchises cost . . . $40 to $60 per square foot. Higher-end clubs cost more than $60 per square foot." That view is echoed by Michael Scott Scudder (2001), who pegs the cost for a build-out of leased space at $40 to $100 per square foot. Table 4.1 gives you a quick look at how much a build-out might cost based on Carter's estimates.

Table 4.1   **Build-Out Cost by Membership Cost and Square Footage**

Club level	APPROXIMATE COST			
	2,500 ft² (232 m²)	5,000 ft² (465 m²)	10,000 ft² (929 m²)	25,000 ft² (2,322 m²)
Low-cost ($30/ft², $323/m²)	$75,000	$150,000	$300,000	$750,000
Midrange ($40/ft², $431/m²)	$100,000	$200,000	$400,000	$1,000,000
High-end ($60/ft², $646/m²)	$150,000	$300,000	$600,000	$1,500,000

Fitness Clubs

Like multipurpose clubs, fitness clubs typically provide weights and cardio equipment. They may or may not include an exercise studio—and that is about all. As a result, they require less money than do multipurpose clubs to start up and maintain.

Special-Population Facility

Special-population facilities include senior fitness facilities and youth fitness clubs. Many personal trainers resist the idea of selecting a specialty for fear of losing out on potential clients. They want people know that they can train most anyone, if not everyone. However, when every personal trainer is a generalist, nobody stands out. In contrast, if you choose to work in a particular niche—or small, defined market—then you may become the go-to person for people who need help in that specific area.

For instance, if you have a heart issue, do you want to rely on a final opinion from your general practitioner? No, you want a cardiologist. Similarly, if you choose to open a place for older adults, or youths, or persons with bariatric issues, you are not limiting yourself. Instead, you are funneling a target market right to your door.

Once you have chosen your niche, it's time to build the right kind of facility and furnish it with the right equipment. For example, if you are focused on the bariatrics population, you don't want a lot of stairs. You also don't want chairs with arms that constrain clients when they sit down, and your exercise equipment had better accommodate your intended clients as well. Otherwise, they will feel that you don't understand their circumstances and needs.

Personal Training Studio

The personal training studio is probably the type of fitness facility that varies most in size and equipment. These facilities can range from 200 square feet (19 square meters) to over 10,000 square feet (929 square meters). Some include a simple weight machine with multiple stations, whereas others provide several lines of equipment and free weights. The size and choice of equipment depends on your training type and style, as well as how you envision the growth of your business. For example, if you wanted to focus on bodyweight and suspension training for small groups of up to six participants, you would need very little equipment or space.

Group Fitness Studio

Group fitness studios provide open space, possibly with a stage and some equipment (i.e., weights, mats, and steps) on the sides. This kind of studio was very popular in the

1980s and has been making a comeback as people move away from larger clubs. This type of facility can be very inexpensive to get up and running.

Boutique Fitness Studio

Boutique fitness studios can offer either personal training, small-group training, group fitness, or all of these options. They are usually developed to have a high-end feel not unlike that of a boutique shop. They can be very specialized—for example, offering only group cycling classes or boot camps. In fact, as I write this, my wife, Heather, and I are opening a boutique fitness studio called Jiva Fitness that will have an artistic flair.

> " One of the goals we have for our boutique fitness studio is to offer personal training and group fitness with an intimate feel and a focus on creating a close community within the membership. "
>
> Heather Stirner Nutting, NSCA-CPT, ACE CPT, AFAA CPT; co-owner, master trainer, and instructor at Jiva Fitness, Easton, Pennsylvania

Athlete Training Facility

There is a large market for providing personal training to athletes, particularly if you focus on kids. Many parents want their child to be the next sport superstar and are willing to pay for specialized training. Most of these facilities start with open spaces, and they often include areas equipped with artificial turf. They may also provide equipment such as sleds, sandbags, medicine balls, tires, and ladders. More advanced facilities may include lifting platforms and Olympic weights.

Small-Box Gyms

This category includes everything from a garage to a warehouse that offers minimal equipment, most often including Olympic weights, kettlebells, pull-up stations, and medicine balls. These facilities often keep decor to a minimum and may consist simply of a building shell containing equipment. This no-frills approach minimizes design costs and attracts members who believe that hardcore training is all about the work—not the aesthetics. Indeed, the first gym in which I worked out was a serious, no-frills, powerlifting hole in the wall.

Location, Location, Location

I know you've heard it before, but location really is *that* important, for multiple reasons. For instance, I've seen a number of facilities that made me think, "The rent must be really cheap." The reasons for this reaction included run-down building appearance, seedy surroundings, and lack of parking. These factors all matter when it comes to picking out a location for your facility because they will matter to your potential clients.

Traffic

Since you are not a "destination" business—one that offers a unique experience worth seeking out and traveling to (such as an ice arena or parkour facility)—you should seek a location that is visible to people driving or walking by. The easiest marketing strategy is simply to have someone see your place and say, "Oh, wow! Just what I was looking for!"

Accessibility

People will always find excuses to avoid going to the gym. If it is too far away, then one of those excuses will be commute time. Generally, your facility should be situated in a convenient location within an 8-minute commute of your primary market and no more than 12 minutes from your secondary market (Plummer, 2007).

Parking

If members will be driving to your location (that is, if your location is not urban), then you must provide ample space for parking. Being unable to find a free parking spot can be a major annoyance for members and a turn-off for potential members. You must also consider local parking regulations, which can vary dramatically for health clubs. Some municipalities require as few as 4 spaces per 1,000 square feet (93 square meters) of facility space (Santa Rosa City Code, 2012), whereas others require as many as 13 spaces for the same facility size (Plummer, 2007). Of course, it is better to offer extra spaces than to have too few, so your safest bet is to go for the higher end. In addition, the Americans With Disabilities Act requires 1 of every 25 parking spaces to be an accessible space (U.S. Department of Justice, 2002).

Demographics

You need to understand your target market and the demographics of the area in which you are looking to open your facility. If you don't, the results could be catastrophic for your business. Imagine, for instance, opening a high-end health club in a neighborhood where the population can't afford to belong or opening a high-intensity interval-training box in a senior residential community.

Competition

Some businesses purposely open next to a competitor, in which case they are knowingly playing a piggyback game. Examples of such competition include Home Depot versus Lowe's, Target versus Walmart, and McDonald's versus Burger King. Being in a cluster gives each store maximum market share between them for a particular location. In addition, the close proximity makes it more likely that consumers will travel to the businesses because they can go to both without additional travel time. If one doesn't have what you want or is too busy, then you can just go next door or across the street.

Although this approach can work for some businesses, it may not be the best bet for a fitness facility as most facilities cannot afford to directly split their market by setting up next door to another fitness center that offers a very similar product or experience. It could work, however, if you offered something that the other facility did not. For example, if the other facility did not offer group cycling classes and you decided to open a cycling studio, you could enjoy the fact that fitness-minded individuals are already in your neighborhood and can easily step over to your studio for a different experience. When looking for the ideal location, determine where the competition is, what it offers as compared with what you will offer, and how it might affect your business.

Franchises and Licenses

Running a franchise involves contracting with an established business to use its business model, operating systems, equipment, logos, and trademarks in order to set up a replication of that business. You also receive coaching and guidance in an ongoing relationship to help make your business successful. Franchises begin with various initial investments, which can see ranges from $3,530-$12,900 for Jazzercise to $853,390-$3,669,150 for Planet Fitness and typically continue with monthly or annual fees. For instance, Snap Fitness had a start-up franchise fee of $29,500 (one piece of the $148,188-$458,458 initial investment) and a monthly royalty of $509. In addition, you might pay the franchisor a percentage of the profits; this figure runs from 5 percent (Planet Fitness) to 20 percent (Jazzercise) (Franchise 500, 2017).

Licenses also provide you with the use of a company's name, branding, intellectual property, and purchasing power, but they generally do *not* provide the operating systems that are part and parcel of a franchise. One example of a licensed fitness club is CrossFit, in which facility owners pay an "affiliate fee" of $3,000 per year ("How to Affiliate," 2017) and can run their "boxes" as they see fit. For this reason, you may see wide variations in how different CrossFit facilities are run.

Franchises are available in almost every type of fitness business you can imagine, from small-group training clubs to big-box gyms. In fact, if you look around your community, you'll probably find one nearby.

> " The benefits [of being a licensed club] included the name recognition and branding, autonomy as to how we ran our club, as well as tremendous discounts on equipment and group fitness programming (Les Mills). The downside is that being a licensed club and not a franchise, we had to create our own operating systems and marketing programs. "
>
> Mike Martino, PhD, CSCS; co-owner of Bodyplex Fitness of Milledgeville, Georgia

Benefits

As a whole, fitness franchises are booming. Listed in Entrepreneur's 2017 Franchise 500 Ranking as the No. 14 top franchise, Anytime Fitness went from 445 franchise locations worldwide in 2007 to 3,617 locations in 2017. Another example at No. 19 is Orangetheory Fitness, which opened its first facility in 2010 and expanded to 668 locations worldwide by 2017. As these numbers suggest, opening a franchise offers definite benefits.

- One of the most obvious benefits is the name recognition that comes with most fitness franchises. For example, names such as Curves, Jazzercise, and Gold's Gym are known even by nonexercisers. Name recognition puts your business high on the list for anyone thinking about joining a fitness facility. Think about it: Most people would choose Gold's Gym over Unheard-of Gym based on name alone.
- Along with name recognition, franchisors usually provide company-branded material and marketing tools to help you promote your business.
- When you are unsure of how to go about planning, setting up, or growing your business, a franchisor provides the needed support.
- Some franchisors even help you find the right location for your facility.
- One of the bigger challenges in running a business is to create and document your business systems. Franchisors can supply you with these systems, thus allowing you to focus on other areas that need your attention.

- A franchiser has a proven track record; otherwise, you wouldn't be considering it! This record of success makes it easier for you to acquire financing for your business.
- Because franchisors often have many franchise units, they tend to wield enormous purchasing power that can be passed on to you as a franchisee.

Challenges

Given that franchising has so much going for it, why would anyone do anything else? Well, owning a franchise also involves some challenges.

- Most franchises are subject to rigid rules of operation, which can reduce your opportunity to be creative. Of course, these rules exist for a reason. Doing things in the same way across facilities ensures that peoples' expectations will be met at every location. For instance, a Curves facility will always have the usual Curves equipment and programming because franchise owners don't get to choose any other equipment or create their own programs. So, when choosing a franchise, make sure that you agree with the various aspects of its brand. In addition, as you research franchise prospects, be aware that many are not set up with the fitness professional as the target franchisee. Many owners are simply investing in a proven model that will make them money, and your knowledge as a personal trainer may even make it harder to follow standard guidelines.
- As discussed earlier, each franchise has its own start-up costs, and some can be quite substantial. Unlike a business of your own design, a franchise does not allow for bootstrapping or cutting back on certain items to make it more affordable.
- Most franchises assess an ongoing monthly fee; they may also take a percentage of your revenue.
- Some franchises run national marketing campaigns for which all franchisees must pay, even though some campaigns may not be appropriate for your specific market or demographics.

Coaching and guidance from an established business can help make your franchise successful.

Getty Images/andresr

- Owning a franchise may involve a longer relationship than you want. Some require a contract lasting 10 years or more (Goldberg, n.d.).

If you do a web search for the top fitness franchisors and licensors, you will find the current opportunities and preliminary costs. This is a great way to see if any of them look like something in which you would want to invest your time, money, and energy.

Contracting With a Vendor

Many multiskilled fitness professionals who open a new business are reluctant to hire someone else to do what they can do themselves. At one club, I was hired as the fitness director, but, because I could, I also built and maintained the club's website, wrote two e-newsletters per month, wrote club protocols and guidelines, trained all club personnel in CPR and AED usage, managed the personal training department, and (at least in theory) delivered at least 20 personal training sessions per week. As you might imagine, I burned out, failed to do a great job at any of these tasks, and ended up resigning the position. The mere fact that you *can* do something doesn't automatically mean that you should. Think carefully about where your time is best spent.

In this light, although the choice to use an outside vendor may not seem ideal when you're trying to keep costs down, the right vendor can make your life as an owner much easier. This was our rationale at Jiva Fitness for licensing an outside vendor to provide high-end, licensed group fitness classes. Heather and I are fully capable of developing fitness classes, but that's not where we need to spend our time. High-quality fitness systems or programs are typically pretested at select clubs for effectiveness and for participants' enjoyment of the music and movements. In addition, they commonly provide staff training in determining the structure and schedule of classes and guidance in promoting and selling the programs.

When choosing an outside vendor for an aspect of your business, ask yourself the following questions:

1. Will this make my work life easier?
2. Who is the company providing the service? What is its history? Who can provide testimonials for it?
3. How much does the service cost? Does it fit my budget? What is the return on investment?

Positive answers typically point to a high-quality vendor who will elevate your business and the programs you offer.

More to Come

In choosing which avenue to pursue in your quest to own a business, start by asking yourself some questions. First, who do you want to help by opening your business? The answer will help you decide what venue might best serve that population.

Next, what part do you want to play in your business? Remember that as a business owner, you won't be able to spend all of your time working *in* the business. You also play the roles of manager and owner, both of which require considerable time and energy, as well as management and business skills. Do you have these skills? If not, you could take a step toward developing them by working in a management role for an established club; you could also take business courses online or at a local college or university. In addition, you can find many wonderful books on business and management.

This strategy is in fact my personal favorite; I have read more than a hundred books on business in the last 10 years, and they have helped me greatly.

Finally, do the benefits of opening a franchise outweigh the challenges for you? If so, is there a franchise that matches what you want to accomplish with your business? Opening a franchise can streamline start-up and management, and it may help you get up and running sooner, with a greater chance of success than if you tried with your own plan.

The following chapters fill in many of the details involved in building and running your business in whatever form it may take.

Part II

Learning and Applying Business Skills

Chapter 5

Creating a Business Plan

Getty Images/DigitalVision/PeopleImages

After deciding why you want to start a business and who it will help, you need to document what it's going to take to make your business work. Writing down your goals makes you much more likely to succeed, and writing out a specific plan helps you consider all variables and thus prepare more effectively. In short, your business plan plays an essential role by helping you know how to begin and then serving as a guide for proceeding into the future.

Importance of Writing a Business Plan

A business plan is a detailed description of your company, its concept, how it will run, what it will cost to run, and where you want it to go. As you learn about the world of business, you may come across varied opinions about how to write a business plan or even whether it's worth it. For instance, you may hear skeptics say that it's just a guess—an educated guess if you've done your homework, but still a guess—so how accurate and useful can it be? What's more, we can't know anything with certainty. The zombie apocalypse could start tomorrow, and wouldn't that throw a monkey wrench into your business plan?

On the other hand, all of science starts with an educated guess in the form of a hypothesis: "I think _____ will take place when I do _____." You then test the hypothesis, and if it pans out—great! If it doesn't, you develop a new hypothesis and try again. And that's what must be done with a business plan. Once you get up and running, you refer back to it, and if things are not going as planned, then you change your plan to reflect your updated best (educated) guess.

Some discussions of how to write a business plan advise you to project your business as far as 10 years into the future. However, the further out you project, the more likely you are to be off the mark. For that reason, I favor extending your business plan only to the point where you can get started, get established, and set a direction for growth, which means about three years for most of the business options we've discussed.

Could you simply bypass the writing of a business plan? Why should you bother putting in the time and effort if you'll probably have to change it anyway? Here are two big reasons:

❶ A business plan enables you to start the business with a good sense of your strengths and weaknesses, the challenges that may arise due to competition or economic factors, and your chances of succeeding. If you can't make it work on paper—that is, in a business plan—then it's not going to make it in real life.

❷ If you need to acquire additional financing, a business plan will show potential investors that you've done your research and are willing to put in the work to make your business succeed. No savvy businessperson will invest in a casual idea that doesn't consider all of the details—good, bad, and ugly.

One final question before getting started: How long should a business plan be? Answers vary widely. Some sources say that a typical plan runs 15 to 20 pages, whereas others say it should be at least 50 pages long. My own belief is that the page count is secondary to the content. Your business plan needs to include sufficient detail in each section for you to know—and show—that you have thought through all relevant variables that can be known at this time. The number of pages then depends on what you need to say in each section. For example, if there is literally no other fitness facility within an 8- to 12-minute radius of your proposed site, then your competitive analysis section will be very short.

You can find a business plan template in appendix A and in the web resource (www. HumanKinetics.com/TheBusinessOfPersonalTraining); you can use it to develop your own business plan. In addition, each section of this chapter fleshes out part of the template. If you are thinking about starting your own personal training business, consider taking notes as you read this chapter and jotting down brainstorm ideas for your own business plan.

As mentioned in chapter 4, my wife, Heather, and I are (as I write this) in the process of opening a boutique fitness studio. Thus I use a business model very similar to ours in the following discussion of the details of writing a business plan.

Components of a Business Plan

A business plan consists of nine key components:

1. Cover letter (optional)
2. Executive summary
3. Business or company description
4. Market analysis and demographics
5. Competitive analysis
6. Management plan
7. Financial plan
8. Capital required
9. Marketing plan

As you put together the necessary information for your business plan, you can gather material for any section at any time. In other words, it doesn't have to be written in order. You may also find yourself working on several sections simultaneously, and that's okay.

Before you get into writing the official business plan, start thinking about what you want to name your company. It took Heather and me much longer than I imagined it would to agree on one. You'll be glad if you start working on yours early in the process.

Naming Your Company

I've had some interesting discussions about naming a fitness business, both with my wife about our own business and in a LinkedIn forum that I run (Fitness Entrepreneurs, www.linkedin.com/groups/909387). Here are some of the options I've come across.

Use Your Own Name

Some people like the idea of using their own name in the company's name. For example, a friend of mine, Vince Mini, calls his place Mini's House of Pain. Using your own name in the name of your business establishes you and your beliefs as the standard for what to expect from the company. This could be a great thing. But what happens if and when you decide to sell your company? In many cases, a business' name and reputation are part of what the buyer is counting on as part of the deal. For instance, Joe Gold opened the first Gold's Gym in 1965, then built the business into a chain before selling it in 1970. Once he sold it, he had no control over how Gold's Gym operated. Then, in 1976, when he decided to get back into the gym game, he had to come up with a new name, which turned out to be World Gym. So, when you're naming your company, consider whether you would ever want your name on someone else's business.

Use Your Location

If you include your location in the name, it makes your business easier to find. Having lived in New York City, obvious examples for me include the 92nd Street Y and the Sports Center at Chelsea Piers. The downside of this approach is that if you ever move or expand to other locations, the business name may be confusing to consumers.

Make It Up

This one is wide open. Your name could be something completely nonsensical or an obscure, unrelated word or phrase that you hope to turn into a household name. Although this approach allows you to create a unique name, it also takes a huge effort to educate the public about your business. Current examples in the industry include Blink, Kosama, and Trumi—three fitness clubs that, by name alone, you would not recognize for what they are.

Choose a Name That Says What You Are

Another approach is to integrate your target market into the name. For instance, if you were creating a club to specialize in working with former athletes, you could call it Athletes Again or Back in the Game Fitness. You might also decide to name your business based on your training philosophy—for example, Full Function Fitness. The best choice is one that speaks to the members of your target market, draws their attention, and makes them want to know more.

In naming our studio, Heather and I played around with words that express energy and found that most were already in use. We then looked at relevant words in other languages and settled on a name that was obscure but held meaning for us and, we hope, for our clients. *Jiva* (pronounced "jeeva") means "vital energy of life" in Hindi. We added *Fitness* after *Jiva* so that our business isn't hard to figure out: Jiva Fitness LLC.

Once you choose a name, it's time to establish your business structure, claim the name as a web domain, and register it with your county clerk or state.

Cover Letter

Ideally, you should present your business plan to a potential investor in person. If that is not possible, then you can use a cover letter as either an introduction or a follow-up to a phone call. If you do use a cover letter, it should be personally addressed to the individual who will make the decision (i.e., not "To Whom It May Concern") and give a brief overview of the business plan—a summary of the plan's executive summary, if you will. Write the letter in standard business-letter format and include contact information for key personnel in your company.

You can find a cover letter template in appendix A and in the web resource (www.HumanKinetics.com/TheBusinessOfPersonalTraining), where you can modify it for your purposes.

Business Plan Example

Cover Letter

Mark A. Nutting
Jiva Fitness LLC
230 Ferry St., Suite 8
Easton, PA 18042
(555) 555-5555
mark@jivafitness.com

John Smith
Business Loan Officer
Smith Bank and Trust
128 Somewhere St.
Easton, PA 18042

Dear Mr. Smith,
As agreed in our recent phone conversation, I'm submitting the business plan for Jiva Fitness LLC in hopes of securing funding of $100,000 from your bank. This funding would provide for the facility build-out, equipment, and monthly expenses until we reach the point when our income meets expenses. As you will see in the financial section of the business plan, we expect to reach that point in month nine.

Almost 70 percent of the U.S. population is overweight or obese, and only 20 percent gets the required amount of physical activity. We, as a society, have a problem with getting and keeping people physically active.

At Jiva, we believe that our great programming, interpersonal connection, thoughtful and caring instruction, and sense of fun will help people who are struggling to become healthier and fitter. Specifically, they will find it easier to both start and stick with an exercise regimen.

Thank you for your time and consideration. I hope that you will review our business plan. I would be happy to hear any feedback and answer any questions that you might have concerning Jiva Fitness LLC.

Sincerely,

Mark A. Nutting

Mark A. Nutting

Executive Summary

The executive summary is often thought of as the most important section of a business plan. If it doesn't grab an investor's attention, then he or she may read no further. The summary should present a one- to three-page overview of the business plan that first addresses your personal expertise and vision for the company and then highlights each section of the plan.

Note: Because it is a summary, this should be the last section written even though it is the first to be presented. You can find a template for the executive summary in appendix A and in the web resource (www.HumanKinetics.com/TheBusinessOfPersonalTraining), where you can modify it for your purposes.

> ## Business Plan Example
>
> # Executive Summary
>
> ## Our Company
>
> Jiva Fitness LLC is a personal training and group fitness studio located in the heart of downtown Easton, Pennsylvania. At Jiva Fitness, we believe that if we can connect with and engage those who are struggling to become healthier and fitter, then they will find the experience both fun and life changing.
>
> With Mark and Heather Nutting as owners, managers, personal trainers, and group fitness instructors, Jiva Fitness is led by uniquely talented, nurturing, highly skilled coaches. Their long, successful track records will draw in and retain individuals who need help to reach their goals.
>
> ## Our Services
>
> Jiva Fitness will offer group fitness classes licensed from MOSSA (a leading provider of group fitness solutions). These classes will include Group Power, Group Core, Group Centergy, and Group Active, among others.
>
> Jiva Fitness will also provide signature classes, including Boot Camp and Living Fit. Our other fitness programming will include one-on-one training, small-group training, and weight loss and corporate wellness programs.
>
> All of these services begin and end with a personal connection with each member. Personal connection with the staff and other members of the Jiva Fitness community will help each individual feel like part of a bigger movement, one that will help each person stay on track and reach his or her personal goals!
>
> ## Our Market
>
> Jiva Fitness' target market will consist of men and women of all ages who need or want high-touch personal programming to help them attain their health and fitness goals. From its physical location in downtown Easton, Jiva Fitness will target the downtown community, both residential and corporate.
>
> Given that almost 70 percent of the U.S. population is overweight or obese but only 20 percent get the recommended amount of physical activity, the average health club is not drawing in the population that is most in need. Big-box clubs lack intimacy, and low-priced alternatives are low-supervision, equipment-access-only facilities, which may be fine for those who already know what to do but are insufficient for an inexperienced individual. Even though Jiva Fitness will certainly draw in experienced exercisers, our desire is to engage those who are timid about entering the realm of fitness. We want to help those who need it most.
>
> ## Our Competition
>
> Five fitness facilities are located within an 11-minute drive of Jiva Fitness. Two of them are large, multipurpose clubs, two are midsize fitness clubs, and one is a small fitness studio. All offer personal training, and three offer group fitness. All but the small fitness studio have lower monthly payments than Jiva Fitness.
>
> ## Our Advantages
>
> Jiva Fitness is differentiated from its competition by our location, our staff, and our classes.
>
> ### Location
>
> Jiva Fitness is located in the heart of downtown Easton. It is within walking distance of city hall, major office buildings, shops, and restaurants.

Our Staff

Mark Nutting is an award-winning personal trainer who received the Personal Fitness Professional 2016 Trainer of the Year Legacy Award and was named 2009 Personal Trainer of the Year by the National Strength and Conditioning Association. Heather Nutting is a national trainer for MOSSA's Group Centergy program. Both are national presenters, and together they have 60 years of industry experience in group fitness, personal training, and health club management.

Our Classes

Partnering with internationally recognized MOSSA, Jiva Fitness will offer MOSSA's professionally developed and tested fitness programs, which will be a unique offering in the Easton area. We will also offer our own signature classes, which, at a previous location, drew 40 to 70 participants per class. All classes are designed for participant safety, results, and fun.

Financial Summary

Jiva Fitness is seeking to secure a loan for $100,000 in order to build out the studio space, purchase equipment, and maintain cash flow until monthly revenues surpass monthly expenses. This break-even point is projected to occur by month nine (for details, please see the Capital Required section).

Table 5.1   **Financial Projections for Jiva Fitness**

Financial factor	Year 1 ($)	Year 2 ($)	Year 3 ($)
Revenues	124,563	301,898	310,082
Expenses	155,936	241,686	246,595
Net	−31,373	60,212	63,487

Start-up costs for Jiva Fitness:	$56,244.00
Accumulated debt before reaching break-even point:	$37,275.42
Capital needed:	$93,519.42

Marketing

Because the company will focus on creating a connected community, Jiva Fitness will rely mainly on various approaches that help establish relationships with potential members. All of the options are low cost or free of cost.

- Social media: Jiva Fitness is already creating a presence on Facebook, Twitter, YouTube, Instagram, LinkedIn, and Snapchat.
- Local events and charities: Jiva Fitness will both sponsor charity events and volunteer in others. We will also seek to participate in local events, such as the Women's Health Fair and the Senior Fest.
- Networking: Jiva Fitness is located in downtown Easton and anticipates that local business employees will make up a significant part of our membership. We will network with other businesses through groups such as the chamber of commerce, the Easton Business Association, and the Easton Main Street Initiative.
- Other: Additional possible marketing avenues include writing a health and fitness column for a local newspaper and hosting an online video program.

Business or Company Description

This section should include a detailed look at your company, your target market, what problem you seek to solve (your *why*), how you intend to solve it, what makes your company unique, and what kind of expertise you bring to the table. In short, this is a place to state your mission statement and mantra.

A mission statement provides a short overview of the *why* that drives you and your company. For example, here is Google's mission statement: "Google's mission is to organize the world's information and make it universally accessible and useful." And here is the mission statement of the National Strength and Conditioning Association: "As the worldwide authority on strength and conditioning, we support and disseminate research-based knowledge and its practical application to improve athletic performance and fitness." For a hypothetical fitness company—let's call it Fit Together—the mission statement might be as follows: "We improve the health and fitness of our community by providing the best fitness instructors and programs in a supportive atmosphere that is a pleasure to be in."

A mantra is even briefer than a mission statement. It is a statement that everyone in the company can easily remember and act on in a way that supports the company's vision. Google's mantra, "Don't be evil," drives everything the company does. Here are a couple of other examples: "Move fast with stable infrastructure" (Facebook) and "Think different" (Apple). The mantra for our hypothetical fitness company, Fit Together, might be, "Change lives through programs and people."

Create a mission statement for your company, then see if you can cut to the chase and find a mantra that fits your company and its mission. You can find a template for the business or company description in appendix A and in the web resource (www.HumanKinetics.com/TheBusinessOfPersonalTraining), where you can modify it for your purposes.

Business Plan Example

Business or Company Description

Jiva Fitness Description

Almost 70 percent of the U.S. population is overweight or obese, and only 20 percent gets the recommended amount of physical activity. We, as a society, have a problem with getting and keeping people physically active. At Jiva, we believe that if we can connect with and engage those who are struggling to become healthier and fitter, then they will find the experience both fun and life changing.

Jiva Fitness will offer group fitness classes licensed from MOSSA (a leading provider of group fitness solutions). These classes will include Group Power, Group Core, Group Centergy, Group Active, and more. We will also provide signature classes, including Boot Camp and Living Fit. Our other fitness programming will include one-on-one training, small-group training, and weight loss and corporate wellness programs. All of these services begin and end with a personal connection with each member.

Personal connection with the staff and other members of the Jiva community helps each individual feel like part of a bigger movement—one that will help each person reach his or her goals! With Mark and Heather Nutting as owners, personal trainers, and group fitness instructors, Jiva Fitness is led by uniquely talented, nurturing, highly skilled coaches. Their long, successful track records will draw in and retain individuals who need help to reach their goals.

Jiva Fitness' Mission Statement

We serve individuals who need to improve their health and fitness through caring attention, co-member connection, and professional instruction.

Jiva Fitness' Mantra

Promoting fitness, fun, and community!

Market Analysis and Demographics

This section strictly defines your market in as much detail as possible. Who is it? What do industry statistics say about your market in relation to your product or service? What are the demographics of your location, and what realistic projections can you make about tapping into that market?

A good place to start is the City-Data website (www.City-Data.com), which is one of the most comprehensive online resources on this topic. It provides an enormous amount of demographic information, such as population, education level, median household income, and even neighborhood-specific data. It allowed me to look up the specific downtown area where Jiva Fitness is located. If you can't find your city on this site, you can still get information through the United States Census Bureau (www.census.gov/quickfacts/).

You can find a template for the marketing analysis and demographics section in appendix A and in the web resource (www.HumanKinetics.com/TheBusinessOfPersonalTraining), where you can modify it for your purposes.

Business Plan Example

Market Analysis and Demographics

Jiva Fitness' target market consists of individuals who need or want high-touch personal programming to help them attain their health and fitness goals. With its physical location in downtown Easton, Jiva Fitness will also target the downtown community, both residential and corporate.

Easton, Pennsylvania, has a population of 27,073 with an average age of 32 years. The downtown area itself measures 0.7 square miles (1.8 square kilometers) with a population of 5,296. Easton also hosts Lafayette College. Jiva Fitness will be located one block away from the Easton Police Department and a new $32 million city hall and parking structure. It will be within a few blocks of the heart of the Easton business district, which includes banks, newspaper publishers, shops, and restaurants.

Due to the prevalence of obesity and inactivity in U.S. society, the average health club is not drawing in the population that may need its services the most. Big-box clubs lack intimacy, and low-priced alternatives are low-supervision, equipment-access-only facilities, which may be fine for those who already know what to do but are insufficient for the inexperienced individual. Even though Jiva Fitness will certainly draw in the experienced exerciser, our desire is to engage those who are timid about entering the fitness realm. We want to help those who need it most.

Through group fitness classes, social events, and a nurturing staff of fitness professionals, Jiva Fitness will create a sense of community, as well as specific experiences that will attract and retain members and clients. Its small, intimate space will enhance the individual's sense of belonging.

Competitive Analysis

List all competitors in your area of operation, as well as their specific target markets. Then address your strengths, weaknesses, opportunities, and threats (SWOT) in regard to these companies. This section is not a place to sugarcoat your offerings as compared with those of your competitors. Investors will see through that approach, and they expect you to face challenges. With that in mind, present an honest comparison that shows how your business' strengths and opportunities outweigh its weaknesses and threats. If you find that this is not the case, then it's time to reevaluate your business approach. What could you do to overcome your weaknesses and threats? It is crucial to generate potential solutions before your business starts and fails.

You can find a template for the competitive analysis in appendix A and in the web resource (www.HumanKinetics.com/TheBusinessOfPersonalTraining), where you can modify it for your purposes.

Business Plan Example

Competitive Analysis

Within a 1-mile radius, where we believe we will find most of our clientele, there are only two clubs. Of course, distance "as the crow flies" is not the same thing as driving distance. When we used a GPS device to chart the route from our potential location to those of our competitors, we found that four of five were 9 minutes away and the fifth was 11 minutes away. The driving distance ranged from 2.5 to 3.6 miles (4 to 5.8 kilometers). Table 5.2 compares the services of Jiva Fitness with those of these five closest clubs.

Table 5.2   **Services and Fees of Jiva Fitness and Its Competitors**

	Jiva Fitness	YMCA	Joe Fitness	Club Fitness	Middle Fitness	Big Fitness
Facility type	Studio	Multipurpose	Studio	Fitness club	Fitness club	Multipurpose
Initiation fee ($)				59	99	99
Monthly fee ($)	69	45	65-129	10	19.99	29.95
Open gym use		✓		✓	✓	✓
Cardio equipment	✓	✓	✓	✓	✓	✓
Weight machines		✓	✓	✓	✓	✓
Free weights	✓	✓	✓	✓	✓	✓
Personal training	✓	✓	✓	✓	✓	✓
Personal training fee ($)	42 (half hour) or 65 (hour)	35 (hour)	75 (hour)	68 (hour)	65 (hour)	78 (hour)
Group fitness	✓	✓	✓			✓
Child sitting		✓			✓	✓
Basketball court		✓				✓
Pool		✓				✓
Online payment	✓				✓	✓
Online scheduling	✓					✓
Distance from Jiva Fitness		9 minutes, 2.5 miles (4 km)	9 minutes, 2.7 miles (4.3 km)	9 minutes, 2.6 miles (4.2 km)	9 minutes, 3.6 miles (5.8 km)	11 minutes, 2.5 miles (4 km)

When considering the other fitness facilities, Jiva Fitness' SWOT analysis is as follows:

Strengths

- Jiva Fitness will offer an intimate space and prioritize personal attention.
- Part of our mission is to create a sense of community among our members and clients. This sense of belonging will enhance their experience, keep them coming back, and help them achieve their goals.
- We will offer high-end, licensed group fitness classes from MOSSA.
- All clients and members will be supervised when working out.
- Our personal trainers and instructors are leaders in the industry.
- Jiva Fitness will be the only non-yoga studio within walking distance of the downtown businesses.

Weaknesses

- Small and unable to accommodate a large membership
- No extra offerings such as a pool or childcare
- Limited hours of operation (access only for classes or by appointment)
- Limited selection of equipment
- Higher price than most facilities
- No street visibility (possible sign on building but city approval required due to historic status)

Opportunities

Jiva Fitness is located in the downtown area just a couple of minutes' walk from many businesses. This location allows us to create various corporate fitness options. The first and simplest approach is to offer businesses a discount on services. We are not big fans of discounting services, but we do have the police station two blocks away and will definitely offer the officers a discount. Other possible corporate offerings include lunchtime talks on health and fitness, weight loss programs, healthy-back programs, and worksite classes.

Some of the competing facilities offer a great deal to their members, but there is little outreach to the community. Therefore, we have the opportunity to partner and cross-promote with many of the local businesses. For example, we could tie in with the local farmers' market (which is only three blocks away). Healthy activity + healthy eating = healthy lives! This effort might include cross-promotion via social media, setting up a booth in order to demonstrate healthy cooking techniques (using fresh produce found at the market), or showing various fitness and exercise options.

There are also opportunities to create a referral network of health and wellness services, including massage therapists, registered dietitians, chiropractors, and orthopedic surgeons.

Because of the exceptional quality and experience of the Jiva Fitness owners, they have the opportunity to become the local authorities, possibly writing fitness columns for the local papers and appearing in segments on local television channels. They are also skilled at creating corporate wellness programs, which will be an advantage because the business is located in the middle of the business district.

Threats

New fitness facilities open across the nation every day, and there is no way to know when or where the next one will appear. Only by maintaining our personal connection with our clients and offering the best service around can we hope to ward off the

(continued)

(continued)

threat of any new fitness arrival. Although the contract with MOSSA doesn't allow any other club in the area to offer its programming, similar programming is offered by a couple of other reputable organizations. If our current or future competitors chose to offer these programs, we would have a more challenging time differentiating our class offerings.

Management Plan

This section outlines the key people and key positions in your organization. Who is your facility manager? What is his or her experience? As we've discussed, this manager is likely to be you. However, you still need to spell out your role and qualifications, both for your own clarity regarding responsibilities and to satisfy potential investors. What other positions exist (or will exist) in your company structure—for example, other managers or maintenance staff? Who else have you hired or will you hire, and what do they bring to the table?

You can find a template for the management plan in appendix A and in the web resource (www.HumanKinetics.com/TheBusinessOfPersonalTraining) where you can modify it for your purposes.

Business Plan Example

Management Plan

Management Team

The initial management team consists of Mark Nutting and Heather Nutting.

*Mark Nutting, CSCS*D, NSCA-CPT*D, ACSM HFD, ACSM CEP, RCPT*E, USAW Sports Performance Coach*

Jiva Fitness co-owner, master trainer, and instructor

Mark Nutting comes to the business with the expertise of 35 years of personal training and health club management. In fact, he is literally writing the book on the business of personal training for industry publisher Human Kinetics.

Mark is an international presenter, and his Fitness Boot Camps for the Masses has been a featured presentation at national and international conferences.

A highly skilled group-fitness instructor, Mark is also an award-winning personal trainer who received Personal Fitness Professional's 2016 Trainer of the Year Legacy Award and the 2009 Personal Trainer of the Year award from the National Strength and Conditioning Association.

Here are some of Mark's responsibilities at Jiva Fitness:

- General management
- Community outreach
- Marketing
- Personal training
- Personal training management and development
- Group fitness instruction

Heather Stirner Nutting, NSCA-CPT, ACE CPT, AFAA CPT, postrehab and senior-fitness specialist

Jiva Fitness co-owner, master trainer, and instructor

Heather Nutting has been a personal trainer for 20 years and a health club manager for 15 years. A skilled national presenter, she is also a MOSSA Group Centergy

National Trainer and runs workshops that cover not only the Group Centergy material but also essential principles of business, marketing, and branding.

Here are some of Heather's responsibilities at Jiva Fitness:

- Group fitness management
- Community outreach
- Marketing
- Personal training
- Group fitness instruction
- Group fitness program management and development

Most of the abilities that one needs in order to start and build a business can be found between Heather and Mark. The skills that will be hired out are accounting and payroll.

Accounting and Payroll

PBC Services LLC will be do our accounting and payroll at a rate of $100 per month.

Facility Maintenance

Mark and Heather Nutting will both be responsible for facility maintenance at no additional expense to Jiva Fitness.

Financial Plan

You need to create an all-inclusive financial plan. It should address all start-up costs, such as renovation, equipment, office supplies, computers, insurance, and licenses. It should also include ongoing expenses, such as payroll, rent, utilities, marketing, and cleaning and maintenance supplies.

Along with the anticipated expenses, you will include your projected profits. Where will your revenue come from? What kind of growth do you expect? What does a profit and loss (P&L) analysis show? When do you project that your monthly revenues will surpass your monthly expenses? What is the outlook three years out?

One tool that helps me organize my thoughts about revenues, expenses, and programs is a mind map (see figure 5.1). You can make a mind map as simply as writing on a

Developing a financial plan helps you consider anticipated expenses as well as projected profits.

Getty Images/DigitalVision/People Images

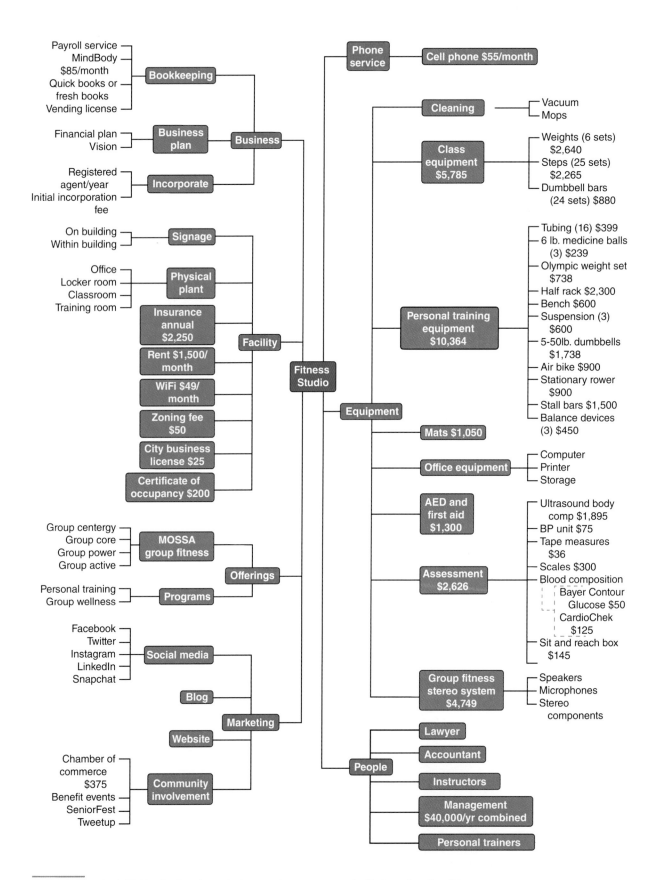

Figure 5.1 An initial brainstorming mind map of expenses and offerings for Jiva Fitness.

napkin or by using any of various online applications; for example, I used MindMeister (www.mindmeister.com). If you go through this exercise, you will be well on your way to getting a good grasp of your expenses. Provide as much detail as you can for each of the branches in the map. This content can then be transferred to the spreadsheets that you create for expenses and income, as shown in table 5.3.

You can find a template for the financial plan in appendix A and in the web resource (www.HumanKinetics.com/TheBusinessOfPersonalTraining), where you can modify it for your purposes.

Business Plan Example

Financial Plan: Start-Up Costs

Table 5.3   **Start-Up Costs for Jiva Fitness**

Budget item	Cost ($)
ONE-TIME FEES (NOT TO BE PAID AGAIN)	
Incorporation fee	534
Zoning approval application	50
City business license fee	25
Certificate of occupancy	200
Equipment costs	
Group fitness weights (4 6-set packs)	2,640
Group-fitness-weight dumbbell bars (24 sets)	880
Fixed weights with various handles (10 @ 4 kg, 10 @ 6 kg)	3,800
Cardio steps (25)	2,265
Wall-mounted stall bars	1,500
Dumbbells (5-50 lbs. [2.3-23 kg])	1,738
Adjustable bench	600
Suspension equipment	600
Tubing	399
Medicine balls	239
Dome balance devices	450
Half rack	2,300
Olympic weights	738
Stationary bike	900
Rowing machine	900
Stereo sound system with microphones and speakers	5,000
Mats	1,050
Cleaning tools	500
Health assessment equipment (e.g., weight scales, body comp tool)	2,626
AED machine	1,300

(continued)

(continued)

Budget item	Cost ($)
Facility set-up	
Phone system	2,000
HVAC	200
Painting	2,000
Wall removal	5,000
Locker rooms	5,000
Lighting	2,000
Stage	500
Signage	300
Fans	800
Furniture	500
Computers, printer, Wi-Fi, backup storage	3,500
ANNUAL FEES (FIRST ANNUAL FEE SHOWN HERE)	
LLC agent fee	235
Insurance	2,250
Music licensing fee	350
Chamber of commerce membership	375
Total for start-up	**56,244**

Now you've figured out what it will cost to open your doors, but what will it take to keep them open? To determine the answer, map out your monthly expenses and revenues. Most expenses are fairly cut-and-dried; others, such as payroll, won't come into play until you're up and running. Do your research by calling the relevant providers to find out what each item costs per month. Revenue projections, on the other hand, require your best guess as to how your business will grow. It's going to take a while to build your business, and you need to project how much growth you will see each month.

Don't get ahead of yourself here. Be realistic, if not somewhat conservative. As a personal trainer, you know that it takes months to build your clientele to the point where your schedule is full. Your business will be no different. The first landmark that every business owner dreams of is the break-even point—the point when your monthly revenues match your monthly expenses. In other words, your business can now start *making* money!

As you create this financial plan, ask yourself how many new members or clients you will pick up each month. How far away is that break-even point? The answer is different for every business and depends on your monthly overhead expenses.

Here is a formula for break-even analysis that calculates the number of personal training sessions or memberships needed to make your revenue meet your expenses:

Break-even point = fixed monthly costs ÷ (price of 1 unit [session or membership] – variable costs [such as % paid to personal trainer])

or

$BEP = FMC \div (P - VC)$

For example, if your fixed monthly costs are $4,233, your average session rate is $65, and your compensation to the personal trainer is 50 percent ($32.50), then your BEP is 4,233 ÷ (65 – 32.5), which simplifies to 4,233 ÷ 32.5 and thus indicates that you need about 130 sessions per month in order to break even.

I realize that most personal trainers tend to think in terms of how many sessions they perform per week rather than per month. To put the calculation in weekly terms, divide the 130 sessions per month by the average number of weeks per month (52 weeks per year ÷ 12 months per year = 4.33 weeks per month). Use that figure to calculate the number of sessions you need per week: 130 sessions per month to break even ÷ 4.33 weeks per month = 30 sessions per week to break even.

Next, make an educated guess at how long it will take you to build up to that point (30 sessions per week) as you create a budget for your business. In the case of Jiva Fitness, we projected that if our prediction of growth happened as planned and we encountered no major surprises in our expenses, then we would be meeting expenses by the end of nine months (the first three months are shown in table 5.4). Remember that the break-even point is specific to each business.

Business Plan Example

Financial Plan: Monthly Expenses and Revenues

Table 5.4   **Monthly Expenses and Revenues for Jiva Fitness**

Budget item	Month 1	Month 2	Month 3
MONTHLY EXPENSES			
Facility and operations expenses			
Rent	$1,500.00	$1,500.00	$1,500.00
Electricity	$200.00	$200.00	$200.00
Loan payment (based on $100,000)	$2,000.00	$2,000.00	$2,000.00
Cable and Internet	$49.00	$49.00	$49.00
Phone	$150.00	$150.00	$150.00
Bookkeeping and payroll services	$100.00	$100.00	$100.00
Water cooler	$40.00	$40.00	$40.00
Online scheduling and payment services	$85.00	$85.00	$85.00
Miscellaneous supplies (e.g., paper, cleaning supplies)	$50.00	$50.00	$50.00
Website maintenance	$59.00	$59.00	$59.00
Payroll expenses			
Management salaries	$3,333.33	$3,333.33	$3,333.33
Instructor compensation ($25/class × # of classes/week × 4.33 weeks/month)	$1,082.50	$2,165.00	$2,165.00
Personal training compensation (50% of personal training revenue)	$363.72	$909.30	$1,363.95
Total monthly expenses	***$9,012.55***	***$10,640.63***	***$11,095.28***

(continued)

(continued)

Budget item	Month 1	Month 2	Month 3
MONTHLY REVENUE			
Membership income			
Class membership fee	$69.00	$69.00	$69.00
Maximum # of class memberships	200	200	200
# of classes/week	10	20	20
Projected # of class memberships sold	10	20	30
Projected monthly member revenue (membership fee × # of memberships)	$690.00	$1,380.00	$2,070.00
Personal training income			
Personal training fee	$42.00	$42.00	$42.00
Personal training maximum sessions/week	40	40	40
Sessions/week	4	10	15
Sessions/month (average of 4.33 weeks/month)	17.32	43.30	64.95
Projected monthly personal training revenue (personal training fee × # of sessions)	$727.44	$1,818.60	$2,727.90
Total monthly revenue	***$1,417.44***	***$3,198.60***	***$4,797.90***
Total net monthly revenue (revenue − expenses)	**−$7,595.11**	**−$7,442.03**	**−$6,297.38**

Now let's look at how some of the numbers used in table 5.4 were determined. The group fitness maximum was set by considering the size of the classroom, which allows for 20 class participants at a time. Thus if we offer 20 classes per week, then we have 400 spots per week; since the average person attends two classes per week, we have space for 200 memberships.

The predictions for revenue growth start with offering 10 classes per week and acquiring 10 group fitness memberships in the first month. Yes, that averages only one person per class. While we could offer fewer classes and charge by the class, we wanted to promote the membership idea from the start. So, we chose to start with 10 classes and build from there. Then we added 10 more classes in the second month and 10 more memberships. In the third month, the class number stayed the same with an expectation of 10 more group fitness memberships.

The personal training maximum per week is essentially 20 sessions per personal trainer per week (the max number that we want to do), and it begins with just Heather and me. This approach gives us a maximum of 40 sessions per week. Of course, both sessions and memberships can increase as we add classes and personal trainers, but that won't take place in the first few months.

The projection for personal training revenue begins by getting 4 sessions per week between two of us for the first month. We build up to 10 per week in the second month and 15 per week in the third month. These predictions are actually a bit on the high side because we want to challenge ourselves to reach that. You may choose to be more conservative in your estimates if you feel that it would help you be more financially prepared for a lower outcome. Either way, you need to realize that you can very easily overestimate or underestimate the actual number. Many people will say that you have to shoot high, but predicting a lower result does not mean stopping when you get there. Instead, you can challenge yourself by asking, "How far can I blow this number out of the water?"

Success results from effective planning.

What assumptions underlie *your* plan? Of course, your growth plan is tied tightly to your marketing plan, which we'll address a bit later. You must also think about the growth of your staff as part of the growth of your revenue. With everything laid out in front of you, you can start to manage by looking at where you might cut expenses and where you might increase revenues. For instance, what other products or services might you offer?

Capital Required

With your financial forecast in hand, and knowing how much funding you can personally bring to the table, how much additional capital do you need? Remember that you are not simply looking for money to open your doors. Covering your start-up costs is not enough, because you will not meet your monthly expenses for some time. For example, in the case of Jiva Fitness, start-up costs totaled $56,244 (table 5.3), and monthly net income was negative in the early months (table 5.4). We projected this additional debt to add up to $37,275.42 over the first eight months of the business' operation. If we left this debt unaddressed, the business would be in financial jeopardy right out of the gate.

As this example illustrates, you need to obtain enough financial assistance both to start up your business and to see you through to the point where the business is self-sustaining (perhaps with a little buffer). That is how much capital you need to give your business a chance to succeed. For Jiva, that's $56,244 + $37,275.42 = $93,519.42 (see table 5.5), which is why the loan amount sought is $100,000. Here it is in the form of a formula:

Start-up costs + accrued debt = capital required

When all goes as planned, each month will bring you a little closer to meeting your monthly expenses. For instance, as you may recall, the Jiva Fitness plan projected meeting monthly expenses by month nine. Table 5.5 shows monthly projections for the first nine months, and you can see the deficit decrease each month. As you consider your projections, you might rethink once again how much you really need in order to get started. Can you find any more places to cut back expenses?

You can find a template for the description of required capital in appendix A and in the web resource (www.HumanKinetics.com/TheBusinessOfPersonalTraining), where you can modify it for your purposes.

Business Plan Example

Capital Required

Table 5.5   **Accrued Monthly Net Losses During Business Growth**

Month	Net ($)
1	−7,595.11
2	−7,442.03
3	−6,297.38
4	−5,152.73
5	−4,008.08
6	−3,404.68
7	−2,260.03
8	−1,115.38
9 (monthly expenses met!)	29.27
Total for months 1-8	**−37,275.42**

Start-up costs:	$56,244.00
Accrued debt before breaking even:	$37,275.42
Total capital required:	$93,519.42

Marketing Plan

In order to build your business, you need to reach your target market; therefore, your marketing plan is critical to your success. To develop your plan, consider your target market carefully, then decide purposefully where to spend your time, effort, and money in order to connect with that market. You might decide, for example, to use social media, create a website, mail out printed items for direct marketing, take out a newspaper ad timed to announce key events or new programs, appear on television (perhaps on a local program devoted to highlighting new businesses), buy a radio ad to play during rush hour, sponsor or host a community activity or event, or use a combination of these options. Map out when your marketing campaigns will happen and how much you will spend on them. Some of your promotions could be timed to address holidays, vacations, key local events, or partnerships with nonprofit fundraisers.

You can find a template for a marketing plan in appendix A and in the web resource (www.HumanKinetics.com/TheBusinessOfPersonalTraining), where you can modify it for your purposes.

Business Plan Example

Marketing Plan

Because Jiva Fitness focuses on creating a connected community, we will rely mainly on approaches that will help us establish relationships with potential members. All of the options are low- or no-cost. They include the following:

- Social media: Jiva Fitness is already creating a presence on social media. Possible avenues include Facebook, Twitter, YouTube, Instagram, LinkedIn, Snapchat,

Pinterest, Tumblr, and others. In creating a connection with potential clients, it is important to create trust and become a valued resource to them. We will do so by providing them with articles on health and fitness from reputable resources, engaging them in conversation, and answering their questions. When trust is built, Jiva Fitness will post offers about personal training and group fitness classes. These advertisement posts will be placed weekly, whereas interaction and information sharing will be ongoing.

- Company website—Jiva Fitness will establish an online presence at www.jivafitness.com that provides a description of our services and important information about our company.
- Grand opening and ribbon-cutting ceremony—This event will be supported by the local chamber of commerce and the Easton Business Association.
- Quarterly open houses—Jiva Fitness will invite the community to join us for free classes, giveaways, and special prizes each January, April, July, and October since those months coincide with the MOSSA quarterly release of new group-fitness material.
- Biannual weight-loss challenge—This free, eight-week challenge will be offered beginning in April and November. Prizes will be donated by local businesses. This effort will require very little management time. Thus it provides an easy way to increase awareness of Jiva Fitness in the community.
- Hosting benefit boot camps—Jiva Fitness will host a Zombie Boot Camp for the whole family on or near Halloween with entry fees benefiting a local charity.
- Networking—Jiva Fitness is located in downtown Easton and anticipates that local business employees will make up a significant part of our membership. We will network with other businesses through groups such as the chamber of commerce, the Easton Business Association, and the Easton Main Street Initiative
- Holidays—Holidays are family events, and Jiva Fitness will offer members free class passes for family members on selected holidays.
- Women's Health Fair—At a cost of $200, Jiva Fitness will rent booth space at the local Women's Health Fair.
- Senior Fest—At a cost of $75, Jiva Fitness will rent booth space at the local Senior Fest.

Guessing the Future

As stated at the beginning of this chapter, a business plan constitutes an educated guess. Therefore, once you have developed your plan, you need to realize that things will not always go according to plan, no matter how carefully you have thought it out. For example, here are two unpredictable developments I've seen:

- Two months after an entrepreneur opened a fitness facility, a similar facility opened just a few blocks away. As you can imagine, the unexpected competition cut into his market and slowed his club's growth.
- Another facility owner projected that her own personal training would account for a major part of the growth of her business. However, she got too busy with running the business and didn't have enough time to take on the number of clients that she had projected.

In a case like this second example, the owner needs to either hire additional personal trainers or outsource her business tasks. The key question is whether the business tasks

can be outsourced. Some tasks—such as data entry, accounting, and facility maintenance—can indeed be given to someone else. However, if what is keeping you busy
involves decisions about your company's brand or vision, then you may be the only
one who knows the company well enough to handle that responsibility. If so, then it's
time to hire another personal trainer.

At the same time, things going differently from what you planned isn't always a bad
thing. Here are a couple of pleasant surprises I've seen:

- One newly opened studio found a huge fan in the owner of a large company
  who sent all of his executives to the studio for training. This windfall boosted
  the studio's growth rate far above the owner's projections.
- Another club benefited when its biggest competitor unexpectedly went out of
  business, thus leaving its entire membership seeking a new place to work out.
  The remaining club gained hundreds of new members in one fell swoop.

More to Come

What I hope you take from this chapter is that writing a business plan is a necessary
part of your business preparation. It forces you to take a fully informed look at your
idea for your business. Each section prompts you to dig a little deeper into the details
that will serve as your guide to building your business.

Here's a summary of those sections. Your *business description* sets the direction
for the key decisions you will make. It explains why you want to create this business,
what problem you will solve, and how you will solve it. The *market analysis and demographics* section documents the fact that your target market exists in the local area in
large enough numbers to make your business viable. The *competitive analysis* examines
your competition and analyzes your own strengths and weaknesses in comparison with
similar businesses in your market. The *management plan* addresses the key players in
your company. Do you have the right people in place to help you build your business?

Next, the *financial plan* presents both the hard numbers indicating what you need
in order to open your doors and the projected numbers for your future income. This
analysis continues in the *capital required* section, where you synthesize the information
contained in the financial plan to determine how much of an investment you need in
order to meet your financial obligations as you work toward your break-even point. The
marketing plan then explains how you will reach your potential market. Specifically,
it indicates where your market can be found, what strategies you will use to create
awareness of your services, how you will establish relationships with members of your
market, and how you will convince them to become members and clients. Finally, the
executive summary pulls it all together, making sure that you can explain your plan
both clearly and concisely.

Once your business plan is complete, you have done your due diligence and are as
prepared as you can be. At the same time, of course, you cannot predict the future,
which means that you should be ready to adapt your plan as the situation changes. If
you allow your plan to be dynamic, it can continue to serve you throughout the life
of your business.

In chapter 6 we'll be discussing the structure of your business. This includes everything
from the legal business entity and whether you should be incorporating to creating a
reporting hierarchy and setting up business systems. Having the right business structure
keeps your business legally safe and running efficiently.

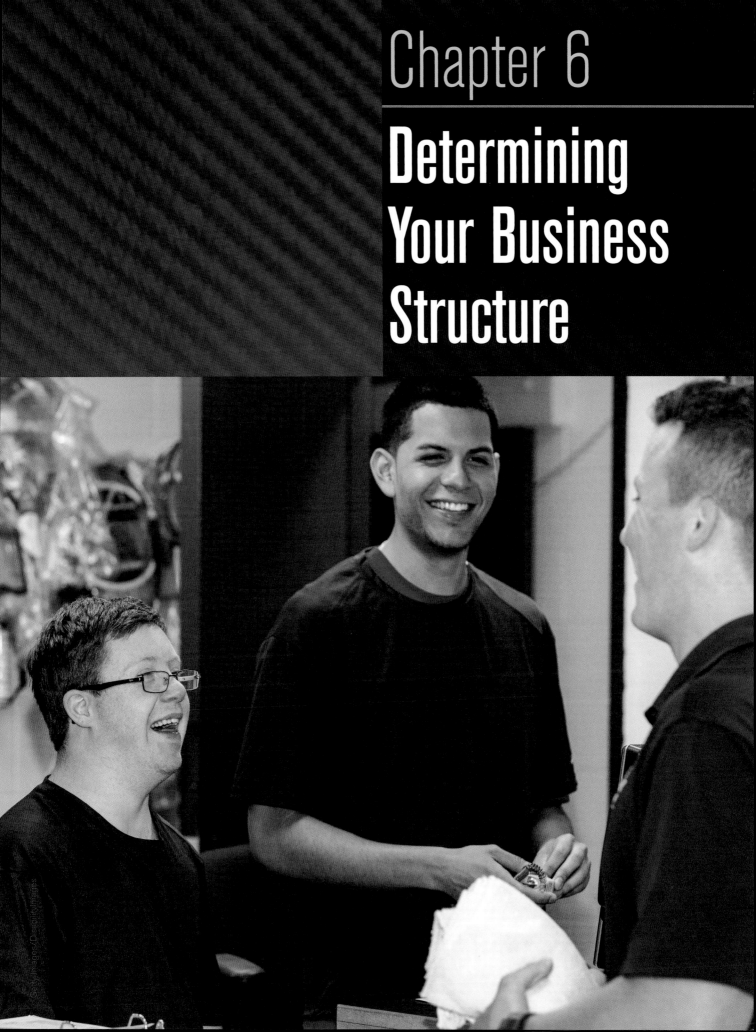

Chapter 6

Determining Your Business Structure

Getty Images/DisabilityImages

Like a house, your business would collapse without an underlying structure. Therefore, this chapter covers the decisions that set the foundation on which your business will operate, regardless of whether you are an independent contractor or a business owner. These decisions address the type of legal entity your business will be, the staffing hierarchy you will establish, and the documentation of the systems you will use to run the business. If you are a personal trainer employed at a fitness facility, then most of the business-related topics discussed in this chapter will not apply to your daily job. However, I recommend that you still read the chapter in order to become aware of how your employer's business has been set up.

Choosing a Type of Business Entity

The type of legal entity that you choose for your business affects how you are protected in matters of law, how you are taxed, and how you run your business. Therefore, you need to consider all of these aspects in order to make the decision wisely. Table 6.1 summarizes the types of entities—sole proprietorship, partnership, S corporation, C corporation, and limited liability company (LLC)—and their primary advantages and disadvantages.

Table 6.1 **Types of Business Entities**

Type of entity	Description	Primary advantage	Primary disadvantage(s)
Sole proprietorship	The business is not separate from the owner.	• It is the simplest type to set up and run. • It is subject to the lowest taxation.	If the business incurs debt, the owner is personally responsible for it.
Partnership	The business has two or more owners.	• It is simple to set up and run. • It is subject to the lowest taxation. • Responsibility is shared.	If the business incurs debt, the owners are personally responsible for it.
C corporation	This structure shields owners from financial liability.	• It can raise money through the sale of company shares. • It allows easy transfer of ownership. • The life of the corporation could be ongoing.	It is more expensive to form and run. It is subject to double taxation. The corporate obligations can be complex and time consuming.
S corporation	This structure shields owners from financial liability.	• It can raise money through the sale of company shares. • It allows easy transfer of ownership. • It is a "pass-through" entity (not taxed as a corporation).	It is limited to 100 shareholders. Shareholders must be U.S. citizens or permanent residents. Dividends must be distributed by ownership.
Limited liability company	This structure shields owners from financial liability.	• It is easier and less costly to form than a C or S corp. • It involves less ongoing paperwork. • It allows flexible distribution of profits. • It is easy to terminate.	It is essentially nontransferable. Owners must pay self-employment taxes and make quarterly payments to the IRS.

Sole Proprietorship

Many personal trainers who are independent contractors or independent personal trainers work as themselves, by themselves, and without giving any special thought to their business as a separate entity. They think, "I'm going out and training people in their homes. They're writing checks addressed to me. I'm just taking care of business." In that case, you are your business, and your business is you. This is a sole proprietorship, which is certainly the easiest way to start a business, because there is no separation between you and the business. It's also subject to the simplest and lowest taxation of any type of business. When filing your tax return, your income, expenses, and losses are reported on IRS Schedule C along with your personal Form 1040.

The ease of setting up and running a sole proprietorship makes it the most common type of business entity. But is it the best one for you? That's the big question, and the answer depends on what services you want to offer and where you want to offer them. As a sole proprietor, you must be personally insured against injury liability claims. For personal trainers, this need is met by obtaining liability insurance through your certifying organization or an insurance agency. Without such insurance, if someone gets injured and brings a lawsuit against you, you could be bankrupt in a heartbeat.

Some other situations may require additional protection. For instance, if, as a sole proprietor, you think you might want to sign a mortgage or long-term lease or purchase equipment on credit, consider the fact that you could find yourself unable to meet your agreed-upon payment schedule. In that case, you could be held personally accountable for the remaining debt. In such situations, a sole proprietorship may not be the best choice; instead, a corporation might be a better option because of the financial liability protection it offers.

Some sole proprietors go one step further to make their business sound more professional by naming it something else—for example, Mark's Fitness rather than simply Mark Nutting—and registering that name with the state as a DBA ("doing business as") or trade name. Creating a DBA gives you the ability to more effectively establish a company brand and allows you to open a business bank account to pay bills and receive income. Understand, however, that simply registering your name doesn't protect you in any way. As sole proprietor, you are still personally liable for all financial obligations.

You must also file for any business licenses or permits required by your state or local government; these requirements differ from state to state. For more information on this topic, see the U.S. Small Business Administration's online resources (U.S. Small Business Administration, n.d.-b & n.d.-c). Examples of forms you are likely to need include the DBA application, state business license, and city business license.

Partnership

Perhaps you don't want to run a business by yourself but you have a friend, colleague, or spouse whom you would like to include in your venture. Businesses shared by two or more individuals are referred to as partnerships. This arrangement allows you to share the responsibilities and benefit from multiple viewpoints regarding how to proceed with the business.

No matter how well you know the other person or persons, a partnership should be formalized by creating a partnership agreement. In it, you must spell out in precise terms how various aspects of the business will be handled—for example, who is responsible for which parts of the business, how finances and profits will be handled, what happens if you go out of business or if one partner leaves, and how business debts will be divided.

Partnerships come in three basic types (U.S. Small Business Administration, n.d.-a):

- General partnerships place equal responsibilities on the owners for operations and liabilities.
- Limited partnerships involve at least one limited or "silent" partner, who provides funds to the business as an investment but carries no responsibility in business operations or liabilities.
- Joint ventures operate like general partnerships but only for a limited time, such as the duration of a special project.

As with a sole proprietor, all partners are personally liable for all financial obligations (with the exception of the limited partner).

Whether you are a sole proprietor or part of a partnership, you are responsible for your own income and Social Security and Medicare taxes. According to the IRS, "As a self-employed individual, generally you are required to file an annual return and pay estimated tax quarterly. Self-employed individuals generally must pay self-employment tax (SE tax) as well as income tax. SE tax is a Social Security and Medicare tax primarily for individuals who work for themselves" (Internal Revenue Service, n.d.). Take care to follow the rules—you do *not* want to mess with the IRS.

Corporations

Corporations are entities that exist beyond their owners. As a result, even though you may be the person who makes legal decisions for the business, it is technically the business that hires, fires, takes on loans, and enters into agreements. In other words, corporations are separate from their owners; as a result, unlike sole proprietorships and partnerships, they provide limited liability protection to their owners or shareholders. This separation means that the owners are liable only for whatever financial amounts they invested in the company.

For example, suppose that my wife, Heather, and I invested $30,000 of our own money in Jiva Fitness. Suppose also that Jiva Fitness couldn't make payments on its business loan and defaulted. Heather and I would not lose any more than the $30,000 we invested. The corporation would be responsible for the rest and would probably need to declare bankruptcy, but that outcome would not reflect on our personal finances.

Corporations also have greater ability to raise money through the sale of shares.

What Do You Have to Lose?

The idea of limiting your liability through an LLC, S corporation, or C corporation is to protect your personal finances and property from liability claims against your company. These approaches create the business as an entity that is separate from the owner (or owners), members, or shareholders. If you do *not* have this legal separation, and litigation is brought against your business, then you face the possibility that any damages awarded could take not only whatever holdings your company has but also anything of value that you own personally, such as your savings, your car, or your home. I strongly recommend that you do *not* take this risk; instead, set your company up as the type of protected entity that best fits your needs and shields your personal assets.

C Corporation

Although the C corporation (C corp) category may be thought of as the "big dog" of corporations because it includes the likes of Microsoft, Apple, Google, General Mills, and Exxon, it is also the default when anyone decides to incorporate a business. In other words, "All corporations are C corporations (under subchapter 'C' of the tax code) unless they file for S status. If you take no action, your corporation is a C corporation" (Wood, 2012).

Many health clubs, particularly chains, are set up as C corps. Others are set up as S corps or LLCs. Your decision about whether to set up your business as a C corp should be based on your long-term vision for the company. How do you want to finance it? How do you want it to be governed?

Here are some advantages of a C corp:

- It allows you to raise money through the sale of shares in the company (which could number in the millions).
- It allows easy transfer of ownership through the sale of shares.
- The life of the corporation can be ongoing (because it is not limited to the life of the owners).

And here are some disadvantages:

- It is more expensive to form and run than are other business entities.
- The corporation is double-taxed; that is, it is taxed on all profits *before* distributing anything to shareholders, who are then taxed again (on the same money) when they receive it as a dividend. This aspect alone usually makes the C corp an undesirable choice for a small business.
- Corporate obligations can be complex and time consuming to fulfill—for example, maintenance of board of directors, regular meetings (with recorded minutes), and substantial paperwork.

S Corporation

An S corporation is so named for the governing rules of subchapter S of chapter 1 of the Internal Revenue Code. Like a limited liability company, an S corp passes the profits through to the owners before they are taxed, thereby avoiding the double-taxation disadvantage of a C corporation. The owners of an S corp are, of course, taxed on their income.

The advantages of an S corporation include the following:

- Like a C corp, it has the ability to sell shares in order to raise capital.
- It allows easy transfer of ownership.
- It is a "pass-through" entity, meaning that it is (usually) not taxed as a corporation. Its shareholders can be paid a competitive salary for the work that they do, and they will pay only the usual income tax on that amount. The S corp can then pay out the remaining net income as dividends to shareholders, and these dividends are taxed at a lower rate than the C corp.

And here are some disadvantages:

- It is limited to 100 shareholders.
- Shareholders must be U.S. citizens or permanent residents.

- Dividends must be distributed by ownership percentage. For example, if you own 10 percent of the shares, you must receive 10 percent of the profits, no matter what level of involvement you have in the company.

Limited Liability Company

Like C and S corporations, an LLC shields its owners from financial liability. Similar to S corps but without the ownership restrictions, LLCs have seen dramatic growth since the IRS first approved them in 1988. In 2013, for instance, more than half of new business registrations in some states were LLCs (Nickels, McHugh, & McHugh, 2013, p. 128), perhaps because an LLC is simpler to organize and administer. It is a hybrid, though, and can file with the IRS as either a corporation or a partnership.

Here are some advantages of an LLC:

- It is easier and less costly to form than a C corp or S corp.
- It requires less ongoing paperwork.
- It allows flexible distribution of profits; for instance, if one owner does more work in the company, that person can receive more of the profits.
- This type of business is easy to terminate.

The disadvantages include the following:

- An LLC is essentially nontransferable without converting to a C corp; therefore, if one of the owners dies or leaves, the LLC probably must dissolve.
- Owners must pay self-employment taxes on income earned and make quarterly payments to the IRS.

LLCs and S corps can both be viable choices for a small-business entrepreneur. I recommend the LLC approach for most fitness-related start-ups because it provides the desired limited liability, is easier to set up and dissolve, and requires less corporate paperwork and red tape. However, when choosing your business entity, consult with a lawyer to make sure that you select what is best for *your* particular needs, the level of liability you are comfortable with, and your vision for your company.

Developing an Organizational Structure

Beyond choosing your legal business structure, you also need to make decisions about the organizational structure. This is where you define staff responsibilities and establish a clear line of reporting. The organizational structure of a business typically depends in large part on its size.

The importance of setting up an effective organizational structure has been recognized for many years. Henri Fayol, acknowledged as one of the founders of modern management, first published his principles of company structure in 1916 in French, and the text was translated into English in 1929 and again in 1949 (Brodie, 1962). The remarkable thing is that what Fayol wrote in 1916 is still being used today.

Let's review Fayol's principles and consider how they might apply to what we do as personal trainers. Many of these principles may seem obvious, but that's because they have become so ingrained in the business world that we now take them for granted. After this review, I'll expand on some options that are more contemporary and more flexible. At whatever level you work—and whether with or within a fitness facility—you'll recognize one or more of these principles and likely see them play out on a daily basis.

1 **Division of work:** When employees are divided into groups or teams and assigned a specific task, they become more skilled and efficient at doing it. Therefore, when you work as a full-time personal trainer, you develop greater skills and become more efficient in working with clients. Part-time personal trainers, of course, do not accumulate as many hours of experience and therefore may be less skilled.

2 **Authority:** Managers must be granted the authority to tell their employees what to do. The managers must accept the responsibility and be accountable for seeing that the task gets done. In the fitness setting, a personal training manager or director must be able to demand certain things of the personal trainers on staff in order to help the company achieve its goals.

3 **Discipline:** For me, discipline boils down to the notion that every employee should pull his or her own weight; when that doesn't happen, an appropriate punishment or penalty should be implemented. I once worked for a facility owner who gave me no way to discipline the personal trainers on my staff when they were late turning in their payroll sheets. As a result, I had to approximate their pay for the bookkeeper, then adjust it during the next pay period. This situation did two things: made more work for me and established that it was okay to not turn in payroll sheets on time. The problem could have been corrected easily by saying, "No payroll sheet, no pay."

4 **Unity of command:** As the saying goes, "Too many cooks spoil the soup." Employees must each report to only one direct manager or supervisor in order to have a clear sense of who is leading them. Of course, this issue can get clouded in our industry. As a fitness director at a previous facility, I was in charge of all of the personal trainers. My wife, Heather, the group fitness manager, was in charge of all classes and instructors. Therefore, when she did personal training, she worked under my direction; similarly, when I taught group fitness classes, I worked under her direction. The key here is that if you work in multiple departments, your duties at the moment dictate who you report to.

5 **Unity of direction:** Under the one manager or supervisor, the organization or department should pursue one shared goal. As you might have guessed, this unity derives from the business' mission statement and mantra (see chapter 5), which move everyone in the same direction.

6 **Subordination of individual interests to the general interest:** Simply put, the company's interests come first. Anything you wish to do must not take the place of,

A clear organizational structure can lead to autonomy, unity, and esprit de corps.

Monkey

or conflict with, the company's priorities. When you work as an employee of a fitness club, you must always support the club's mission and do nothing that undermines it. If you are an independent contractor or independent personal trainer working within multiple facilities, then you need to follow the rules and guidelines set by the specific facility in which you are training a client at the moment.

❼ Remuneration: Employee compensation must be fair and act as a motivator for productivity. Compensation doesn't always have to come in the form of money, but it does have to be reasonable in order to retain an employee. Of course, if you are an employee yourself, then this principle supports *your* getting paid a fair wage.

❽ Centralization: This concept refers to how close employees are to the decision-making process. Fayol seemed to favor centralization, or keeping employees relatively far from the decision-making process. This approach might be likened to the classic top-down style of management, in which all decisions are made at the top of the hierarchy and passed down through the ranks. This system of "What I say goes!" provides certain advantages for those at the top, but it may not be best for employees on the front line—or even for the company itself—since it leaves the people doing the work out of the loop of deciding how that work is to be done. Nowadays, many companies use a more decentralized structure that allows for a much freer flow of ideas and solutions from all employees. For me, the best approach is to involve your employees sufficiently to give you a sense of what they have to deal with and then make the decision that is best for all involved—including the company and its employees. And if you are an employee, speak up and provide your opinion when you feel you have something of value to say.

❾ Scalar chain: The word *scalar* simply refers to establishing a clear chain of command or structural hierarchy and ensuring that employees understand where they stand in that chain. They must know, in other words, who to go to if an issue arises with a club member that they don't have the authority to handle. This topic is discussed further in the next section.

❿ Order: This item has been translated in different ways. It seems to include everything from keeping the workplace clean and safe to minimizing the waste of effort and materials. For our purposes, it means that operational systems found in a health club should be followed closely in order to maximize both safety and efficiency.

⓫ Equity: Managers should treat all employees equally, with both kindness and justice, and all employees should treat their supervisors with kindness and respect.

⓬ Stability of tenure of personnel: Employee turnover costs the business money, and management should seek to retain productive employees. In fact, turnover constitutes a huge expense because of the time, effort, and financial drain involved in training a new employee. It happens both with service desk employees and personal trainers.

⓭ Initiative: Management should empower employees to use their own initiative as it benefits the organization. This principle may seem a bit at odds with Fayol's notion of centralization, but employees who are empowered feel better about doing their jobs. As a result, they can help make the company more efficient and help more people in the moment. Heather and I saw a negative example of this principle while checking out a class at a nearby club. It turned out that the club's website had listed the wrong time, and the class was already starting when we arrived. In addition, the service desk attendant said that we had to see a salesperson before we could take the class, but the salesperson was busy at the moment. When we asked if we could see her after we took the class, the attendant said, "I can't let you do that. I would get in trouble." We left.

⓮ Esprit de corps: Fayol understood that a company's success depends on company spirit and unity among employees. This principle is even more highly valued today.

Every company wants its employees to be happy team players, and every employee wants to work in a positive environment. Realizing this vision depends in large part on establishing a strong mission statement and mantra and hiring individuals who share those values. Doing so creates a team with united purpose and camaraderie as members work toward achieving the same goal.

Setting a Chain of Command or Reporting

A staffing hierarchy is essentially an established chain of command, or reporting structure. In Fayol's terms, it is the scalar chain. A classic hierarchical structure for a sizable company includes many levels between the owner or president and the front-line workers (that is, those who deal directly with customers). A flat organizational structure, in contrast, contains fewer steps from the owner or CEO to the frontline workers. One school of thought holds that it is better to use a flatter organization that is more in touch with workers. This really depends on the size of the organization. I used to work for a health club company that employed more than 1,700 personal trainers. Can you imagine the chaos if all of them had reported directly to the CEO (not to mention all of the employees of other departments)? That just doesn't work; there has to be a hierarchy.

Having said that, the idea of being in touch with the front line is great. Who knows better than frontline workers whether our clients like our programs, classes, and equipment? One way to hear from these workers is to encourage them to provide honest feedback about what clients and members are saying. You can also empower these employees to offer solutions to any issues that arise. Adopt the ideas that are viable and give credit to the employees who come up with them.

Another way of being more in touch with frontline workers is to engage in "management by wandering around," a practice made famous by the 1982 book *In Search of Excellence* (Peters & Waterman). This technique is used by many department managers, general managers, and owners. The idea is to get out of the office and be

Employee chain of command is important no matter the size of your club.

Getty Images/Disability:Images

more accessible to the employees who work for you: talk with everyone you can at all levels, ask for their suggestions, and answer their questions. For this technique to be valuable, you must make it a regular routine, not a one-time deal. If you are an employee and are approached in this manner by a manager or supervisor, be outgoing and responsive. It's a chance for you to make a good impression and show that you are a valuable member of the company!

Common Hierarchical Structures

Figures 6.1 through 6.4 lay out some common business structures using health club examples: a departmental structure (figure 6.1), a target-market segmentation structure (figure 6.2), a geographic-region structure (figure 6.3), and the flat structure of Jiva Fitness. These examples are fairly straightforward, but in actual practice a company's structure may involve a combination of types. Imagine, for instance, a company with global reach. It may include departments assigned to specific geographic regions but also separate management units for certain product types within each region. For example, fitness equipment companies typically have regional representatives and, if they have multiple lines of equipment, they may have different representatives for each line, in each region. Companies may also use separate management for functions such as marketing and sales within each segment (what marketing works in the United States may not work in Asia). The key is to find out what structure will best suit your company.

Figure 6.1 shows the classic, hierarchical reporting structure of a health club separated by departments.

In contrast, figure 6.2 shows the hierarchical structure of a health club separated by target clientele. This approach is less common, but I have seen it used in some clubs where each client group, or membership category, has its own director, marketing team, and program coordinator.

Figure 6.3 shows the hierarchical structure of a health club chain separated by geographic regions. This model is typically found in larger organizations and usually integrates the classic structure shown in figure 6.1 as you go down the levels of the hierarchy.

Figure 6.4 shows the flat organizational structure of Jiva Fitness. This model is very common among small studios. My wife, Heather, and I share ownership but separate

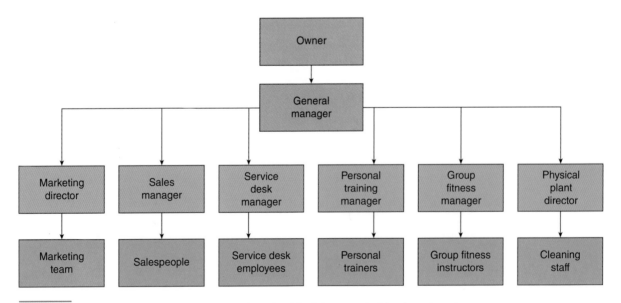

Figure 6.1 Hierarchical reporting structure for a health club separated by departments.

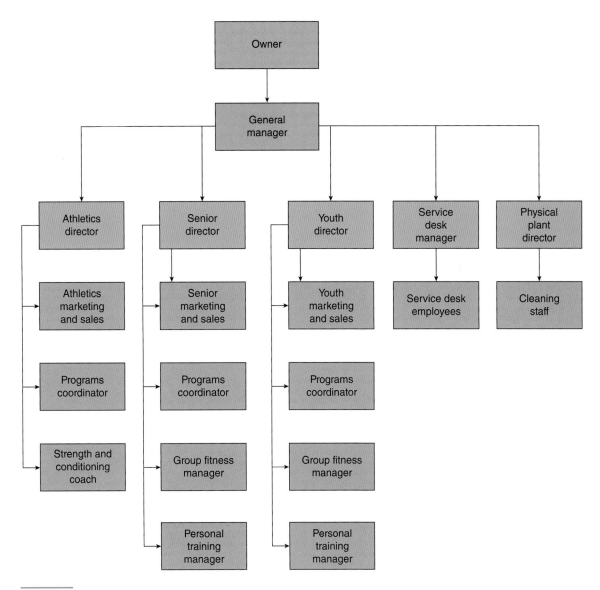

Figure 6.2 Hierarchical reporting structure for a health club separated by target clientele.

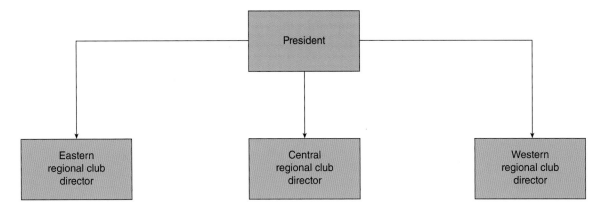

Figure 6.3 Hierarchical reporting structure for a health club chain separated by geographic regions.

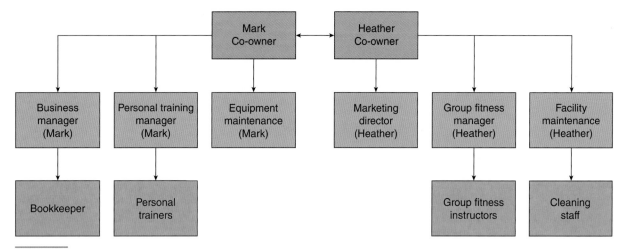

Figure 6.4   The flat organizational structure of Jiva Fitness, in which each person fills several roles.

the responsibilities to prevent confusion about who does what. Our business doesn't have a classic breakdown because I play various roles, including co-owner, business manager, personal training manager, and handler of equipment maintenance. Heather also serves as co-owner while playing various other roles. Thus we, the owners, are connected directly to the frontline staff and sometimes *are* the frontline staff. If you decide to create a fitness start-up, you may find that this management "stacking"—in which one person wears many hats—works best for you, too, at least in the beginning.

Developing Systems

Let's say that you have spent years becoming a very good, in-demand personal trainer. You have a way of putting people at ease and eliciting the strongest commitment and effort from them; as a result, your clients tend to reach their health, fitness, and performance goals. That's your reputation, and it's true (you're just being honest!). Now you want to help more people, but you have only so many hours during the day to work with them. What do you do? Hire more people, right? But, how can you do that if you are the only personal trainer who can do what you want done in the way that you want it done?

In the old days, skilled tradespersons would arrange for an apprentice to learn the nuances of the work and help with the business. Then, on completion of an apprenticeship, the learner was free to either continue working with the same boss or start a new business. The problem with apprenticeships is that they are very time consuming for the teacher; therefore, if you're already running short on time, then you need to find another way.

One solution is to develop systems that teach others to replicate what you do. In fact, you've already developed systems that you use to do your own work. You know exactly what to do and how to do it. What you may not have done is document what you do in a way that others can digest and learn. To begin this process, document everything you do in a day. Here's an example:

❶ Arrived at 5:45 a.m. to open the studio.

❷ Unlocked the front door.

❸ Turned on the lights.

❹ Turned off the auto-answer for the phones.

❺ Turned on the computer.

❻ Flipped the sign from "Closed" to "Open."

❼ Answered the phone.

❽ (Re)scheduled a personal trainer's client.

❾ And so on . . .

This is a great start, but to get exactly what you want from a new hire—or to replicate the process for a second location, you should take it further. Here is the same list annotated with questions to help you flesh out your documentation:

❶ Arrived at 5:45 a.m. to open the studio. *What does arriving at this time allow you to do? Why is it important to be there at this time?*

❷ Unlocked the front door. *Is there anything else someone needs to know about this in order to do it right? For instance, I once had a set of double doors that required me to unlock the first door with a key, then flip a top lever and a bottom lever in order to open the second door.*

❸ Turned on the lights. *Where are they located?*

❹ Turned off the auto-answer for the phones. *Where is it? How do you turn it off?*

❺ Turned on the computer. *Where is it? How do you turn it on?*

❻ Flipped the sign from "Closed" to "Open." *On the front door? Why is this done after everything gets turned on?*

❼ Answered the phone. *What greeting do you want your employees to use? What should their tone of voice be?* (The answer may seem obvious, but it will not be clear to everyone. Spell it out.)

❽ (Re)scheduled a personal trainer's client. *How do you do this? What's the procedure?*

❾ And so on . . .

Ultimately, you're creating an operations manual. The more you document, and the more detail you include, the easier it will be to train a new hire or to help current employees move to a different role. You can also get more creative if you like. For instance, go beyond paper and video-record what you do. Make it as easy as you can for people to do what you want. If something changes in a procedure, make the corrections in the manual and retrain the appropriate staff as a group so they can hear each other's questions and your answers.

Most companies maintain a general employee manual that discusses matters such as the company's history, mission, general rules, and benefits. In addition, every department should have its own operations manual. For instance, procedures used at the service desk differ greatly from procedures used by the group fitness instructor, and these differences should be reflected in the content of their respective manuals.

One good starting point for creating a department manual is to state the department's purpose within the company and how it relates to the company's mission. Next, include a position or job description for each employee in that department, documenting the position's specific responsibilities and expectations. The rest of the manual should mainly address how to do the required tasks in that department—for example, how to dress (such as wearing a uniform), how to greet people, or how to structure a workout. The more you want things done in a particular way, the more detail you should include in the manual.

More to Come

If you're thinking, "This is not what I signed up for," don't worry! This is the sometimes tedious process of setup, and it pays off in the long run. Choosing the right business entity sets you up to protect yourself and keep as much as possible of what you earn. Clarifying your organizational structure defines responsibilities and lines of reporting. Developing and documenting your procedural systems simplifies the process of training new employees to do what you want them to do in the way you want it done. All of this work sets the stage for an easier entrepreneurial life. But don't kick back just yet—plenty of additional challenges lie ahead!

With your company structure determined, it's time to think about your employees. Maybe you need a full staff right at the start or maybe you are small enough that you may not need or want to hire. Doing it all yourself can last only for a short time. Building your business requires that you spend time working on the business and not in the business. At some point, you will have to delegate daily tasks to others so that you can work on the big picture of where you want to take your business. The next chapter will take you through the process of hiring your staff.

Chapter 7
Screening and Hiring Your Staff

Getty Images/Morsa Images

Have you ever gone to a store, restaurant, or fitness center where the staff was inattentive, or even rude? How did you feel about the company? Experiences like that lead me to wonder if the owners know how bad their staff is. I also lose interest in ever going go back there. Now think of a time when you had a good experience with a company's staff. For instance, every time I walk into an Apple store, I leave wanting not only to come back but also to work there.

As these scenarios illustrate, hiring and training the right people for the right jobs is one of the most important roles you will play as a business owner. Getting the right people doing the right work creates a positive experience for your customers and helps them want to come back.

But what if you don't have your own staff? What if you're part of someone else's staff? This chapter still is relevant for you! If you understand what an employer looks for in a new hire, you have an advantage when you look for a job and go through the interview process. The guidelines presented here will give you valuable insight into how a potential boss defines your target job and uses certain criteria to evaluate you during an interview. This perspective will enable you to anticipate questions and plan your answers. As a result, you'll make it easy for the employer to choose the best person for the job: you!

Determining Your Staffing Needs

In the chapter 6 discussion of common hierarchical structures, the specific positions described happen to be positions that are common in our industry. That doesn't mean, however, that you have to hire for those positions. Hiring staff is not about filling standard roles. It's about hiring for your particular needs. In other words, if you're thinking about hiring someone, then you have identified some required tasks that you either can't do, don't want to do, or don't have time to do. Therefore, you need to find someone else to do them. What exactly are those tasks? Make a list of them. What type of ability or expertise is needed to do them well? Add that information to your list.

Typical Tasks That Need Doing

Here are some common positions and tasks:

- **Ownership, general management, vision:** With rare exception, this is you. It's your job to set the foundation and directions of your company and to be accountable for making sure that it performs how you want it to.

- **Marketing:** You will make no sales if people don't know about you and care enough to check you out. The person who does your marketing drives interest in your company and should possess a savvy understanding of marketing media (including social media). He or she must also thoroughly understand your company and its mission.

- **Sales:** Salespeople need to be personable, warm, and caring individuals. They also need to be knowledgeable about the company's values and products and skilled at helping people discover how your facility can help them solve their problems.

- **Member services:** At some level, providing service to your members is every employee's job, but the specific role referred to as member services typically applies to a reception or service desk manager and his or her employees. In my view, the most important function of this role is to greet members as they enter and wish them well as they leave. These employees are the gatekeepers of your business, and they determine the first and last impressions that your members and clients have of your facility. Therefore, it is essential for you to fill these positions with people who are warm, friendly, and outgoing. They should also be able to smoothly handle any questions or issues that members may have.

- **Personal training management:** In the beginning, you may be your business's only personal trainer, but as soon as you have multiple personal trainers working, someone needs to be in charge of their ongoing education and performance. This person must not only understand personal training but also be able to coach personal trainers to help them reach their full potential, both in your club and in their careers.

- **Group fitness class programming:** If you offer classes, then you should hire someone who understands your club demographics, group fitness options, and how to structure a balanced program to meet your members' needs. This individual should also be skilled at coaching group fitness instructors on technique and presentation.

- **Facility care and upkeep (operations):** It is crucial to keep your facility clean, the equipment functioning, and all walkways clear and safe. To help meet these needs, you may decide to contract with an exercise equipment maintenance service and an HVAC service. Even so, you also need a person to handle facility care and upkeep, and this person should take pride in how the facility looks, be able to fix common facility problems, be attentive to details, and be warm and friendly. Yes, like everyone else in your facility, this person too should be warm and friendly, partly because these qualities make anyone easier to work with and also because this person will interact with members and therefore affect their relationship with your company.

- **Childcare:** If you offer childcare, the person in charge of it must love kids, love parents, and be able to skillfully manage both—oh yes, and be warm and friendly! (See a theme here?)

- **Bookkeeping (accounting):** This individual could work either on- or off-site. Either way, he or she should be highly skilled at accounting for businesses and, preferably, have specific experience in health club accounting.

Depending on the size of your staff and facility, some individuals may hold more than one of these positions. For example, figure 6.4 (in chapter 6) illustrates how I play the roles of co-owner, business manager, personal training manager, and equipment maintenance manager while also working as a personal trainer and group fitness instructor. My wife, the other co-owner, also plays multiple roles. As our company grows, we will hire others to take over some of these roles. Similarly, as you start out, you may find yourself needing to do as much as you can on your own. Do not, however, attempt something that you're not ready for or that requires you to sacrifice time and energy needed for other crucial tasks, such as making an income. In short, hire others when you need to.

Full-Time, Part-Time, or Contracted Staff

Another thing to consider is whether the position requires a full-time or part-time staff person or can best be handled by an independent contractor. For positions where you want something done in a certain way because it is integral to the success of your business, hire employees. As for the question of full-time or part-time, simply determine how much time is required to do the job. Hiring a full-time employee generally means that you agree to pay for 30 or more hours of work per week. Do you need that many hours? Can you afford to pay for a full-time employee?

Only you can answer that question for your business. My standard for personal trainers is to hire part time with the potential to build to full time. This approach gives you the option to limit the person's hours initially (thus minimizing overhead). Then, as the personal trainer builds clientele and fills more hours, he or she can achieve full-time status. With other staff positions, you might start by having them work part time, as needed. That could be someone to manage social media or to manage client relations—or whatever you need.

Thus if you are not an owner but are hired to work as a personal trainer, then you may find that you're offered part-time hours at first. However, if you strive to excel in your role, then you could be looking at full-time hours in no time.

It is common, especially in the early years of a new club, to hire a third-party company to provide cleaning services on a part-time schedule (e.g., every other day) or to process biweekly or monthly payroll checks for staff. Independent contractors can be a good choice for such tasks because they simply do what they are hired to do (usually off-site, in their own office), and you don't have to manage how they do it. In addition, your business pays employment taxes only for employees, not for independent contractors, thus saving you money.

Defining Staff Duties and Roles

For every position in your business, you must define its specific roles and duties. Clarifying expectations in this way enables new employees to confidently give you the help you need in order for your business to succeed, which makes everyone happier. For example, if you need a personal trainer who can provide one-one-one training *and* teach group fitness, then define the position that way. To avoid potential confusion, you might name the position something other than the usual title of "personal trainer"—for example, "fitness all-star." Then, lay out precisely what is expected from an individual who hired as an "all-star" in a job description that is clear, enticing, and empowering. Here is an example:

> Fitness all-stars are confident, outgoing, talented fitness professional hybrids who excel at personal training, group fitness, interpersonal communication, and teamwork. They are expected to build their personal training clientele to a minimum of 20 client sessions per week and to teach at least three group fitness classes per week. All-stars make themselves available 10 minutes before and 10 minutes after each class that they teach in order to connect with and answer questions from class participants. They also proactively schedule three half-hour meet-and-greet sessions per week. These sessions are intended to welcome members as they enter the club, ask how the member is doing, and answer any questions that the member has.

The job description should explain the responsibilities associated with the role played by the position in your company. It should not, however, go into too much depth. When you fill the position, the person you hire will find the nuts and bolts of how to do the job in the relevant operations manual (as described in chapter 6). This detailed description will help the employee complete daily, weekly, and monthly tasks in the way that you would like.

As for the "fitness all-star" job title and description, I just made them up. (I do like the idea and may use it. If you would like to use it as well, please feel free to do so.) The point is that you can define each role or position in exactly the way you would like and then title it whatever you like. For instance, Roseanne Barr referred to her television role as that of "domestic goddess." And you can call yourself, or any position you create, by any name you like; in fact, many companies are exploring this kind of creativity. You can even use crazy titles, such "growth hacker" or "dream granter," as long as you clearly define the associated roles and responsibilities.

Hiring to Fit Your Business Culture

Your mission statement and mantra should set the direction for your staff, but these two elements alone do not make up the company's culture. That culture, or flavor, is more a question of what "feel" you want your business to have. If this line of thought strikes you as too touchy-feely, fear not—it's more than that. In fact, it needs to be a main consideration in your hiring process, because any new employee should enhance your company's flavor.

In Lorraine Grubbs-West's book on Southwest Airlines, *Lessons in Loyalty* (2005, p. 11), she quotes a Southwest employment ad: "If you want to have fun, this is the place to work! This is a place where you can be yourself, where it's okay to be irreverent, where you will be loved and valued, where Elvis has been spotted ([founder] Herb Kelleher in costume, no less), and where 'wearing pants is optional!'" Of course, some sort of outer clothing is required, but it's not unusual to see Southwest flight attendants wearing khaki shorts and polo shirts. The Southwest ad gives a sense of what it would be like to work for the airline and indicates that its culture values being free to have fun, as well as being loved and valued by the company. Of course, the company expects its employees to extend that fun, love, and value to Southwest's customers.

Advertising Open Positions

At this point, you've defined the work that needs to be done, determined the expertise and time required to do it right, decided what to call the position responsible for doing

It's important to hire employees that fit the culture of your business.

it, and developed a clear job description. Now it's time to communicate this information to potential employees by advertising the position. The more clearly you lay out your expectations, the less time you will spend wading through interviewees who don't have what you're looking for.

Some posting venues restrict how much information you can provide or charge by the word or line. For these outlets, create an abbreviated but still-descriptive version of your advertisement. Other venues offer affordable full-page ads that allow you to provide a great deal of information. In these cases, include both the full job description and a company overview to give prospective hires a good sense of what it would be like to work for you. See the sidebar for short and long examples of the same ad.

Short and Long Ads

Before advertising an open position, develop both a short version and a long version of the job description. At Jiva Fitness, we might describe an open "fitness all-star" position as follows.

Abbreviated Ad

Jiva Fitness is looking for confident, outgoing, talented fitness professional hybrids who excel at personal training, group fitness, interpersonal communication, and being team players. These fitness all-stars are expected to build their personal training clientele to a minimum of 20 client sessions per week and teach at least three group fitness classes per week. We want our employees to feel like we are a big family. We want them to have fun and enjoy themselves, feel valued and supported, and pass on the same kind of feeling and experience to our members.

Long Job Description

If you are an experienced, passionate fitness professional who wants to be part of an exciting fitness company, join the Jiva Fitness team!

OUR STORY

Jiva (pronounced "Jeeva") Fitness is a boutique fitness studio located in the Easton Arts building in downtown Easton, Pennsylvania. It was founded by nationally experienced fitness presenters Mark Nutting and Heather Stirner Nutting. We are a fitness couple with nearly 60 years of combined experience in the fitness industry. Having worked in health club management for larger clubs, we are now building a fitness solution that focuses on human connection and nurturing support while delivering the most current and effective programs available.

At Jiva Fitness, we create an environment where members are guided, encouraged, and challenged—all while having fun! If people enjoy their workouts and receive sound fitness guidance and support, they are far more likely to continue and to achieve the results they seek. Jiva Fitness provides a high-touch workout experience that can make all the difference.

We're now seeking a "fitness all-star" to help us grow our community of fitness participants. This person needs to be a confident, outgoing, talented fitness professional hybrid who excels at personal training, group fitness, interpersonal communication, and teamwork. We want our employees to feel like we are a big family. We want them to have fun, feel valued and supported, and pass on the same kind of feeling and experience to our members.

A Note About Diversity

The process of screening and hiring staff will be affected by the question of diversity. If your staff is too homogeneous, some people may feel less comfortable. For example, if your staff members are all males, then potential clients who would feel more comfortable working with a woman will look to join another club. The same could be true if your staff members are all very young, or all one race, or religion, or—you get the point. Thus you might consider hiring someone from a demographic in which you are weak or who reflects your target audience in order to help draw in more clients and members. Thankfully, you've already done research in this area when you worked on

A qualified Jiva fitness all-star is

- an experienced personal trainer who currently holds a third-party-accredited certification,
- an experienced group fitness instructor,
- CPR and AED certified,
- a fitness evangelist who loves sharing the gift of health and fitness with others,
- comfortable speaking in front of groups of people,
- organized and attentive to details,
- a team player who looks for the chance to help fellow teammates,
- a natural salesperson who knows that selling is our opportunity to help others,
- skilled at building relationships both in person and through social media, and
- lighthearted and fun!

A Jiva fitness all-star will

- build his or her personal training business to a minimum of 20 client sessions per week;
- teach at least three group fitness classes per week;
- be available 10 minutes before and 10 minutes after each class to connect with and answer questions from class participants;
- lead monthly intro classes;
- proactively schedule three 30-minute meet-and-greet sessions per week to welcome members as they enter the club, ask how they are doing, and answer any questions they have;
- attend biweekly staff meetings; and
- attain eight continuing education credits per year (ongoing education is a priority at Jiva Fitness).

COMPENSATION

Fitness all-stars receive a competitive hourly wage, a continuing education stipend, and opportunities to earn bonuses.

If this description sounds like you, then join the Jiva Fitness team and become a fitness all-star!

your business plan. The information gathered in your market analysis yielded demographic data about the local community and your target audience that should help shape your decisions about staffing.

Getting the Word Out

Now it's time to get the word out that you are looking for help. In the old days, we would simply place an ad in the Help Wanted section of the local newspaper. You can still do that, but, generally speaking, people nowadays are less likely to read the paper (though it depends on the local community). Instead, most people tend to get information from websites and social media. The same holds true for job seekers in particular; that is, most people now search online.

If the type of person you're looking for may not be working in the fitness field, then you could use a general job site, such as Monster, Indeed, CareerBuilder, or Simply Hired. If you're looking for fitness-related personnel, then you might use GymJOB, FitnessJobs, ExerciseJobs, or Healthclubs.com (IHRSA's consumer website, which includes a jobs section). I also see more and more clubs placing ads on Craigslist because doing so is cost free and the site attracts local applicants. Finally, if you want the employee to hold a particular fitness certification, you may able to post a listing on a job board maintained by the certifying association. For example, the American College of Sports Medicine and the National Strength and Conditioning Association each maintain a job board.

My own favorite place to start is the realm of social media. For instance, LinkedIn, though more social than it used to be, still focuses primarily on networking for business. Other viable venues for announcing open positions at no cost include Facebook, Twitter, Google Plus, Instagram, and even Snapchat. As with the Southwest Airlines ad described earlier, a creatively written ad piques interest and may attract a special candidate who would not otherwise consider your open position. In addition, if you describe your company with flair, job postings can create curiosity among potential clients and members. The use of social media is discussed further in the chapter devoted to marketing.

Connecting Face to Face

There are, of course, other ways to connect with future hires. These options—job fairs, internships, and club members who end up joining the staff—are typically more time consuming and usually not as useful for a start-up business. However, if your business continues to grow, you will continue to need to hire more help. Therefore, you should always be looking for great new people who might fill future positions. The methods discussed here offer good ways to start a recruiting process for your company.

Job fairs, often held at colleges and universities, can be an effective means for meeting prospective hires. Some job fairs narrow the field—focusing, for example, on health professionals—but they often address all professions. The organizers of a typical job fair at a university may charge you $150 for the right to set up a booth or table during the three to six hours that an average fair runs. In addition to the table or space, the fee often includes Wi-Fi and power access, but ask to be sure; the details of what your fee buys you will vary from one fair to another. The fair's hosts usually promote a list of the participating businesses, and that in itself can provide you with good visibility among job seekers.

If your facility is located near a college or university, consider offering internships for students. This option not only lets you give back to the industry by providing on-the-job training for up-and-coming fitness professionals; it also gives you direct access to potential employees. I've hosted quite a few interns and found it to be a great way to "try before you buy," so to speak. Some of my interns were not right for our company, but others became great employees.

Last, though it may seem backward, we've also invited select members who had the right stuff—that is, they were smart and social, enjoyed the club and its members, and loved the fitness world—to "graduate" to becoming a staff member. You can guide such individuals to the right certifications, coach them through the learning process, and hire them once they are certified. They tend to become dedicated, loyal employees.

Interviewing Prospects

Interviewing potential hires is a crucial step in the process of getting the right people in the right positions to allow your company to grow as you want it to. I can also tell you, based both on personal experience and on reports from managers all over the United States, that hiring and retaining the right employees is one of the biggest challenges faced by fitness facilities on a regular basis. This challenge derives in part from the fact that potential employees can put on their best face during an interview and then, after being hired, let down their guard and let their true colors show. Possible negative results can range from habitually showing up late to showing every emotion they feel to members and clients. There are also some hires who have good potential but leave because it takes too long (in their eyes) to build their business. This outcome, of course, leaves the employer looking to fill the position yet again.

The step-by-step process I use for interviewing is designed to apply increasingly specific criteria in order to determine whether a potential hire is the right one for the job. If you've gone through the job description process described earlier in this chapter,

Having a clear interview process is essential when looking to hire new staff.

Getty Images/Morsa Images

then you'll come to the interview with a clear idea of what the right person should know and be able to do.

Reviewing the Resume and Cover Letter

The first screening tools at your disposal are the applicant's resume and cover letter. Use them to get an idea of the person's education, professional experience, and longevity with previous employers. The cover letter can also reveal certain basic skill levels, such as the ability to express oneself with a good vocabulary, use proper grammar, and communicate in a formal and respectful manner.

In addition, the applicant should provide three to five professional references (if the applicant is just out of school, then he or she may present references from instructors). You can check the references before speaking with a candidate, but I usually wait until after we meet face to face. This approach saves you the time you would otherwise spend checking on applicants who end up not making it to the in-person interview stage.

Conducting a Phone Interview

Candidates who make it past the first step qualify for a brief phone interview to determine whether they have the personality and speaking ability to warrant bringing them in for a face-to-face interview. Ask about anything that raises a question in your mind when you read the applicant's resume and cover letter. I also like to ask, "What was your favorite job and why?" and "What was your least favorite job and why?" The answers to these questions give you an idea of what excites and motivates the person and what turns him or her off. You should also check whether the applicant is comfortable with your pay scale; it's very disappointing to find out at the end of an interview that the candidate won't work for the pay you are offering.

Scheduling and Prepping for an In-Person Interview

If the candidate makes it through the phone interview, set up an in-person meeting. Begin your preparations for this meeting by creating a list of questions that will uncover the individual's knowledge, skills, and abilities (KSAs). At Jiva Fitness, the following KSAs are important:

- Confidence
- Outgoing personality
- Talent for personal training
- Talent for group fitness instruction
- Interpersonal communication skill
- Team-player mentality
- Mind-set of having and being fun

When the applicant arrives, the first few seconds can say so much. Is he or she on time? There's nothing as telling as showing up late for an interview. Does the person smile, look you in the eye, walk right up to you, initiate an introduction, and extend a hand? Doing these things portrays initiative, confidence, and ability to connect with others and set them at ease.

Next, how is the person dressed? Preferably, the look at least meets the standard of dressed-up casual. For men, a suit and tie aren't necessary (though they do impress me); clean, pressed pants with a dress shirt, sweater, or polo shirt make for a good look. For women, a professional dress or suit looks nice but certainly isn't necessary. Really, the guideline here is the same as for men—it's about knowing that appearance does make a difference and caring enough to make the effort. In contrast, I've seen interviewees show up in tank tops and baggy sweat pants, as if the interview is something to do on the way to a workout. For me, that alone rules out a second interview.

After greeting the applicant, invite him or her to join you in the room or other space you have designated for the interview. Be ready with a written list of questions to avoid getting sidetracked by casual conversation. In the case of Jiva Fitness, the list of KSAs makes it easy for me to pose relevant questions and scenarios. Next, take the applicant to the fitness training floor to check his or her skills as a personal trainer and group fitness instructor. The other, softer skills—such as judgment, discernment, decision making, and customer service—tend to be harder to assess.

For help in this area, visit the Monster website for a list of interview questions that will help you get an overall sense of the applicant (Peterson, n.d.). Here's an example: "What is one thing about yourself that you wouldn't want me to know?"

This question presents the interviewee with the challenge of revealing something uncomfortable, which makes him or her vulnerable. At the same time, it gives the person the opportunity to illustrate his or her capacity to learn and grow (Conlan, n.d.). If need be, adapt the Monster questions to be more specific. A question like, "How would you go about establishing your credibility quickly with the team?" could be made more specific for a personal trainer by asking, "How would you go about establishing your credibility as a personal trainer quickly with our members?"

However you generate your questions, have them ready when you conduct the interview. Score each response from the applicant on a scale of 1 to 6 (the absence of a middle score forces you to choose either higher or lower than center). If you intend to use practical assessments—such as having the applicant teach you how to do a perfect squat—have those ready as well. There again, score the applicant's performance on a scale of 1 to 6.

Beware of Illegal Questions

The U.S. Equal Employment Opportunity Commission (n.d.) states, "It is illegal for an employer to discriminate against a job applicant because of his or her race, color, religion, sex (including gender identity, sexual orientation, and pregnancy), national origin, age (40 or older), disability or genetic information." In light of this law, certain questions cannot be asked during an interview. Review your list of interview questions and eliminate any that address these issues.

Checking References

After I select the top candidates from the in-person interviews, I contact their references. You may choose to take this step earlier in the process or use it as a final hurdle before you hire. Just be sure to do it *before* you offer the job.

Some companies won't comment on a past employee beyond confirming that he or she worked there. If a former employer *is* willing to talk about the candidate, one of the big questions to ask is, "If you had the opportunity to hire him or her back, would you do it?" If the answer is yes, follow up with, "Why?" You want to hear all of the person's positive qualities. If the answer is no, ask, "Why not?" It may *not* be that the person wasn't good at the job. Perhaps he or she just wasn't a good fit for that company but would be the right fit for yours. It is also useful to ask what kind of relationships the candidate had with co-workers and members. We are a social profession, and creating strong relationships indicates that an applicant's interpersonal skills are probably good.

Meeting One More Time

No matter how much you like a candidate, go through at least one more face-to-face meeting and include another person for a different perspective. Sometimes, at a previous club we worked at, I got along great with a potential hire but when I had them interview with Heather, she'd tell me that the individual wouldn't look her in the eye or seemed uncomfortable talking to a mature woman. (Heather is not old! Let me be clear about that right now. However, she is older than many of our hires.) Since half of our members were women and many were mature, this was a problem. Possible people to bring into a second in-person interview include managers, personal trainers, group fitness instructors, and other higher-level staff members. These individuals can provide additional opinions about the candidate, and their presence in the meeting gives you a chance to watch how the candidate interacts with others.

The Tried-and-True Process for Interviewing Job Candidates

This step-by-step process applies increasingly specific criteria to help you find the best candidate for the position.

1. Define your needs (i.e., the tasks that need to get done).
2. Based on those tasks, write a detailed job description and an abbreviated but enticing ad for the position.
3. Announce the opening through various media, including social media, job boards, and other appropriate avenues.
4. Collect resumes and applications.
5. Conduct phone interviews with qualified candidates.
6. Narrow the field.
7. Prepare scorable questions and assessments for use during in-person interviews.
8. Interview candidates who make it beyond the phone interview.
9. Narrow the field.
10. Check references.
11. Narrow the field.
12. Conduct second interview with each remaining candidate and include other staff members to gain more insight.
13. Narrow the field.
14. Hold additional interviews as necessary (i.e., if you have more than one good candidate)
15. Narrow the field.
16. Offer the position to the best candidate.

Selecting the Right Fit

There's a philosophy in the business world that advises, "Hire slow, fire quick." In other words, take time, as much as you can, to assure yourself that you have found the right person for the position. On the flip side, do not let the wrong person—who can bring down the morale of others—linger in a position.

So, let's say that you've narrowed your search down to two individuals. Double-check your list of the absolutes that you need in the position and make sure that both candidates meet them. Next, compare total scores for the interview questions and tasks and give the job to the winner. It can be that simple.

In my opinion, however, if the scores are close and you feel disappointed about which candidate has the higher score, you should hire the other person. Why? Because your preference for the candidate with the lower score is probably driven by an intangible factor that is important. Go with your instinct. There are no guarantees either way.

Once you make a hire, train the person in every aspect of the job to ensure that he or she has all of the tools needed in order to succeed. Remember, employees who succeed help you succeed.

Noncompete Agreement

Many fitness-business owners are concerned about employees building their *own* business, then quitting, taking their clients with them, and opening a new place across the street. Thus was born the idea of requiring a new employee to sign a noncompete agreement. Should you require your employees to sign one?

The idea, of course, is to protect your business, and there's no harm in that line of thinking. Before taking this step, however, consider the following factors. First, in some states, noncompete agreements are difficult to enforce because you can't prevent someone from making a living. Therefore, if you required a personal trainer to sign a noncompete agreement that prevented him or her from providing personal training to anyone within a 20-mile radius of your club for a period of five years, it wouldn't hold up in court because it would require the individual to move or change professions in order to make a living.

Therefore, if you're going to use a noncompete agreement, it must be reasonable in what it protects, where it tries to protect it, and how long the protection lasts. Typically, for a fitness business, a noncompete is aimed at protecting yourself from clients or members being drawn away from your club and at keeping proprietary information (trade secrets) secure and used only with your permission. These priorities—and the agreement developed to uphold them—require input and direction from an attorney. In addition, your noncompete agreement must be tailored to your specific business; don't just find a generic form online or swap out the business name on a form used by another club and consider it done.

My professional opinion regarding noncompetes is that if you take good care of your employees, as you should, then they won't want to leave—and if for some reason they do leave, they won't want to hurt your business. From this perspective, unless you really do have a secret formula that generates a lot of your income, asking your employees to sign a noncompete seems like an act of mistrust. And when you treat your employees as if you don't trust them, they are less likely to trust you.

More to Come

I hope this chapter has given you some additional confidence about hiring employees—or, if you are an employee, insight that will help you excel when applying for a job. The hiring process begins with defining the company's needs, translating those needs into a job or position description, and using various media to get the word out to prospective candidates. The next step is to review resumes and applications in order to determine which candidates warrant a phone interview and—after preparing an interview format that includes both general and task-specific questions and assessments—bringing the appropriate individuals in for an in-person interview. Use a scorable interview process and conduct at least two face-to-face interviews (one including other staff members) to make a final selection for your new hire. Adding new members to your business family—or joining a new one—can be an exciting time. Good luck!

Of course, another important piece to get in place before you open your doors is insurance. Every personal trainer, fitness instructor, and business owner needs to protect themselves from the events that could cripple your ability to make a living. This could range from a client or member getting injured and filing a lawsuit, to heavy snow that collapses the roof of your facility. Chapter 8 will describe the kinds of insurance that you will need to consider for your business.

Chapter 8

Obtaining the Right Insurance

Getty Images/Mikolette

Chapter 2 discusses the importance of liability insurance for personal trainers, whether the premium is paid by the personal trainer or by a club. If you own your own fitness business, you'll need both more and different types of insurance. Making the right decision requires you to become informed about the possible pitfalls of owning a club and the insurance options available to you.

Why Insurance Matters

Lawsuits can be brought against health clubs, personal trainers, and instructors. If you'd like to get a taste of the possibilities, a simple web search will provide you with many examples (see, for instance, Eickhoff-Shemek, 2013). Regardless of whether a given lawsuit is valid, it involves you in legal action rather than in running your business. Even if you have never been sued for anything and don't anticipate having to deal with legal action, it is crucial for you to think about insurance for your business in the same way that you think about health insurance.

There was a time when I didn't have health insurance. I stayed fit and was never sick, and health insurance was expensive, so I decided that I didn't need it. Eventually, I got a job that not only provided health insurance but also paid 100 percent of the premiums (a great deal, especially these days). Now that I had insurance, I started to use it, and I realized that everyone should have it, just in case. For example, I recently needed to have a full shoulder replacement. My injury had gotten to the point where I couldn't even lift my arm, and that's a big problem for a fitness professional. A quarter-of-a-million dollars later, I have a brand new shoulder. Imagine if I didn't have health insurance! My shoulder replacement could have wiped me out financially. It takes only one "thing" to change your life.

It's the same with liability insurance. The fact that you have never been sued doesn't mean that it can't or won't happen tomorrow. What's more, lawsuits rarely stop at $250,000 (the price of my shoulder surgery). And here's another reason for obtaining liability insurance: "Maybe you were negligent, maybe you weren't. Either way, to defend yourself will cost you more than you have" (Leve, 2015). When even the cost of defending yourself could put you out of business, do you really want to take the risk of going without coverage?

Thus there are many reasons to get insurance, but these stand out:

- It is sometimes required by a governmental body.
- It helps offset the risk of owning a business or providing services to others.
- It protects your physical assets, such as fitness equipment and furniture.
- It provides a defense against claims related to injuries and damages resulting from professional mistakes.
- It helps you recover from a dramatic event and safeguards you from a resulting loss of income.
- It attracts and maintains high-quality employees.

Types of Insurance

Many types of insurance are available, and your decision about what type (or types) to obtain depends on your role—personal trainer for a fitness facility, self-employed

Special thanks to Jennifer Urmston Lowe, from Sports & Fitness Insurance Corporation, for providing insights used in this chapter.

Yes, You Need Insurance

If you find it tempting to begin your business operations without liability insurance, consider these examples:

- In a group fitness class at a Manhattan fitness club, a 35-year-old woman suffered eye injuries when exercise tubing anchored by her feet slipped off, snapped back, and struck her in the face. She sued for $1 million, claiming that the broken band had blinded her (Ross, 2014).
- A 62-year-old woman was awarded $750,000 in a suit against a gym in Branford, Connecticut (Schoenfeld, 2015). She fell and broke her hip and wrist when her personal trainer had her get on the platform side of a domed balanced device during their fourth session.
- A 58-year-old woman claimed that her ACL was torn when she was pressured to jump from a 10-foot wall during the first session of a fitness boot camp (Boniello, 2015).
- A California health club paid $2.9 million to settle an employee lawsuit related to overtime wages and meal breaks (Turner, 2015).

personal trainer, or facility owner. If you own a facility, your decision also depends on the types of personal trainers and instructors you employ.

No matter which of these paths you choose, if you work with clients in any capacity then you need professional liability insurance. Period. The question of whether to obtain any additional insurance—and how much it will cost—depends on your individual situation. In all cases, however, you should always look into what type of insurance is required by federal, state, county, and local governments.

Let's look now at the different types of insurance you may need.

Professional Liability

Though it was mentioned earlier, let's briefly revisit professional liability insurance, which is also referred to as "errors and omissions insurance." Like malpractice insurance for doctors, professional liability insurance covers the acts that you undertake as a fitness professional. You can be held responsible for any injury resulting from an exercise, movement, or act that you show, teach, or explain. You can also be held liable for things that you should have done but didn't—for example, failing to spot a client who gets injured while doing an exercise that calls for spotting. For these reasons, professional liability insurance is the one type that personal trainers and group fitness instructors *must* have in order to protect themselves.

General Liability

General liability can be thought of as environmental liability. In our case, a physical facility and all of its equipment have the potential to cause injury. To cover this possibility, general liability insurance protects business owners against having to make payments for injuries that result from equipment malfunction, slipping or falling, or any other cause at their facility that is related to a person's surroundings. In fact, so-called premises liability claims are by far "the most common type of personal injury claims and suits" (Heermance, 2013, p. 4). Therefore, if you have a space or equipment, you need general liability coverage. Moreover, if you own the building, then you also need to cover the area from the parking lot to your space.

Your insurance needs to cover your space and equipment.

If you lease your space, check your lease (and have your insurance agent check it) to determine what you would be liable for and what the landlord would be liable for. Sometimes a landlord asks to be named as the "additionally insured" on your policy and even dictates the amount of coverage, such as $2 million or $5 million aggregate coverage. Don't make assumptions about who is responsible for what. For example, you may might think that an HVAC (heating, ventilation, and air conditioning) breakdown would be covered under the landlord's policy, but that's not necessarily true; you could be required to replace or fix it yourself.

Because general liability insurance is more of an overarching type of insurance, you can choose to purchase additional aspects of insurance (called "riders") to cover losses from such causes as nonpaying clients and offenses caused by efforts to market or advertise your services—for example, defamation, copyright infringement, and invasion of privacy. In this day of social media, you need insurance to cover what you say, what you don't say, pictures you post, and more. You need to be covered for personal and advertising injury, as well as sexual impropriety. Be aware, though, that general liability insurance typically does not cover employee discrimination lawsuits or damage to your business property.

Building and Property

If you own your building, make sure your investment is protected by insurance. Building insurance protects you, as owner, from losses resulting from damages to the building, the foundation, or permanently installed fixtures—for example, the electrical system and the HVAC system.

If you have a fitness room, office, or both in a home-based personal training business, do not assume that your general homeowner's property insurance covers any losses to those parts of your house. For example, if your home catches fire from a short circuit in the treadmill, your homeowner's insurance is unlikely to cover any resulting damage. To cover such events, add a rider that specifically provides protection from that type of loss. To determine exactly what coverage you need, consult your insurance agent.

If you lease the property, the building owner should have the building insured, but take nothing for granted—ask the owner about the policy. Make sure that your business's contents (which include everything portable) in the structure are covered through property insurance. That way, if, say, the building burns down, your insurance will cover the cost of replacing the equipment and other items you own in the building. Such policies can be purchased to cover building only, contents only, or building and contents.

Natural Disaster

Depending on where you live, you may also want to consider coverage for natural disasters. Regular property insurance usually does not cover natural events such as flooding, earthquakes, hurricanes, tornadoes, and lightning strikes. If you live in a location where one or more of these events may occur, it could be devastating to your business. Even if a storm does not cause structural damage, it can create indirect damage—for example, by activating a sprinkler system or causing it to malfunction, thereby flooding your building.

Insurance that protects you from natural disasters can be very expensive. To help you decide whether to obtain it, ask other business owners in the neighborhood and city officials when a natural disaster last occurred, then consider whether the insurance premium is worth it. How much would 10 years of premiums add up to? Could you repair or replace any business losses for that amount of money? Of course, the best protection is to avoid locating your facility where you would run significant risk of a natural disaster.

Business Interruption

The problem with property damage goes beyond the physical loss. Even if property insurance covers what's in the building, the loss of precious time needed for working and making money can also become a real hardship. For this reason, business interruption insurance helps cover your ongoing bills and your payroll for salaried employees. If you consider buying this type of insurance, find out when it would take effect (it often doesn't kick in until a month or more after the causal event). Business interruption policies for rental spaces usually cover a three- to six-month period. If you own the property, the policy may cover a year or more.

This type of insurance usually must accompany other insurance that covers the cause of the damage. For example, if you do not have earthquake insurance and your business is interrupted because of an earthquake, then your business interruption insurance may not cover the resulting income loss.

Workers' Compensation

Workers' compensation insurance covers employees, as well as independent contractors who work on-site, if they get injured at the workplace or become sick because of it. For instance, a friend of mine contracted Legionnaires' disease from his work environment. This type of insurance typically covers medical expenses, lost wages, and rehabilitation and even provides death benefits.

Premiums may vary somewhat based on the risk involved in the particular profession or position. Desk workers, for instance, are on the low-risk end, whereas Cirque du Soleil performers are on the high-risk end. Because personal trainers do physically demanding work, we fall somewhere in the middle. You may be able to reduce your premiums by putting safety guidelines in place.

Regulations related to this type of insurance vary from state to state; therefore, you need to find out what your state requires. Most states do not require you to carry workers' compensation for the owners; in those states, you need it only when you hire a non-owner employee.

Accidents happen even with the best of personal trainers. Make sure you have the appropriate insurance.

Getty Images/Mikolette

Surety Bonds

Back in the 1990s, there was a rash of health clubs selling prepaid, long-term memberships and then closing abruptly, thus leaving members stranded with no way to recover what they had paid. Laws were then put in place to make sure that, should a club close unexpectedly, members would have a way to recoup their investment. Surety bonds are a guarantee and require either a significant amount of money be placed in an escrow account or surety bond insurance. Escrow costs could range from $50,000 to $150,000 (New York State, 2016, p. 4), depending on the amount of "up front" money the club takes in through either membership fees or high volume personal training packages. Surety bond insurance can range from $270 to $2,550 per year (Tucker, n.d.).

Shopping for Insurance

Some insurance companies have experience with insuring fitness facilities, and I would absolutely go with one of those companies. In the same way, if I need to go to an orthopedic surgeon, I want one who works with athletes. If an insurance agent is not familiar with your circumstances, then he or she will not know what questions to ask in order to set up an effective policy. Here are a few companies that are familiar with covering clubs:

- Sports & Fitness Insurance Corporation: www.sportsfitness.com
- Philadelphia Insurance Companies: www.phly.com/productsfw/default.aspx
- K&K Insurance: www.kandkinsurance.com/HealthFitness/Pages/Exercise-Personal-Training-Studios.aspx

This list is by no means exhaustive, but it will help you get started.

What Affects the Price?

The cost of insurance is based on a number of factors. One is the maximum payout (the "coverage limit"), which is typically set "per incident" and is subject to review and approval by the insurance company. For example, if you have $1 million in professional liability insurance, the insurer will pay up to that amount. Your premium will also be affected by the amount of your deductible—that is, the portion that you must pay if you file a claim and the insurance company has to pay out. Know from the start that if you cannot afford to pay a high deductible, then the cost of your premium will be higher. Ask your agent for a variety of deductible-versus-premium scenarios. Your premium also depends on various other factors, such as the size of the facility, whether you have wet (surface) areas, whether the owner is on-site, whether clients or members are allowed to work out without direct supervision, and what types of programs you offer.

Once the premium is determined, it is not static; rather, it will go up as your business grows. If you have more members or clients, then you have more exposures (people exposed to risk), and you need more coverage. Your rates may also rise if you offer new programs, such as childcare or martial arts; therefore, before adding anything, check with your insurance agent to find out how it would affect your coverage. In addition, in order to get coverage for certain things (such as obstacle courses and climbing walls), you will have to implement more safety precautions.

Fortunately, there may also be some things you can do to decrease your rate—for instance, adding proper signage, putting emergency procedures in place, and purchasing an on-site AED. Check with your agent and ask, "What can I do to reduce my premium?"

How Should I Choose?

You absolutely need professional liability insurance (did I mention that?). If you own the space, you also need building insurance. And if you have employees, you need workers' compensation insurance. The rest depends on your individual needs, offerings, and budget. To get the most appropriate coverage, talk with your insurance agent about your entire business situation. Also make sure to shop around. Specifically, get recommendations from unbiased sources; get quotes from several companies; and compare coverages, premiums, and deductibles to get the best deal for the coverage you need.

Then What?

After you've purchased insurance, take another positive step by organizing your policy paperwork and keeping it in a secure but easily accessible location. Then, at least yearly—or whenever something changes in your business or job duties—review the details of your policy to be sure that it still matches what you do and provides the coverage you need. It's also a good idea to periodically schedule a meeting with your agent to see if you are still getting the best deal for the needed coverage.

Minimizing Risk to Help Avoid Claims

Beyond getting the right insurance, you can also take steps to avoid or at least minimize claims. After all, the best insurance is prevention. Here are some actions that can help keep your clients and members safe:

- Keep all employee certifications up to date.
- Stay within your scope of practice and refer to other professionals when necessary.
- Provide training in avoidance of sexual harassment.
- Get all personnel certified in CPR, AED use, and first aid.
- Keep first aid supplies and an AED available.
- Establish and regularly practice emergency procedures.

- Require and thoroughly review a Physical Activity Readiness Questionnaire for Everyone (PAR-Q+) for all clients and members. Note: PAR-Q+ is a minimum requirement, which might be all you can do with a drop-in class participant. However, if the situation allows it, it would be better to have a more in-depth medical health history as a requirement.
- Have all clients and members sign waivers and informed consent forms.
- Fix or replace equipment early, maintain equipment repair logs, and remove any defective equipment from use (put an "out of order" sign on it) or remove it from the floor.
- Keep pathways clear and dry.
- Clearly display all appropriate signage, from warnings about wet areas to a sign for an automated external defibrillator

More to Come

You are building your business, which takes a huge amount of time, effort, and money. You must also take the right precautions to protect your business from unforeseen events, and that requires you to understand your insurance choices. Professional liability insurance addresses instances when what you do, or don't do, causes injury. General liability insurance covers incidents that happen within your space, as well as things you say or post that affect your clients. Building insurance protects you from building damage, whereas property coverage protects your belongings. If your business is located in a place where it could be affected by a natural disaster, then you should also consider insurance to cover that possibility.

If your business has to close (either because something happens to your building or for another reason), you will experience hardship caused by loss of income. In this case, business interruption insurance can help cover bills and salaries. If you have employees, you also need workers' compensation insurance in case an employee becomes ill or gets injured at your facility.

Even with the information provided here, you still need to consult an insurance agent who is experienced in working with health clubs and studios to fully determine what coverage, and how much of it, you need. Make sure you get the right insurance to keep your business safe.

So, with most of what I think of as the "less fun stuff" figured out, it's time to determine your precise offerings (what you are selling) and what you are going to charge for them. There are a lot of variables that can make or break the success of each of these options. The next chapter looks at these variables and explores how to create the right product with the right price for your particular target market.

Chapter 9

Determining Your Offerings and Their Pricing

Most businesses provide something that somebody wants or needs in exchange for some form of payment. A fitness business is no different. We provide things that the public is willing to pay for. These offerings can be tangible or intangible. Tangible offerings are items that can be touched, such as equipment, t-shirts, and supplements; intangible offerings are things that cannot be touched, such as the services of a personal trainer or group fitness instructor.

There are also hybrid offerings, such as club membership. On one hand, membership provides the tangibles of a contract, an ID card, and perhaps a t-shirt. On the other hand, it's also a kind of rental agreement that allows a person to use the facility for a given period of time. In fact, members of low-priced clubs are often said to be "renting equipment," because they get access to equipment but little else.

What you decide to offer your target market can vary greatly, and it may evolve over time. In the beginning, however, you should start with your basic programs, such as one-on-one personal training and group fitness. These are the ones from which future programs may build on. Create a clear pricing structure for these offerings and it will give you a reference point to help you determine the pricing of other products in the future.

Types of Offerings

The first step is to determine exactly what you will sell so that you can price it and market it to your target clientele. Start by revisiting your reasons for starting your business. Who are the members of your target market, and how are you going to help them? If, for example, you want to help individuals with postinjury rehabilitation conditioning (sometimes referred to as retraining or reconditioning), then you may focus on one-on-one personal training to help them regain their functional abilities. At the same time, you would decide against offerings such as memberships, small-group training, and group fitness classes because those items do not serve the best interest of a reconditioning client.

Membership

For club owners, the most common offering is membership paid for by monthly or annual fees (typically called "dues"). At a typical health club, membership dues account for 61 percent to 76 percent of revenue (International Health, Racquet & Sportsclub Association, 2015), which makes sense because most club users feel (whether rightly or not) that they know what they are doing with their workout and just need a place to do it. You give them that option by selling memberships, which also gives you a sizable revenue stream.

If you do offer memberships, you set your hours of operation for each day of the week and are then obligated to be open and staffed for those hours (unless you have a keycard-entry facility). Does that fit your vision for your business? It does for most club owners. It may not fit, however, if you see your facility as more personal, focused on fully supervised exercise, and offering services by appointment only. Of course, this kind of facility must make up for the loss of potential dues revenue through other offerings.

One-on-One Personal Training

This is our staple, our wheelhouse. Although other options exist, almost all personal trainers continue to offer one-on-one personal training. In addition, this type of service is where we can have the greatest effect on our clients, through proper health and lifestyle interviewing, goal setting, program design, and progression. Of course, this model depends on finding clients who are comfortable with being the sole focus of a personal trainer's attention. Not everyone wants that approach, and you must consider that reality as you try to match an individual with the right offering.

Semiprivate and Small-Group Personal Training

When the global financial crisis happened in 2008, most people became very conscious of how they were spending their money. As a result, semiprivate and small-group personal training came to the forefront as a way of getting instruction and guidance at a fraction of the cost of one-on-one personal training.

These approaches also offer other benefits, such as being more comfortable and motivated when others (whom you likely know) are working out beside you. This social aspect helps alleviate the anxiety that some people feel when working one-on-one with a personal trainer. Shared exercise experiences create camaraderie and attachments to others in the group. I continue to be amazed by the friendships created in semiprivate and small-group personal training (and in group fitness classes, for that matter). This approach also gives participants a sense of accountability to the group for their own workouts. This accountability makes them more likely to show up and do the work because they don't want to let down their fellow group members. Often, in fact, if someone misses a session, others call or text to make sure that he or she is okay.

If you decide to offer semiprivate or small-group personal training services, take care to define them clearly. For example, semiprivate personal training may include two or three participants, whereas small-group personal training may include four to ten participants. For the personal trainer, these sessions provide a way to help more people and make more money per hour than is possible with one-on-one training. This is as it should be. That is, personal trainers *should* make more money in this model, because it takes more work to monitor and train a group than it does to train a single person.

Group Fitness Classes

Back in the 1980s and 1990s, group fitness classes were widespread, and their popularity was enhanced by movies such as *Perfect*, starring John Travolta and Jamie Lee Curtis. Everywhere you turned, you saw "studio" facilities focused solely on group fitness classes. As time progressed, larger health clubs jumped on the bandwagon and started to offer classes that rivaled those of the stand-alone studios, and, since the clubs had more to offer members than just classes, many studios gradually died out. Recently, however, group fitness classes have seen a resurgence. The cause for this revival is, I believe, the same cause that boosted small-group personal training. That is, group fitness classes are less expensive per class, offer camaraderie, promote accountability to other participants, generate energy from a larger group, and usually allow participants to work out to musical accompaniment.

Some personal trainers worry that group fitness classes will cannibalize their personal training sessions. I don't believe that's true. In fact, I think group classes can help you *build* your personal training business. If people get to know and trust you as you lead them through group classes, then they will come to you first for personal training.

On the other hand, I do think that a strong group fitness program can cannibalize a small-group personal training program, because the difference between training with 8 people and training with 20 people may not seem significant (in a participant's mind) as compared with the price difference. Therefore, if you offer both types, then you must clearly differentiate them for your potential clients and participants. For instance, if your small-group personal training sessions can have no more than 10 participants, then group fitness classes could pick up from there, allowing 11 to, say, 80 participants (or whatever number your space and supervisory capacity allows).

Your decision about whether to offer group classes also depends on the amount of available open space. For instance, if your area measures 900 square feet (about 84 meters)—for instance 30 by 30 feet, or 18 by 50 feet (9 by 9 meters, or 5 by 15 meters)—then you may decide that you won't offer anything larger than small-group personal training. Your decision may also be dictated by your equipment. For instance, if you want to hold a kettlebell class, do you have enough of the right weights for everyone?

More generally, do you have a sound system that is appropriate for group fitness? You don't *need* to have music for classes, but it sure helps, as does having the right music for the demographics of your participants. Remember also, however, that playing music by the original artists requires you to pay for a music license from BMI (Broadcast Music, Inc., 2016) and ASCAP (American Society of Composers, Authors and Publishers, 2016).

Boot Camps

Boot camps fall into a few categories, including small-group personal training, group fitness, and special programs. Nowadays, boot camps exist for almost every imaginable area in life: business boot camps, relationship boot camps, data analysis boot camps, and, of course, military boot camps for new recruits. Any boot camp is expected to be intense, challenging, and oriented toward getting a lot done in a short time.

For fitness boot camps, the perceived benefits include exercise diversity and the camaraderie that typically characterizes exercising with others. Even within the category of fitness boot camps, many styles exist—for example, sport specific, age specific, and general sessions for a variety of participants. They can also be done either circuit style or in unison. If you decide to offer a boot camp, take care to clearly define the size, style, and intended participant group.

Group fitness is a great way to engage and build relationships with members.

Specific Goal-Oriented Programs

These programs pursue a specific goal for a certain length of time. They typically begin and end with assessments that measure performance related to the program goal. The limited duration (often 6 to 12 weeks) may help potential participants commit to the program: "Oh, I can do that for 8 weeks." The content of such a program may consist of any of the previously mentioned offerings, either alone or in combination with others. For example, you might offer a one-on-one weight loss program, a small-group weight loss program, a beginning runners' club, or even a mud-run preparation program. To set the framework for a program, choose a focus, a duration, a day of the week and time, a modality, and an assessment method.

For example, let's say that you want to create a My First 5K running (or run–walk) program. Eight weeks may not be the ideal length to prepare for a race, but it is long enough for participants to experience positive change, and many people will perceive it as a reasonable length of time to commit to a specific goal. You could begin and end the program with the Cooper 12-minute run/walk test (Quinn, 2016) in order to track participants' improvement (which will help you promote the program next time around). You could also have everyone complete a 5K race at the end of the program. For scheduling, then, you would find a local race and start the program eight weeks earlier.

What about the program's content? It could, for instance, include a weekly treadmill-running class (and if you have 12 treadmills, then you've also determined the program's maximum enrollment). It could also include a weekly track run (you can get the local high school's permission to use its track at a designated time) and a weekly longer run or walk. To summarize, you now have assessments at the start and end, as well as a 5K race and three workouts per week for eight weeks. Thus you have created a specific goal-oriented program!

Other Sources of Income

Beyond memberships and fitness services, consider other potential sources of income, such as drop-in childcare and pro-shop sales (including items such as apparel, fitness equipment, food, and supplements). Drop-in childcare is a common service for clubs because it allows parents to leave children in a safe, supervised location while they work out. It's a great service for people who cannot exercise in any other way, but it requires you to have a safe, secure space equipped with toys, books, and games to keep kids entertained, as well as enough qualified staff to take good care of them. Check your state's regulations to find out what requirements you must meet—for example, a minimum caregiver-to-child ratio.

Additional income can also be derived from pro-shop or service-desk sales. Because this activity involves selling retail items, you will probably need to collect and pay sales tax. You can find a direct web link to your state-required licenses and permits at the website of the Small Business Administration ("State Licenses and Permits," n.d.). Selling such items can add more than just another revenue stream. If you brand the items with your name (or your facility's name) and logo, then they also serve a marketing purpose anytime a client, member, or guest uses them. The obvious choice here is apparel, but you can also carry branded water bottles, shopping bags, workout journals, equipment, and even private-label supplements, to name a few possibilities.

This option can also work for independent personal trainers who travel from client to client. For example, you could keep your items in the trunk of your car. Don't go crazy, though. For each item you offer, you have to carry it in stock, which means that you pay for it up front in hopes of selling it. Evaluate your cash flow to determine how much you can afford to tie up in inventory.

Factors That Affect Pricing

Price is a critical factor in selling your offerings. It's not just a random number that you pick out of the air. To price effectively, the first thing you need to consider is how much your business needs to make in order to stay in business. Everything else aside, if you don't cover expenses, you won't be around long. Additional pricing factors include your target market, the local demographics, your competition, your unique selling proposition, the perceived value of what you're offering, what *you* believe your time is worth, and how much time you commit to your offerings. These factors are discussed separately in the following paragraphs, but in practice they overlap, and interplay will occur between them as you determine your prices. You considered these factors when you wrote your business plan, and now is the time to address them with precise pricing in mind.

Your Operating Expenses

Whatever your prices, you must be able to cover your expenses after you build your base of members or clients. This base will take time to build. You know that, and you have (I hope!) planned for it. In the long run, however, your operating expenses must be covered by your prices in order for your business to survive. Your basic operating expenses consist of your monthly financial obligations, such as rent, utilities, licensing fees, payroll, and marketing expenses. The revenue that you receive in return for your offerings must, at a minimum, cover your operating expenses. Minimum, however, is not the goal for most of us. In order to succeed in business, we need to become profitable. So, let's look now at key factors for determining how much more we can charge.

Target Market

Here you consider pricing to match your target market. Ignoring other target market factors, the key for the moment is whether people can afford what you offer. For instance, if you are pursuing a lower-income, underserved market, then your prices need to be in line with that financial reality. In contrast, a higher-income target market allows you to charge higher prices.

For 15 years, I worked as a personal trainer for various clubs and organizations in New York City. During this time, I also maintained a side business of training people in their homes and apartment-complex gyms as an independent contractor. For that work, I set my own prices. It was an ongoing education for me to learn what I could charge that was still perceived as reasonable by my target market. I worked with affluent people, which allowed me to set my prices at the top end of the scale.

Local Demographics

As we look at local demographics with pricing in mind, the key is to know your target market and whether it includes enough individuals close enough to your location. Typically, close enough means within a radius of 5 to 8 miles (8 to 13 kilometers) from your business (Pire, 2013). If you are surrounded by a dense population of your target market, then you have the option of lowering your prices because you can make it up in volume. If your target market is affluent, it's unlikely that you would need or want to lower your price, but if you are seeking a lower- or middle-income market, then price will matter. Specifically, if lowering your price increases your volume and still allows you to make the income that you need and want, then lowering the price might work in your favor.

Competition

People shop around for everything, including their gym. Who else is nearby who can be perceived as doing the same thing you do? What do they offer, and what are their prices? Go check them out and maybe even try them out. Find out what you need to do in order to stand out from them. If the competitor is a club, how big is it, what equipment does it have, what are its offerings, what is the aesthetic feel of the club, and who are its members? If it's a big-box club with a ton of equipment, loud music, and an average member age of under 30, whereas you are a small, quiet studio catering to the over-50 population, then your prices don't need to be in the same ballpark. You and your competitor are two completely different animals, and people will readily make that distinction. On the other hand, if you're very similar to each other, then it will be very challenging if your prices are much higher than your competitor's.

Your Unique Selling Proposition

Does the lower price always win? If people aren't knowledgeable about fitness offerings and fitness facilities, then a gym is a gym and they may simply look at the price. In that case, yes, the cheapest one wins. This is a big reason that low-cost clubs tend to have a huge member base. They are simply too cheap to ignore. If you're not going to match their price, then what are you going to do or offer that makes you stand out? Savvy fitness entrepreneurs know that, in order to distinguish ourselves from our competitors, we must go beyond the *what* of our offerings and also consider how we offer it. The answer is that we can create member and client experiences—and these experiences are something that people will pay more to get.

Picture this: I'm sitting at the counter of a diner with a cup of coffee that was very cheap. It's bitter and cold when I get it, the waiter is rude when I ask him to heat it up, and I feel pressured to leave when I finish it. Contrast that scenario with the Starbucks experience. There, I get a very expensive coffee from a very friendly barista, sit at a comfortable table, listen to very pleasant background music, and can spend all day there using their Wi-Fi if I so choose. Do you go for the cheaper coffee? I definitely do not. The Starbucks experience wins my business every time. For a personal trainer, it may be as simple as being friendly, caring, and attentive and having a little sense of humor. These factors can make all the difference between you and another personal trainer who is equally knowledgeable.

Perceived Value

This factor relates closely to your unique selling proposition. What do people *believe* is the value of what you offer? Here, we are talking about the consumer's belief—not yours, and not the industry's. If you price yourself higher than your target market believes you are worth, then your marketing must prove that value to them. What is your audience looking for? How would they like to receive it? What would they be willing to pay more for? These are questions you must answer in order to create a higher perceived value for your offerings.

For example, say that you are trying to reach elderly new exercisers. They may be afraid of getting hurt, unsure that "working out" is the right thing to do, and afraid of looking foolish. If you are able to connect with such a person by listening attentively and offering assurance that the exercise program you've designed is very safe and will produce results—and if you present all of this in a caring manner—then the potential client will assign a much higher perceived value to what you're offering. Again, look to create experiences that stand out from the crowd and offer greater perceived value.

Your Own Believed Value

What *you* believe you are worth also matters. If you work hard and feel that you are not receiving what you are worth, then you will begin to resent it, and that resentment will inevitably show through to your clients and hurt your business. Conversely, if you or your employer have set a price higher than your own believed value, then you will communicate that difference to your potential clients, who will be unlikely to buy what you are offering.

What Went Wrong? Reevaluating an Offering

Let's say you created a group fitness class, boot camp, or goal-oriented program and not enough people participated to make it profitable. What went wrong? In order to find the answer—and make your next venture profitable—you must objectively evaluate each aspect of your offering.

Target Market

- Does the program fill a real need for the target market?
- Can your target market afford the cost of the program?

Local Demographics

- Are enough members of your target market located within a radius of 5 to 8 miles (8 to 13 kilometers) of your facility?
- Is your location accessible to your target market? For example, is sufficient parking available, or is your location within walking distance of your target market?

Competition

- Carefully compare the price you advertised with what your competitors charge. Is your price reasonable?
- If your competition is very well established and you are new to the area, how might you get participants to experience your program? For example, could you create special offers?

Your Unique Selling Proposition

- Is your offering truly differentiated from that of the competition?
- Is your offering differentiated in a way that is meaningful to your potential members and clients?

Perceived Value and Believed Value

- Is there a conflict between the value you see in your program and your target market's perception of its value?
- If so, how can you bridge that gap? Do you need to adjust your own valuation of the program, or do you need to educate potential clients in order to increase the program's perceived value?

Marketing

- Are you marketing where your target market will find you?
- Are you marketing the benefits that your program offers specifically for your target market?

For example, once when I was presenting a personal training sales session at a conference, I asked the attendees who charged a higher-end price. One person, whose club charged $60 per hour, thought that price was too expensive. I then went to the next person, and he was charging $180 per hour. I asked him if he was worth $180, and his response was, "Absolutely!" Either way, you have to charge something that is close to your believed value, or the difference will likely affect your work satisfaction and ultimately rub off on your clients.

Your Time

We have a limited numbers of hours in a day, and we need to recognize that all of our time is valuable. This applies not only to the time spent with the client but also to the time it takes to prepare and, if we are traveling, the time it takes to get to the client. Consider an hour-long personal training session with a client who wants to train for an obstacle course race. Your work in this case consists not only of the hour during which you train your client. You also have to prepare by deciding what progressions will take place during the session; you may also have set up special equipment, such as climbing ropes or vaulting boxes. All of this time should be considered in setting a price.

Packages, Discounts, and Billing

It is a commonly held view that every new sale provides an opportunity for clients to rethink whether they want to continue training. To reduce these opportunities for people to change their minds, packages were created—that is, groups of personal training sessions purchased for one overall price—in order to get people to commit to training for a longer period of time. To make a package seem more attractive, it is often discounted as compared with the single-session rate; in addition, the per-session discount typically gets bigger as the number of sessions in the package goes up. For example, if your single-session rate is $75, then a 24-session package could be discounted 20 percent to a rate of $60 per session.

What is the ideal package size? I know of one club that will not sell anything smaller than a 24-pack. In fact, the club requires all potential clients to go through a "strategic planning session," during which a consultant generally recommends personal training for at least 24 sessions in order to create good habits and develop proper technique. Other clubs offer packages with a maximum of 10 sessions because they believe it is easier for people to commit to smaller packages and then sign up for more once they experience the value. Thus the decision depends on the viewpoint of a given club's management.

Meanwhile, personal trainers often debate whether sessions should *ever* be discounted. The arguments usually have to do with the diminishing perceived value of a personal training session when it is discounted. I've heard many personal trainers say, "Your doctor never gives you a discount." Personally, I don't like to discount, particularly for larger packages, because if a person can afford a 24-session package with me, then he or she doesn't need a discount. I'm more likely to give away sessions to people who need the help but can't afford it.

For exercise classes at a large fitness facility, the cost of participating is often included in the price of the membership. Thus you receive no additional income for these classes, and, as a result, when you pay your instructors, you are operating at a loss. This arrangement can be justified, however, as a cost of doing business and set against the income from membership dues. These days, some clubs do charge an additional fee (either per session or as part of a multisession package) for specialized exercise classes or for those taught by a high-level or very popular instructor.

Smaller studio owners typically sell a "drop-in" pass, which offers a single class at one rate or a package of 10 classes at a discounted rate. (It's almost always a 10-class card, probably for no other reason than "that's how we did it in the old days.") Alternatively, you could offer a monthly rate that allows a person to attend up to a certain number of classes per week. At Jiva Fitness, we offer both a drop-in rate and a monthly unlimited-class rate. For fitness studios located in urban areas, another trend involves becoming part of a consortium of studios (such as ClassPass) that sells a monthly pass allowing members to take a certain number of classes at any of the participating facilities.

Another approach is known as bundling, which involves combining two or more offerings to create a new one. This practice can be applied readily to specific goal-oriented programs. For example, you could offer a Get Started Right! program that combines a two-month membership with two personal training sessions per week. Another idea would be a mud-run preparation program offered as a bundle that includes two boot camp classes per week, one personal training session per week (to work on obstacle strength and skills), and the registration fee for the mud run scheduled at the end of the program. Your bundle offerings can be as varied as you want to make them. Just ensure that all of the bundled components are specifically geared to help your client reach the goal set for the program.

One question that often arises in relation to small-group personal training is whether participants will commit and adhere to the class schedule. For example, if you offer a four-week package of eight sessions scheduled for 8:30 a.m. on Tuesdays and Thursdays, what happens if someone misses a session? Do you allow that person to make up the missed session when everyone else showed up as scheduled? If you do offer a makeup, will it be a one-on-one session? These questions need to be answered before the program begins, and the answers need to be announced so that everyone knows up front how missed sessions will be handled. Often, a personal trainer or club includes the schedule in the program's promotional materials. That way, if someone signs up for the program (knowing the schedule) and later has to miss a session, he or she understands that the session is forfeited because there are no makeup sessions.

Another common practice intended to remove the repurchase decision from the client's mind is to use electronic funds transfer (EFT). In this billing system, dues and fees for personal training, babysitting, and other offerings are automatically charged to a person's checking account, credit card, or debit card. In personal training, clients are billed monthly on the basis of an assumed number of weekly training sessions that the personal trainer and client agree on, and the appropriate amount is calculated based on the average number of weeks in a month (52 weeks per year ÷ 12 months per year = 4.33). For example, if a client agrees to do two sessions per week, then he or she is billed monthly at two times the per-session rate multiplied by 4.33.

To make this monthly package more attractive, EFT payments are sometimes discounted as well. Some clubs charge the full amount per month regardless of any sessions missed by the client. Other clubs allow makeup sessions. If you take this route, it can be challenging to keep track of missed sessions and determine how to make them up. This quandary used to pose an issue for my clients and me. They would train with me multiple times per week, then go away on a business trip for a week or two, and scheduling makeup sessions would become a logistical nightmare. As a result, I decided not to sell personal training via EFT on the basis of anything more than one session per week. For other personal trainers, however, EFT billing works very well. The key is to think through how it might work with your clients.

Another way to minimize the repurchase decision came to my attention when I attended a roundtable of fitness directors from around the United States. When talking about packages and package sizes, a couple of the directors said that they charge only by the session. When I asked why they took that approach when everyone else was offering larger packages and monthly billing, the answer was so perfect that I instituted it at the club where I was working as soon as possible. Those clubs got permission to charge the client's credit card (which was on file) each time the client had a session.

As for the decision to continue, the personal trainer and client scheduled the upcoming sessions for the following week with the expectation that they would continue. If the service you are providing has great value, why would it ever stop? This was exactly the mind-set my clients and I had when I was charging by the session back in the day. It works.

Consider these various options for packages, discounts, and billing. Find what works best for you, your business, and your clients.

Pricing Recommendations

Now, let's get down to pricing considerations for the specific offerings we have discussed.

Membership

If you're offering memberships, what benefits do they provide to members? What is a reasonable amount to charge for monthly dues? Somebody will have the lowest price in town, and somebody else will have the highest. Low-priced clubs provide memberships without much more than that; thus members essentially pay for access to fitness equipment. For savvy users who already know how to use the equipment, this option may be perfect for their needs; it also happens to be a very successful business model. Sadly (at least in my mind), it also draws in novice exercisers because of the low price. Since they are mostly left to their own devices, they rarely succeed. In contrast, higher-priced clubs usually include many other benefits with membership. Common features include access to saunas, steam rooms, group fitness classes, and use of a pool or basketball court.

To help you decide what to include with membership at your club, start by checking out other clubs in your area. (This process is covered in chapter 5.) How do their offerings compare with yours? If you offer less than they do, how would you justify charging more?

At Jiva Fitness, our membership is strictly for group fitness. We anticipated that the average class participant would attend two classes per week, which, based on the average of 4.33 weeks in a month, translates to 8.66 classes per month. If we round down (to be conservative) to eight classes per month and say that the low end of the per-class price spectrum is $10, then participants would still be paying at least $80 per month. From there, we considered the effect of perceived price—that is, financial break points that make the difference between a price seeming more expensive and seeming less expensive. With that effect in mind, we adjusted the $80 figure down to $69 for our monthly membership price.

Of course, participants could take classes at the big multipurpose club for only $29.95 (see table 9.1, which presents an excerpt of table 5.2). However, we are a smaller

Table 9.1 **Comparison of Monthly Fees Across Types of Fitness Facilities**

	Jiva Fitness	YMCA	Joe Fitness	Club Fitness	Middle Fitness	Big Fitness
Facility type	Studio	Multipurpose	Studio	Fitness club	Fitness club	Multipurpose
Monthly fee ($)	69	45	65-129	10	19.99	29.95

and more intimate facility that offers exceptional and tested classes, which we believe elevates our perceived value. Therefore, we feel justified in charging more—but not so much more that we price ourselves out of the market.

Initiation Fee

Typically, when someone joins a fitness club, he or she must pay a "processing" (or "initiation" or "enrollment") fee. Essentially, these are different names for a one-time fee that members pay separately from membership dues. According to Thomas Plummer (2007), this fee "should be equal to one month's dues, but no more than $89 for most clubs" (p. 144).

What this fee pays for is up to you. I believe that an initiation fee is often levied simply to have something to discount for sales purposes. How many times have you seen a club say something like, "Sign up now and we'll waive the initiation fee!"? Of course, you may give them some printed material (such as class schedules, "How to" sheets, or "What to expect" handouts) or a new-member gift package (may include a branded towel, a water bottle, or a t-shirt) in return for the fee. A new-member gift package certainly goes at least a little way toward justifying the fee. However, I prefer partnering with other local businesses to offer giveaways and discounts, because it is less costly and helps support the business community.

So, are you going to charge an initiation fee? If not, maybe that's a point of differentiation between you and your competition.

One-on-One Personal Training

The main considerations in setting your price structure for personal training are usually the session length and the experience level and credentials of the personal trainer. In the old days (I know you love it when I start a sentence that way!), there were only hour-long sessions and only one level of personal trainer. It was a simpler time. Now, sessions are commonly offered at lengths of either 60 minutes or 30 minutes, and some facilities also offer 45-minute and 75-minute sessions. The first time I discussed adding the 30-minute option with some other personal trainers, we were all skeptical that we could fit everything we needed to cover in such a short time. Turns out, we can. Not only that, but it's easier to sell and to get people to participate because it costs less and requires less time commitment.

I like the idea of designating different levels of personal trainers so that the more experienced, better-educated ones command a higher price and, in turn, make a higher hourly wage. Some clubs also grant higher status (and a higher hourly rate) to personal trainers who train more clients, whereas other clubs may compensate personal trainers based on one or a combination of these factors, but only identify one level of personal trainer and price for service to the membership.

Let's start by considering pricing for an hour-long session with a single level of personal trainers. According to the *IDEA Fitness Industry Compensation Trends Report* (Schroeder, 2015), 62 percent of personal trainers are paid by the session or by the class, and 50 percent of those are paid a certain percentage of what the club charges the client. The average split between the personal trainer and the club is 60 percent and 40 percent, respectively, which has been about the same each time the annual survey has been conducted since 2004. In 2015, the average compensation for personal trainers was $30.50 per hour, and the average cost to the client was $60.75 per hour-long session (Schroeder, 2015). (Remember, these averages reflect the fact that half of personal trainers are paid a flat amount—that is, *not* a certain percentage of what the

Getty Images/Mikolette

One-on-one personal training offers the greatest amount of personal attention.

club charges the client. That's why the $30.50 average paid to the personal trainer and the $60.75 charged by the club don't match up with the 60–40 percent split.)

How do you decide what to charge? Well, what do your competitors charge? How do you compare with them? What is your perceived value? Your believed value? Determine those answers and adjust your price as you see fit. Then use the standard fee for a one-on-one, hour-long session as a guide in determining your prices for other personal training offerings.

This is not to suggest that you make everything exactly proportional; that is, don't think that the price of a 30-minute session needs to be exactly 50 percent of the hour-long price just because it's half as long. Fitting everything into a half hour is more challenging for the personal trainer; therefore, he or she should be compensated at higher rate for doing it. In fact, the fee for 30-minute sessions generally ranges from 60 percent to 70 percent of the hourly fee—or, more precisely, 62 percent on average, according to numbers presented in the 2015 IDEA report (Schroeder, 2015). This range means that doing two half-hour sessions back to back delivers hourly income that is 120 percent to 140 percent of the standard one-hour session fee.

Semiprivate and Small-Group Personal Training

Again, delivering a multiperson training session involves more work than does a one-on-one session. Therefore, the personal trainer should be compensated at a higher rate for a multiperson session than for a one-on-one session of the same length. The result of paying a personal trainer more may impact what is charged to a group of clients (multiperson group participants pay less as they receive less personal attention, but personal trainer compensation may affect how much less) or what the club profits from each group session, or both.

For example, let's say that you are going to train two clients at the same time (that is, semiprivately). If you simply let them split the hourly rate for one-on-one personal training and then the club pays you a greater percentage of that rate, the club makes less. This would be a good deal for the clients—that is, paying only half of the full one-on-one rate. But they should understand that it's more work for you to train both of them at the same time and that each of them should therefore pay more than 50 percent of the hourly rate so that you will earn more. For example, you could charge each of them 60 percent of the full one-on-one personal training rate. This way, you make more, the club makes more, and the clients still get a deal by paying less than the full hourly rate.

Let's flesh this example out with some numbers. Specifically, let's say that the club's standard rate for one-on-one personal training is $64 per hour and that you split this fee with the club at a ratio of 60 percent for you and 40 percent for the club. Here's how much each party would get paid for a one-on-one personal training session:

Hourly cost for one-on-one personal training session = $64

Personal trainer compensation = $64 × 0.60 (60 percent) = $38.40

Club compensation = $64 × 0.40 (40 percent) = $25.60

Now, instead of charging each of the two semiprivate clients 50 percent of the hourly rate, you raise the cost to 60 percent each. Here's how much you and the club would get paid for a semiprivate personal training session:

Hourly cost per client for semiprivate session = $64 × 0.60 (60 percent) = $38.40 (instead of $64)

Hourly income for semiprivate session = $38.40 × 2 clients = $76.80

Personal trainer compensation = $76.80 × 0.60 (60 percent) = $46.08 (instead of $38.40)

Club compensation = $76.80 × 0.40 (40 percent) = $30.72 (instead of $25.60)

Everyone wins! Also, as with the 30-minute, one-on-one personal training session, the fee per person for a 30-minute semiprivate session is usually 60 percent to 70 percent of the normal hourly fee. This again means that the income per hour is 120 percent to 140 percent of the standard hourly fee for a one-on-one session.

It works a little differently for small-group personal training. The more people in the group, the less personal attention they get—therefore, the *lower* the fee they should pay. Most clubs charge one low price whether you have three people or ten. You need to charge enough to pay the personal trainer at least the same, if not more than, you would for a semiprivate session. Since what you really need to consider is the minimum cost for which you can provide this service, let's price it out for three participants.

Using the previous semiprivate personal training example of $76.80 in total income for the hour, what would it look like if we simply took that amount and divided by the three participants in the small group? Instead of each client paying $38.40 per hour for a semiprivate session, they would each pay $25.60 (that is, $12.80 less per hour) for a small-group personal training session. That will certainly seem like a good deal for the three clients, but it won't allow the personal trainer and the club to make more than they would for a semiprivate personal training session. Remember, however, that this example addresses the minimum number of participants. Let's look now at the maximum number.

If a small-group personal training session costs each client $25.60 per hour and you have a maximum-sized group of 10 participants, then the total income for the hour would be $256. Given that total, here's how much you and the club would get paid:

Personal trainer compensation = $256 × 0.60 (60 percent) = $153.60

Club compensation = $256 × 0.40 (40 percent) = $102.40

So, small-group personal training has the potential to bring in considerably more money for both the personal trainer and the club.

I know that many clubs and studios charge less than $25 per person for small-group personal training. And of course a lower price makes it more appealing to clients. However, if you set a low price, then you also need to set a higher minimum number of participants in order to guarantee that you will not make less than you would for a semiprivate personal training session.

Group Fitness Classes

Now let's consider the pricing of group classes not included with a membership. In the late 1980s, classes typically cost $10 each or $90 for a 10-class card. Oddly, the same price is charged today by most places I see. Of course, some elite studios charge more; for instance, I know some indoor cycling studios that range from $15 to $34 per class. So, how should you set your price? Start by considering what you pay your instructors and how much space you have. Also, are the classes your own, or do you pay a licensing fee for the right to offer them?

Let's think through these considerations. Regarding instructor pay, the average hourly pay for a group fitness instructor is $27.50 (Schroeder, 2015). Next, let's look at capacity. Say that your studio can hold 20 participants and you offer 20 classes per week. That's 400 potential spots per week. Based on the average of 4.33 weeks per month, you offer 87 classes (with a total of up to 1,732 participant spots) per month. Therefore, your monthly payroll for instructors is $87 \times \$27.50 = \$2,392.50$.

Divide that figure by the per-class fee in order to determine the number of participants you need per month in order to meet payroll. So, if your per-class fee is $15, then you need 160 participants per month. Divide that number by the number of classes to get the average number of people you need in each class in order to meet payroll: 160 (participants) ÷ 87 (classes) = 1.8 (we'll call it 2) people per class. Note, if you offer an unlimited class membership, the minimum number of participants needed to cover the instructor fee would be more because of the cost per class discount. Now for the upside: If you were to ever meet capacity for all classes in a given month, you'd earn quite a bit: 1,732 (participant spots) × $15 (per-class fee) = $25,980!

Specific Goal-Oriented Programs

It is generally easier to price goal-oriented programs because all you need to do is total the time and services. Most clubs discount a fixed-length program, as compared with the cost of an ongoing program, but in my view that's like discounting a larger package. I believe that a specific goal-oriented package has an inherent attractiveness that doesn't need a lower price.

For an example, let's return to the earlier case of our fictional eight-week program titled My First 5K and add up the time for each component:

- Two Cooper 12-minute run/walk tests: 15 minutes × 2 = 30 minutes
- Registration for 5K race: 15 minutes to register plus race cost of $35
- Eight weekly 30-minute treadmill classes: 4 hours
- Eight weekly 30-minute track classes: 4 hours
- Eight weekly 60-minute runs or walks: 8 hours
- Total: 16.75 hours and $35

Since this offering is like a small-group personal training program (limited to 12 participants because there are only 12 treadmills in our example), let's use our previous small-group cost calculation of $25.60 per participant per hour. The total time is 16.75 hours, and multiplying that by $25.60 produces a total of $428.80. Add the race registration fee of $35, and you end up with a total price of $463.80 per participant for the eight-week program.

More to Come

Your offerings and prices are critical factors in making your business viable. What you offer to your target market can vary greatly and may evolve over time. When you are starting your business, ask yourself what offerings will best suit your clients and help them effectively reach their goals. For instance, memberships are great for individuals who are self-motivated; one-on-one personal training offers the most direct attention; and semiprivate, small-group, and group fitness classes provide diminishing levels of attention from the personal trainer or instructor but increasing levels of social connection and accountability, as well as a diminishing price. You can also consider other possible sources of income, such as selling apparel or nutritional items.

Once you decide on your offerings, it's time to price each one. This process involves a complex interplay between the cost to you, your target market, the demographics, your competition, your unique selling proposition, the value perceived by your clients, your believed value, and how much of your time is involved. When these details are all pulled together, you have something ready to market and sell.

I want to send you off to the next chapter with one cautionary note: Unless you are opening a low-cost club, do not compete to offer the lowest price. If you undercut the lowest competitor, it will then undercut you, and that process will continue until you can't pay your bills. Instead, be better and charge more. Compete on quality and value. That's a game you can win.

Now that you know what your offerings will be, it's time to develop the forms and contracts that you will need to keep the appropriate records of the transactions and interactions that occur. Everything from medical history forms to independent contractor contracts are discussed in chapter 10.

Chapter 10

Developing Forms and Contracts

Getty Images/iStockphoto/Ralph Nestel

Chapter 6 discusses the importance of documenting your business. This chapter, in turn, introduces you to the most common forms and contracts used in the fitness industry. Using these forms is essential for you as a business owner, manager, or personal trainer because they can help you run a fitness business or facility that is safe, effective, and professional.

Standardizing and Clarifying Through Forms and Contracts

Forms are simply informational tools on which club members, clients, or staff fill in blanks to provide the club or personal trainer with details that enable better service. Official forms require at least a signature from the person filling out the form in order to acknowledge understanding and agreement. Some forms for members and clients help you provide care and protection—for example, the PAR-Q+, health history, and physician's clearance forms. Others protect you (as a personal trainer)—for instance, informed consent and waiver forms. And still other forms (or handouts) provide members and clients with information about the club or about you and your offerings.

Forms for staff members range from initial employment forms (such as the W-4 form for federal income tax withholding) to daily maintenance and cleaning checklists. Other staff forms document policies and procedures to enable staff members to properly perform tasks and follow procedures. In other words, these forms provide a way for everyone to be consistent. Specifically, if you have a staff (or just want to document key information for yourself), you should write out procedures for various tasks, such as opening and closing the facility, handling emergency situations, running a class, and meeting with a new client. The person who performs a given task can sign such a form in order to acknowledge his or her understanding of how you want it done; the signed form can be filed in the employee's personnel file.

Contracts are typically longer and are legally binding. Some common elements of membership contracts and personal training contracts are explored in later parts of this chapter. On the business side of things, the chapter also addresses real estate leases, equipment leases, and independent contractor contracts, which all have their own particular requirements.

Confidentiality and Contracts With Minors

All forms and contracts should be kept confidential, especially ones that contain personally identifiable information such as a Social Security number, debit or credit card information, and preparticipation medical forms. Such forms should be kept in a locked file. Be aware that forms such as informed consents, waivers, and contracts are *not* legally binding when signed by a legal minor (check state law regarding the age cutoff). Therefore, if a minor wants to use your facility or work with a personal trainer, all forms and contracts must be signed by a parent or legal guardian. In addition, if you apply different rules or guidelines for legal minors, make sure that both the individual and the parent or legal guardian are informed of those differences at the time of joining or signing up for participation.

Forms for Members and Clients

Forms can serve as a way to communicate information and set expectations. They should be used both with members and clients and with any staff involved in providing services. Forms that can help you serve members and clients include those relating to health and wellness, assumed responsibilities, and waivers. In each case, the form must be completed before an exercise program is developed and, ideally, before an initial fitness assessment is performed. Many of the forms can be found in appendix B and in the web resource (www.HumanKinetics.com/TheBusinessOfPersonalTraining), where you can modify them to fit your purposes.

PAR-Q+ Form

The Physical Activity Readiness Questionnaire for Everyone (PAR-Q+) is a risk assessment that serves as a minimal screening tool to help you determine whether a physician's clearance is needed before a given individual begins an exercise program. The previous version, the PAR-Q, led to many false positives, which unnecessarily directed individuals to obtain a medical referral. This flaw cost both time and money and created a barrier to starting an exercise program (Bredin, Gledhill, Jamnik, & Warburton, 2013). To address this problem, the new version does not send individuals to a physician if they merely answer yes to one of the seven questions. Instead, it leads the individual to answer additional questions that allow for a more detailed look at his or her readiness to participate. Thus it avoids restricting a low-risk individual from beginning a low- to moderate-intensity exercise program.

Thanks to this revision, and the fact that the PAR-Q+ is quick and easy to complete, it now serves as an effective screening tool. It should be completed by all clients, members, and guests who want to exercise. (Of course, if you wish, you can use a more in-depth screening tool such as a health and activity history.) The PAR-Q+ is included in appendix B and in the web resource (www.HumanKinetics.com/TheBusinessOfPersonalTraining).

Health History and Activity History

A health history is a crucial form that helps you determine whether an individual needs to be seen by a physician before starting an exercise program. If the person can start now, the history form also informs you of any physical conditions the personal trainer needs to consider when creating a program for the individual. The form typically includes questions about cardiovascular risk factors, such as age, family history of cardiac issues, smoking, hypertension, cholesterol, blood glucose, obesity, sedentary lifestyle, and HDL levels. Other questions may inquire about such topics as any surgeries experienced, musculoskeletal issues, respiratory conditions, and current medications.

You might also use a lifestyle questionnaire or activity history form to ask about topics such as the individual's exercise programs (past and current), dietary practices, and health habits. This form may also ask about the client's goals, as well as successes and challenges experienced in any previous attempts to reach those goals.

Although the health history and the lifestyle questionnaire are often used as two separate forms, I find that combining them allows a smooth transition and connection between the two topics. This connection helps both the client and the personal trainer see the whole picture. If you use a combined form, give it a user-friendly title, such as Personal Wellness Profile; an example is given in appendix B and in the web resource (www.HumanKinetics.com/TheBusinessOfPersonalTraining).

Physician's Clearance Form

If either the PAR-Q+ or the health history indicates that the client needs medical clearance before beginning an exercise program, then you will need yet another form—specifically, a standardized form to document the physician's full approval, approval with restrictions, or nonapproval. Given the possibility that the physician will give approval with restrictions, the form should provide space where he or she can note exercise recommendations and limitations. See the Physician's Clearance Form in appendix B; it is also included in the web resource (www.HumanKinetics.com/TheBusinessOfPersonalTraining).

Informed Consent Form

An informed consent form and a waiver are not the same thing; they cover different aspects of risk management, and each one needs to be completed. Informed consent, sometimes referred to as "primary assumption of risk," describes the program or activity, summarizes its inherent risks and benefits, includes a confidentiality clause, and states the participant's responsibilities. In order for the informed consent to protect you as a defense strategy, the participant (potential plaintiff) must "know, understand, and appreciate the inherent risks, and voluntarily participate in the activity" (Eickhoff-Shemek, 2007). In other words, you need to inform the person of what the activity entails and obtain his or her acknowledgment of understanding and accepting everything described. Ideally, you review the form with the individual and answer (and document) any questions that he or she has about its contents.

For example, I created a kids' parkour and freerunning class, for which the informed consent form stated, "We run, climb, and jump up, down, and over objects; roll; crawl; chase; and do anything else that kids may do on a playground. While riskier activities will be spotted and mats will be used where appropriate, it should be assumed that the same kinds of injuries that could occur on a playground could occur in this class." That description spelled out the activity, and parents had to sign the form to acknowledge their willingness for their child to participate.

In a general fitness facility, of course, an informed consent form would include a broader blanket statement, such as, "Joe's Gym offers free weights, weight machines, cardio machines, group exercise classes, and other programs and services. Inherently, all physical activities carry physical risks. These risks will vary between individuals based on their current health status; their knowledge of the particular activity; and their own choice to participate in, or continue to participate in, any particular activity." At the bottom of the form, the member would sign and date a statement that says, "I have read, understand, agree with, and assume the risk of participation in any or all of the activities at Joe's Gym. I waive my rights to litigation in the event of injury, even if the injury is caused by negligence on the part of an employee of Joe's Gym."

An informed consent and release form is included in appendix B and in the web resource (www.HumanKinetics.com/TheBusinessOfPersonalTraining). Before committing to using this or any other informed consent form, you should get it approved by your lawyer for your facility according to your needs and all applicable laws.

Waivers

Rather than covering inherent risk, waivers cover against claims of negligence, whether from not doing something one should have done or from doing something one should not have done. Examples include injuries that occur when a personal trainer fails to spot a client during a resistance training exercise or provides improper spotting. "Waivers, if written and administered properly, can protect health/fitness facilities from negligence in most states" (Eickhoff-Shemek, 2005).

In signing a waiver, the client or member releases the club and its employees from legal responsibility for negligent acts. The release language should—and in some states, must—use either the word *negligence* or the word *negligent*. It should also state explicitly that the signer releases the business for its negligent acts. A very good waiver

Informed consent forms should be specific to the activity and should summarize the activity's inherent risks.

of liability is available to members of the Association of Fitness Studios through the organization's website.

Guest Forms

Guest forms serve multiple purposes. First, they obtain informed consent and a liability waiver to cover any activities in which the person engages at your facility. They also gather contact information that you can use to follow up with the guest. Specifically, you should gather the following information:

- Name
- Mailing address
- City
- State
- Zip code
- Primary phone number
- E-mail address
- Date of birth
- Age
- Sex
- Description of how the guest heard about your club
- Summary of the activities or training the guest plans to perform—for example, lifting on his or her own, working with a personal trainer, participating in small-group personal training, taking a group exercise class
- Emergency contact name and phone number

The contact information enables you to follow up with the guest about membership, programs, or personal training. The description of how the person heard about you helps you understand how well your marketing efforts are working. And the summary of the person's activities or training at your facility gives you an idea of his or her interests. You could also include a question asking about the person's exercise goals.

Assessment Forms

Many types of fitness and wellness assessments are available for you to use with your clients and members. They often include activities (tests or procedures) that go beyond what is typically experienced when a person exercises in a facility. Therefore, you need to create a separate informed consent form that spells out the nature of the assessments, their purposes, and the risks they involve. I would also create a specific waiver for these activities, although you can check with your lawyer to see if the general waiver would cover your assessments.

The list of possible forms goes on and on (another common form is the photo and video release form). However, keep in mind that you don't want to overwhelm your clients with forms. If they sign too many forms, they may never remember what they've signed. (We sold our house not long ago, and the required forms stacked up to look like *War and Peace*. I've never signed so much and understood so little of what I was signing.) So, you might choose to combine some forms for simplicity's sake. For example, Jiva Fitness' informed consent and waiver for our group fitness program are simplified and combined on one sheet of paper.

Appendix B includes a general assessment recording form that includes areas for recording vital signs, body composition measures, and fitness test results. You can also find it in the web resource (www.HumanKinetics.com/TheBusinessOfPersonalTraining), where you can modify it to suit your purposes.

Forms for Staff

As with member forms and contracts, the purpose of staff forms is to create clarity and understanding—in this case, about what is expected and how to perform one's duties. Copies of all relevant documents should be kept in each employee's file. Although I discuss these forms as relating to your staff, they are also for you. Even though you may know what you want done and how, you can benefit in two ways from documenting your own activities. First, it gives you a record of the activity taking place; second, it shows your employees that you are part of the team and hold yourself accountable to the rules.

Initial Employment Documentation

Although each facility or club is a unique business, all new employees in every business complete certain standard forms when they are hired. A comprehensive list of these forms is provided by the Internal Revenue Service (2017). The three primary forms are as follows:

- Compensation agreement spelling out how much, and how, the employee will be paid
- Form W-4 (Employee's Withholding Allowance Certificate)
- Form I-9 (Employment Eligibility Verification)

Emergency Procedure Protocols

As you have seen, risk management consists partly of taking legal precautions, such as obtaining informed consent and waivers. Another important part of risk management involves ensuring that proper training and care are provided in the first place. Thus it is crucial for you to establish emergency procedures that are understood and practiced by all employees. These procedures should cover both facility emergencies (such as fire and earthquake) and personal emergencies (such as a member going into cardiac arrest). This documentation should indicate in detail what needs to be done in order to handle the given situation in your specific facility with your specific staffing.

Examples of Emergency Protocols

In Case of Member Collapse

1. Check to see that the scene is safe.
2. Check for responsiveness.
   a. **If the individual is unresponsive,** call 911 (there is always a mobile phone on the premises) and put the phone in speaker mode. Proceed to step 3.
   b. **If the individual is responsive** after collapse, call 911 and stay with the person until paramedics arrive.
3. Appoint another staffer or a member or client to retrieve the AED located by the studio front door; if you are alone, retrieve it yourself.
4. Send another staffer or a member or client to the building's front door to guide paramedics into the studio when they arrive.
5. If the AED is not yet available, check for signs of circulation for 5 to 10 seconds.
6. Make sure that the victim is on a firm, flat surface. Move them to one if needed.
7. Follow AED directions and perform CPR as needed.
8. Continue until paramedics relieve you.

After paramedics arrive and take charge, fill out and file an incident report (the forms are located at the service desk).

In Case of Fire

If a fire is discovered, the studio staff must do the following:

1. Get the attention of all staffers, members, clients, and other guests and direct them to the emergency exit and then to the designated meeting area (through the courtyard to the sidewalk across the street). The group should be led by a staff member if more than one staffer is in the facility.
2. Call 911 and notify the fire department.
3. **If the fire is small and contained,** staff should access the fire extinguisher (located at the front-door entry) and use it to extinguish the fire. If the fire continues to burn, staff should do a final check to ensure that everyone has left the facility, then proceed to the emergency exit, closing fire doors along the route.
4. **If the fire is not small or is spreading,** immediately do a final check to make sure that everyone has left the facility, then proceed to the emergency exit, closing fire doors along the route.
5. After exiting, meet with others and ensure that all are accounted for.

After fire officials give the okay to return to the facility, fill out and file an incident report (forms are located at the service desk).

Accident and Injury Reports

When an accident or injury occurs, document it in detail so that you can refer back to your records if needed—for instance, if a lawsuit is brought against you as a result of the incident. This documentation should include the following information:

- Injured person's name
- Injured person's contact information
- Date of accident or injury
- Description of how the accident or injury occurred
- Where the incident occurred
- Name of person(s) who witnessed the accident or injury
- Contact information for each witness
- Description of relevant actions taken, including by the person(s) involved
- Name of staff member who filled out the report

Other Forms

You may also want your staff to use or fill out additional forms, which can cover all of the systems discussed in chapter 6. Here are some examples:

- Fitness consultation procedure
- Daily opening checklist
- Cleaning checklist
- Equipment maintenance log
- Phone scripts

You can find two such forms—a facility and equipment maintenance log and a cleaning checklist for floors, walls, and ceilings—in appendix B. They are also included in the web resource (www.HumanKinetics.com/TheBusinessOfPersonalTraining), where you can modify them to suit your purposes.

You should also document certain employee situations by creating one or more of the following forms:

- Employee discipline form
- Employee dismissal form
- Exit interview form (for employees who leave voluntarily)

Types of Member Contracts

For our purposes, contracts are legally binding written agreements made between two or more entities. They describe what is and what is not included in the dealings between the entities. In addition, through signatures, they acknowledge understanding of an agreement's expectations and limitations. Because contracts are meant to be legally binding, you should have them reviewed by your lawyer before using them.

Please note that most people don't like filling out paperwork and almost nobody reads long agreements. Think about the last update for your smartphone. You could read through the technical, ultralong user agreement or just hit the "I agree" button. I know I just hit the button. The fact that a document serves as a legal contract does not necessarily mean that it must be long or written in legalese. Keep your language clear and the contract as short as possible; after all, the real purpose is to create understanding.

Membership contracts can help explain the responsibilities of both the members and the staff.

Getty Images/iStockphoto/FatCamera

Membership Contracts

Membership contracts serve the valid purposes of clearly providing information and establishing obligations; unfortunately, they can also be a source of ill will. For instance, they often bind the member to a certain length of time and a certain amount of financial obligation. They may also include financial penalties for early termination of the contract. If a member moved or became ill, imagine how this continued financial obligation may make them feel about your business. As a result of restrictive contracts, if you do a web search for "health club membership contracts," most of the hits address how to get out of them. In response to this problem, the Division of Licensing Services in New York (New York State, 2011) created a document about health club licensing in order "to safeguard the public and the ethical health club industry against deception and financial hardship."

The point of a membership contract should not be to trap or lock members into something that they no longer want to be part of. In recognition of this fact, many of the more enlightened clubs are doing away with time commitments in their membership contracts. This change makes it easier both for potential members to decide to join the club and for members to leave it if and when they so choose.

Why would you want to make it easier for them to leave? Well, if someone chooses to leave your club, for whatever reason, and experiences a hassle in doing so, then that person leaves with a bad feeling about your club. This type of departure makes the person less likely to join again and more likely to complain about you to others. On the other hand, if the person experiences an exit that is smooth, friendly, and hassle free, then not only might that person come back at a later time but also he or she may refer others to you. With these considerations in mind, my recommendation is to limit the time commitment of your membership agreement to a month-by-month approach.

Now, it's time to consider what should be included in your membership contract. Let's go through the necessities.

General Member Information
- Full name
- Date of birth
- Home address (street, city, state, zip)
- Home phone
- Mobile phone
- E-mail address
- Emergency contact name and phone number
- Physician's name and phone number

Membership Information
- Type (if you offer multiple options)
- Fee
- Membership start date
- Membership end date
- Payment options (payment in full or periodic payments, via cash or credit or debit card)
- Automatic payment information, if applicable (automatic billing permission, name on credit or debit card, card number, expiration date, card verification number)

Member or Client Contract for Personal Training

A personal training contract for a member or client spells out the expectations and guidelines of employing a personal trainer. It should include your booking and cancellation policies, session time expectations (we've all had clients show up late and still want their "full time"), how to get in touch with the assigned personal trainer, and anything else you want the member or client to know about personal training before getting started. The contract should include at least the following information:

Member or Client Information
- Name
- Phone (home)
- Phone (mobile)
- E-mail
- Address
- Preferred method of communication (phone, e-mail, text, other)

Personal Training Policies
- Fees
- Cancellations
- Late arrival by client
- Late arrival by personal trainer

Other Information or Expectations (Optional)
- Proper attire
- Ongoing open communication as it relates to any changes in the client's health and wellness status

Personal Trainer Information

- Name
- Phone (club or studio)
- Phone (mobile)
- E-mail
- Personal trainer's signature (dated)
- Member or client's signature (dated)

Although some of these details could be handled as part of an informational hand-out, I like to include them in the signed document. That way, the member or client can keep a copy as a reminder of the expectations, and I can refer to it if, down the line, the person protests that I never said he or she would get charged for late cancellations.

Types of Common Business Contracts

At this point, we've covered various documents addressing relationships between your business and its members, clients, and employees. Whether you operate as a sole proprietor or a corporation, you will also enter into other kinds of contracts that you must understand before signing on "the dotted line." Three examples are real estate leases, equipment leases, and independent contractor contracts.

The following discussion is intended only to give you some general insight into what can be expected with these types of contracts. They are legally binding agreements made between parties; as such, they should always be reviewed by your lawyer. Securing a real estate or equipment lease will likely require you to provide your personal and business credit ratings, as well as current financial records. If your status is deemed not suitable, then you may be required to find a co-signer.

Real Estate Leases

If you are not working in someone else's facility, home, or office, then you will probably either buy or lease your space. Leases can be as variable as the spaces they are written for. Here are the most common elements:

- Name and contact information of the landlord
- Name and contact information of the tenant
- Definitions of common contract terms, such as *rent*, *additional rent*, *common areas and facilities*, and *leasable area*
- Definition of the leased space or premises
- Term or length of the lease (typically 5 to 10 years, which prevents you from having to move every year)
- Rent amount, when it is due, and any required deposit (such as first or last month paid in advance)
- Intended use of the space by the tenant
- Renewal option if any (desirable as a way to provide a future location for your business)
- Improvements to space allowed to be made by the tenant and whether they must be approved by the landlord
- Responsibility for repair of built-in items (tenant possibly responsible for existing HVAC system, for example; worth checking with your insurance agent)

- Insurance requirements (how much and what is covered; worth checking with your insurance agent)
- Lease termination conditions (very important for issues such as noise from music or dropped weights)
- Subletting options (that is, options for subleasing a portion of the space to a complementary business, such as a registered dietitian)
- Other provisions or items for which the landlord or tenant wants agreement
- Dated signatures of the involved parties

Please note that requirements can vary from state to state and even from property to property.

Equipment Leases

When you set up your business, you go through the process of deciding what equipment to put in your facility. That equipment can be either bought or leased. Buying it outright could diminish your cash flow, perhaps to a dangerous level, because equipment can be expensive. Leasing, in contrast, offers a couple of advantages. One, of course, is that it allows you to keep a larger cash reserve. It also enables you to save on taxes because payments to lenders are made with pretax dollars. The typical down payment consists of one or two advance payments, or approximately 2 percent to 5 percent of the total cost. You also need to consider the other up-front costs—sales tax and shipping and installation fees—but they can be added into the total lease price (Nolan, 2015).

Equipment lease contracts include at least some of the following components:

- Name and contact information for the lessor
- Name and contact information for the lessee
- Term or length of the lease
- Monthly lease amount, when it is due, and any security deposit required
- Requirements for the lessee to maintain proper care and upkeep of the equipment
- Requirement for the lessee to obtain proper insurance on the equipment
- Restrictions on transfer of the equipment and payments to another party (i.e., selling your business) without approval
- Disposition of the equipment if the lessee files for bankruptcy
- Dated signatures of the involved parties

Independent Contractor Contracts

Whether you work as an independent contractor or are preparing to use one to provide services to others on your behalf, you should know what goes into an independent contractor contract. This document sets the expectations of working as an independent contractor and the boundaries that the company will enforce with the independent contractor. This delineation can be a bit tricky because, as you may remember, in a true independent-contractor arrangement, the person is hired to perform a service but cannot be told *how* to perform it. At the same time, the club may require certain items to be included in the contract. Here are typical components of an independent contractor contract:

- Name and contact information of the business
- Name and contact information of the independent contractor

- What services are being contracted
- Location where the contracted services are to be offered or provided
- Who may be trained by the independent contractor
- Term (time period) for the contracted services
- Defined fees for the independent contractor, how payment will be received from clients, and how the independent contractor will be paid
- Certifications required for the independent contractor
- Proof of liability insurance by the independent contractor
- Assumption of risk by the independent contractor
- Noncompete and nondisclosure agreements to protect the business
- Dated signatures of the involved parties

More to Come

Forms and contracts provide clarity, enable understanding, and serve as documentation of key actions. To serve these goals, keep the language clear and as simple as possible. These documents offer you and your facility protection from lawsuits and assurance that things are being done in the way you prefer.

Member forms can help inform us about the readiness of an individual to participate in a fitness program and what the person hopes to achieve. Examples include the PAR-Q+, the health history and lifestyle questionnaire, and the physician's clearance form. In addition, informed consent and waiver forms can protect personal trainers, instructors, and the business overall from being found guilty in a liability lawsuit.

Forms for staff range from employment forms such as compensation agreements, W-4s, and I-9s to documentation of what to do and how to act while working for the club. Other crucial documents include descriptions of emergency procedures and accident and injury reports. Every form should serve as a tool for performing or understanding how to perform a key task at the facility or for the business.

Contracts are more formal documents that establish agreements with clients or members or with outside parties—for example, leases and independent contractor contracts. Contracts typically go into great detail. Because of that, and because they are legally binding documents, you should always have them written or reviewed by your lawyer.

The forms and contracts addressed in this chapter do not constitute a complete list. You will come across others and will want others, and you will need to adapt and add forms and contracts as you go along. This part of owning a business is always a work in progress.

Now it's time to look at the details of becoming financially profitable. In chapter 5, we went through the process of predicting ongoing expenses and income. Tracking and managing expenses and income (as well as a few other key performance indicators) is critical to maximizing your business' profitability. In the next chapter, you will learn what to do when your predicted numbers don't match your actual numbers.

Chapter 11

Becoming Financially Profitable

Getty Images/iStockphoto/monkeybusinessimages

We enter the health and fitness field to help people change their lives for the better. That does not mean, however, that we don't want to make a good living while we're at it. Whether you're running a large club or providing personal training in clients' homes, you must understand the financial aspects of running a business and how to make that business profitable. Even organizations classified as nonprofits need to be profitable; they just reinvest their surplus funds in the organization.

Accounting Software

To track your financial statistics (often referred to simply as "financials"), you need to become intimately familiar with reading and manipulating spreadsheets. Yes, you can have someone else do the data entry, but you still need to be able to review and understand the information—after all, it's your money! Many software programs are available for producing these financial reports, including spreadsheet programs such as Microsoft Excel, Google Sheets, and Numbers (for Apple devices). These applications are infinitely adaptable, and it may take you a while to learn how to use them. I now use Excel for many purposes, but in my earlier days it took me quite a while to learn how to fully use it. If you want something simpler and quicker while you get up and running, you might prefer a more complete, guided program such as QuickBooks, FreshBooks, Xero, Zoho Books, or Wave Accounting (Angeles, 2016a).

The best choice depends on what tasks you need the software to perform. To help you choose, create a needs analysis and consider only programs that meet those needs. Your list might include factors such as simplicity of use, on-demand access to account information, legal compliance, ability to generate various kinds of reports, and mobile access. Another consideration, of course, is price. Many top programs are cloud based, and they often charge a monthly fee ranging from $10 to $40 (Angeles, 2016b).

Even if you use an accounting app, I encourage you to use an accountant at least for your tax returns. You should also get a recommendation from your accountant about which app he or she prefers clients to use and make sure that the app can meet your business needs.

Profit and Loss Statement

At the most basic level, you need to learn to use a profit and loss (P&L) statement, or a business income statement. A P&L statement provides a look at how your business is doing financially. As you may recall, the financial information you generate for your business plan should include a projected budget for the first three years (refer to chapter 5, as well as the financial plan template provided in appendix A). Once you start operations, that budget can be compared with the actual numbers for certain periods of time, usually the last month, quarter, or year. The point of this comparison is to adjust your plans as needed to maximize revenues and minimize expenses.

Jiva Fitness Example

Table 11.1 shows an example in which figures in the Budgeted column are taken directly from table 5.4 (Monthly Expenses and Revenues for Jiva Fitness) in chapter 5. This column, of course, shows what you predicted would happen. To its left, the Actual column shows the reported numbers at the close of the month. To the right, the Variance column shows the difference between what was predicted and what happened.

As you can see in the example, some expenses, such as rent, are regular or relatively unchanging. Others vary from month to month—for example, electricity (table 11.1,

Table 11.1   **P&L Statement for Month 1 at Jiva Fitness**

Budget item	Actual	Budgeted	Variance	Explanation of change (where applicable)
MONTH 1				
MONTHLY EXPENSES				
1. Rent	$1,500.00	$1,500.00	$0.00	
2. Electricity	$150.00	$200.00	$−50.00	Less electricity used
3. Loan payment (based on $100,000)	$2,000.00	$2,000.00	$0.00	
4. Cable and Internet	$49.00	$49.00	$0.00	
5. Phone	$150.00	$150.00	$0.00	
6. Bookkeeping and payroll services	$100.00	$100.00	$0.00	
7. Water cooler	$20.00	$40.00	$−20.00	Less drinking water used
8. Online scheduling and payment services	$85.00	$85.00	$0.00	
9. Miscellaneous supplies (e.g., paper, cleaning supplies)	$15.00	$50.00	$−35.00	Fewer cleaning supplies used
10. Website maintenance	$59.00	$59.00	$0.00	
Payroll expenses				
11. Management salaries	$3,333.33	$3,333.33	$0.00	
12. Instructor compensation ($25/class × # of classes/week × 4.33 weeks/month)	$866.00	$1,082.50	$−216.50	Lower payroll to instructors
13. Personal training compensation (50% of personal training revenue)	$454.65	$363.72	$90.93	Higher payroll to personal trainers
Total expenses	**$8,781.98**	**$9,012.55**	**$−230.57**	**Lower total expenses (you saved on expenses)**
REVENUE				
Membership income				
14. Class membership fee	$69.00	$69.00	$0.00	
15. Maximum # of class memberships	200	200	0	
16. # classes/week	8	10	−2	Fewer classes held
17. # of class memberships sold	3	10	−7	Fewer memberships sold
18. Monthly member revenue (membership fee × # of memberships)	$207.00	$690.00	$−483.00	Lower class revenue
Personal training income				
19. Personal training fee	$42.00	$42.00	$0.00	
20. Personal training maximum sessions/week	40	40	0	
21. Sessions/week	5	4	1	More sessions held
22. Sessions/month (average of 4.33 weeks/month)	21.65	17.32	4.33	More sessions held
23. Monthly personal training revenue (personal training fee × # of sessions)	$909.30	$727.44	$181.86	Higher personal training revenue
Total revenue	**$1,116.30**	**$1,417.44**	**$−301.14**	**Lower total revenue (you made less)**
Total net revenue (revenue − expenses)	**$−7,665.68**	**$−7,595.11**	**$−70.57**	**Lower net revenue (greater loss)**

line 2), regarding which you may find opportunities to conserve energy (and thus money). These are the expenses that you need to manage actively and keep as low as you can in order to maximize your net revenue. You can also see that expenses were lower than expected for drinking water, miscellaneous supplies, and instructor compensation (payroll) (lines 7, 9, 12). Unfortunately, it's not enough simply to say, "Yay, expenses are down!" You need to understand *why* they are lower than expected (more on that in a moment).

Now let's take a look at revenues. In the revenue portion of the P&L statement, the first variance consists of holding fewer classes than planned (line 16). Of course, fewer classes held means less need for instructors, which explains why the instructor compensation expense (line 12) was lower than expected.

In many cases, a reduction in expenses is a positive change, but for your offerings (such as classes) you need to engage in ongoing analysis. For instance, offering fewer classes means that you pay less in instructor fees, but if you offer *too* few classes per week, then you also reduce the perceived value among members of buying an unlimited-class membership. Imagine two unlimited group-fitness memberships that each cost $69, one of which provides access to 35 classes per week while the other provides access to only 5 classes. The membership that offers 35 classes provides members with the opportunity to take more classes, or different ones, or at various times. As a result, it will have a much higher perceived value.

At Jiva Fitness, we determined that 10 classes per week was the minimum we could offer and still create value for our unlimited group fitness membership. (Although, you'll note in table 11.1 we only actually taught an average of 8 classes/week in the first month. This was due to scheduled classes that had no participants.) This package gave Jiva Fitness a chance to build the group fitness program without draining too much net revenue while we worked toward covering instructor costs. That said, you could still choose to reduce the number of classes or eliminate the monthly membership fee entirely and change to a class-by-class payment system.

The second variance involves number of class memberships sold (line 17). Specifically, we sold seven fewer memberships than we had projected. This is definitely not a positive variance! It means that we brought in $483 less than projected through memberships (line 18), which outweighs the $216.50 saved in instructor compensation for the month. So, for this month, the group fitness program is $266.50 in the hole.

As for monthly revenue from personal training, we projected selling four sessions per week but actually sold five (line 21). Given the average of 4.33 weeks per month, that extra membership means that we sold 4.33 more personal training sessions than projected for the month. This difference translates to $181.86 more revenue than projected (line 23). Of course, because personal trainers are paid 50 percent of what they bring in, we saw a corresponding increase ($90.93) in the personal training compensation expense (line 13). Thus, in this case, more income means more payroll. In other words, when personal training compensation goes over budget, it means that the personal training revenue did so as well (assuming that you compensate only for sessions delivered). That's a good thing!

Now let's look at the items that show a savings in the expense section. With the exception of lower instructor compensation expense (line 12), the other changes can be attributed to fewer people coming to the facility than planned. Less electricity is used because lights, treadmills, and so on were needed less than expected. Fewer people also means less drinking water needed and fewer cleaning supplies used. Thus you can see that lower expenses don't necessarily make for a better financial outlook.

Recognizing the interplay between expense and revenue items sets you up to understand your profit or loss for the month when you look at total net revenue. The projected loss for this month was $7,595.11, but the actual loss turned out to be 7,665.68, or a $70.57 greater loss than the budgeted amount.

Ideas for Maximizing Net Revenue

Based on the information presented in a P&L statement, you can decide what actions to taken in order to improve net revenue. Optimally, you should try to limit expenses *and* increase revenues.

Regarding the expenses that are not fixed, you could look for less expensive supplies or ways to use fewer resources. For instance, what if you install motion sensors on your lights so that they turn off when nobody is in a given space or room? You might also shop around for the best prices for cleaning and office supplies. Another option is to reduce the percentage of income paid to personal trainers. Many facilities choose this path, but those payroll cuts will also reduce the motivation and loyalty of the personal training team.

You could also change the compensation structure for management from a straight salary to a percentage of actual total revenue. In the Jiva Fitness example (table 11.1), management salaries were budgeted at $3,333.33 to reflect the combined salary for two managers who each earn $20,000 per year. This amount is 299 percent of the actual total revenue of $1,116.30. You might agree that paying your managers three times your actual income could be a challenge for your budget in the early stages of a start-up! If, instead, you paid the managers a percentage of actual total revenue—say, 100 percent—then the combined salary amount for management would be $1,116.30, which would save you $2,217.03.

Why would managers want to take the percentage option? Well, they wouldn't make as much at first, but down the road, as total revenue increased, they could make a lot more. For instance, if total monthly revenue rose to $4,000, then they would make $666.67 more than they would have with the $3,333.33 straight salary (that's $4,000.02 more per year for each manager). That's an attractive offer for them, and it provides an incentive to get those revenues up as quickly as possible. It also benefits you as the business owner by lowering the management expense until the facility achieves more financial security.

Becoming financially profitable requires you to be able to understand and adapt to variances in profits and losses.

Getty Images/Image Source/Natalie Faye

If you take this route, put a cap on the arrangement to ensure that it doesn't get out of hand. For instance, suppose that your total revenue rose to $20,000 per month. Management would make their 100 percent, or $20,000, which would make their annual combined salary $240,000! Set your payroll cap at a level that is attractive enough for management to choose that option, but keep it in proportion with industry standards. For fitness directors and group fitness directors, the averages range from $41,332 to $56,203 per year (International Health, Racquet & Sportsclub Association [IHRSA], 2015, p. 11).

From an income standpoint, how can you increase the sales of your services? Without giving away all of the ideas covered in the next chapter, here are two methods to get you started:

- Boost or change your marketing efforts. You may need to get your brand in front of more people in your target market. This work might include getting out into the community and meeting people face to face or creating a direct mail campaign. In addition, consider whether your current efforts are sending the right message to the right target audience.
- Change your product offerings. For example, rather than simply offering group fitness or personal training as separate items, you could bundle them as a packaged product. For instance, you could offer a package that includes unlimited group fitness and two personal training sessions per week.

The concepts underlying a P&L statement apply to businesses at all levels, whether you manage or own a facility or work as an independent contractor. Systematic tracking enables you to see how much income you make, where it comes from, and where you spend it. By continually seeking ways to limit expenses and increase revenues, you will be able to maximize your net revenue.

Understanding Cash Flow

A cash flow statement helps you understand the ins and outs of accessible funds for your business. The key word here is *accessible*. Being able to pay an unexpected bill can make the difference in whether you are able to stay in business. Imagine, for example, your HVAC system breaking down on a sweltering summer day. If you don't get it fixed right away, members will stop coming and will look for another place to work out. Often, however, getting immediate service requires you to pay the repair company with cash or a check. You won't be able to do so if you just spent your available cash on items for the pro shop to help you earn income down the road. In that case, you're stuck until you can get more cash.

Here's another example. Suppose that a company contracts with you to deliver a fitness program. In order to deliver the program, you need certain equipment, and you use most of your available cash to buy it, knowing that you will make it up when the company pays you for the program. However, many companies require you to invoice them and may then take up to 90 days to pay the invoice. (In addition, it's not unusual for the invoice amount to be based on how many people attend the program. In that case, you will have to deliver at least part of the program before you even know what you will charge.)

Now, imagine that during this time of having to pay out for equipment but wait for your invoice to be paid, you receive a bill for landscaping at your facility that is due within 30 days. Here again, you find yourself without the funds. Even though you know that the money for providing the corporate fitness program is coming soon, it could arrive 60 days too late for you to pay the landscaping bill. As you can see, being "cash poor" is something you need to avoid.

One tool for staying on top of your available cash is the cash flow statement. Here is the formula for calculating cash flow:

Net revenue + asset investment + savings and financing = cash balance

Let's start with the total net revenue on your P&L statement. Asset investment is the net balance of what you spent on investments (e.g., buying pro shop items to resell) and the income you made from them (e.g., total pro shop sales). It could also include investment in new equipment; this item is frequently, but not always, included in a P&L statement. The savings and financing element consists of the net balance of any savings you invested in the business, any business loans, and any lines of credit you secure. Although loaned money constitutes debt and using a line of credit creates debt, they still count as cash that you could use if needed.

Your cash flow sheet can help you make spending decisions that enable you to keep cash on hand for paying both normal and unexpected expenses. Returning to the preceding examples, given that cash flow was low, you should have held off on purchasing the pro-shop inventory. In the example of the corporate fitness program, if you were aware that purchasing the needed equipment would deplete your available cash, then you might have chosen to negotiate with the company to purchase the equipment, make the invoice payable within 30 days, or insist that the company pay for the program before you deliver it.

As these examples illustrate, understanding your cash flow makes it clear when you can safely tie up cash in a new investment—and when you cannot. A good rule of thumb is to generate a cash flow statement every month, as well as any time that you are considering a major investment. An example of a monthly cash flow statement is presented in table 11.2.

Table 11.2   **Sample Cash Flow Statement**

Jim's In-Home Personal Training	
MONTH OF JUNE	
Operating costs (from P&L)	
Income	$4,583
Expenses (e.g., marketing, transportation)	$−280
Net revenue	$4,303
Asset investments	
Apparel inventory purchased for resale	$−150
Apparel inventory sales	$50
Yoga mats and carrying straps (2) for resale	$−48
Net cash from asset investments	$−148
Savings and financing	
Savings account balance (personal investment)	$5,000
Bank loan	$3,000
Bank loan payments	$−500
Net cash from savings and financing	$7,500
Cash balance	
Net revenue	$4,303
Net cash from asset investments	$−148
Net cash from savings and financing	$7,500
Net cash balance (or total cash available)	**$11,655**

Key Performance Indicators

Key performance indicators, or KPIs, are certain tasks or items that can be quantified and tracked to reveal how well things are going for you or your company. As management guru Peter Drucker is often credited with saying, "What gets measured gets managed." In other words, if you determine what you're doing (by measuring it), then you can figure out what to change in order to get better results.

You can measure almost anything, but is it necessary or advisable to spend your time trying to actively manage everything? In this regard, I'm a believer in the Pareto Principle (also called the 80/20 rule), which holds that 80 percent of the results (or effects) come from 20 percent of the inputs (or causes). Or, for our purpose here, 80 percent of the improvement in your business results will come from 20 percent of the possible things you could change. In other words, you don't need to manage all possible metrics—just the 20 percent that will give you the biggest results.

The following sections address some common KPIs that can be used regardless of whether you run a health club or fitness studio or work as an independent personal trainer.

Conversion Rates

Conversion rates indicate how well you are able to sell memberships, group fitness programs, personal training sessions, and whatever else you offer. These rates are based on the number of sales closed as a percentage of the number of opportunities given. For example, if you meet with 10 people and 5 of them join your club, then you have a 50 percent conversion ratio. Here are some other key conversion opportunities:

- Number of walk-ins and percentage converted to members
- Number of telephone, e-mail, and social media inquiries and percentage converted to in-person meetings
- Number of fitness consultations and percentage converted to purchased personal training sessions or programs
- Number of free-trial attendees and percentage converted to members

You can also track the frequency and the conversion rate for other means of drawing in potential clients and members, such as social media offers and radio ads. In each of these scenarios, you are looking to determine both the effectiveness of your marketing (to get the individual to take some kind of action) and your ability (or that of your staff) to move people to the next level of commitment.

Client and Member KPIs

For fitness facilities and personal trainers, clients and members are the lifeblood of business. That's where you get the majority of your income, so what more meaningful KPIs could you have? Here are some key KPIs in this category.

- **Total number of clients or members:** This KPI enables you to get an idea of your current total of personal training or membership income. However, you also need to look at other KPIs to get the whole picture. The total number of clients or members will fluctuate throughout the year, and it's important to know what is going on at a deeper level and, ideally, the reasons for the ups and downs.
- **New clients or members acquired this week (or quarter or year):** This indicator reflects how well you are doing at getting new people signed up. Two key sub-

KPIs are sales opportunities and conversion rates for those opportunities. Sales opportunities are chances to sign up a new client or member, whether in response to a phone, e-mail, or social media inquiry or a walk-in visit.

- **Members or clients lost this week (or quarter or year):** Attrition is ongoing. People leave personal trainers, studios, and clubs for many reasons. Some can't be helped (such as moving away), but others fall within your control (such as poor service and dirty equipment). Therefore, it is extremely important to understand the reason for the loss of a member or client. To find the answer, conduct an exit interview if at all possible; it may be as simple as a brief conversation. Keeping clients and members is less expensive than acquiring new ones; therefore, retention is crucial.

- **Average length of membership or personal training relationship:** These statistics show you how well you retain your clients and members. At the first club where I worked, in Boston in the early 1980s, the owner didn't care about members' success. He cared only about making money. The club had plenty of members, and if that was the only number you looked at, you'd think the business was in good shape. The philosophy was to sell as many memberships as possible, hope for people to decide that it was too crowded and fail to show up, and then sell more memberships. The club didn't measure retention, but I'd bet that it averaged only a couple of months. That doesn't work in these days of social media, when someone can instantly warn thousands of people about a business that wrongs its clients or members. Such a business will soon find itself running out of customers.

Key Performance Indicators (KPIs) can help you track aspects like club attendance that reflect your business's relative success.

Getty Images/iStockphoto/monkeybusinessimages

Group Fitness KPIs

If you offer a group fitness program, the following numbers can help you judge your program's success.

- **Weekly visits to the facility:** This number indicates how many people walk through the facility door each week. Though not specific to group fitness, you can still use it as a piece of the puzzle in understanding the level of success of your group fitness program.

- **Average weekly class attendance:** Group fitness programs are typically set up by the week. In other words, you offer certain classes on Mondays, on Tuesdays, on Wednesdays, and so on. Therefore, a week gives you a good look at your whole program. Average weekly class attendance helps you see whether the program is growing.

- **Percentage of weekly visits:** This indicator shows the strength of your group fitness program as compared with the rest of the club's offerings. To determine this figure, divide the number of weekly group-fitness visits by the number of weekly club visits, then multiply by 100 to translate it into a percentage. For instance, if 100 people take classes in a particular week and 1,000 people check in at the service desk, then you would make the following calculation: $100 \div 1,000 = 0.10 \times 100 = 10$ percent. In other words, 10 percent of club visits for the week included participation in group fitness.

- **Average individual class attendance:** Even if your group fitness program is doing well, there are always certain classes that struggle to draw attendees. You should establish a minimum number of participants as a cutoff to indicate when a class is not performing well enough to remain on the schedule.

Personal Training KPIs

You also need to know how your personal training program is doing, regardless of whether you manage only your own program or that of a team of personal trainers.

- **Number of personal training sessions delivered per day (or week or month):** How much personal training are you doing? You can also break it down into types of personal training, either by session length (such as 30-minute versus 60-minute sessions) or by style (such as small-group versus one-on-one sessions).

- **Percentage of weekly visits:** As with group fitness, you can find out what kind of penetration your personal training achieves as compared with other facility offerings.

- **Percentage of weekly personal training sessions:** You can also take a more specific look at your own personal training business within the overall business of the fitness facility. What percentage of the total number of personal training sessions are you delivering?

Revenue per Square Foot

Revenue per square foot shows how efficient you are at using your space. According to the Association of Fitness Studios (2016, p. 39, figure 43), smaller studios (those 5,000 square feet or less, or 465 square meters) are generally more efficient at using their space than are larger studios (5,001 square feet to over 10,000, or 465 square meters to over 929), as indicated by their average revenue rates of $104 per square foot versus $47 per square foot, respectively. Space that isn't used to its full potential reduces the overall profitability of your business.

Revenue per Client or Member

Tracking revenue per client or member can help you identify which individuals use more particular services, such as personal training, nutritional coaching, group fitness, or massages. Equipped with this information, you can target others like them in marketing your products. Members that use more of the available services can also get better results when they get assistance in different areas. Imagine how much change can happen if someone works with a personal trainer, a nutritionist, and a meditation coach. Good for them and good for your business.

Client or Member Satisfaction

This indicator is also referred to as Net Promoter Score (NPS), which can range from −100 to 100. Probably the best indicator of client or member satisfaction is the answer to the question, "How likely are you to recommend us to your friends?" Answers can be structured on a scale of 0 (not likely at all) to 10 (extremely likely). Individuals who answer with 9 or 10 are termed Promoters, those who answer with 7 or 8 are termed Neutrals or Passives, and those who respond with 0 to 6 are termed Detractors. The NPS formula subtracts the percentage of Detractors from the percentage of Promoters to arrive at a score for your business (Net Promoter Network, 2016).

If you are an independent personal trainer, you might ask 25 clients to answer the key NPS question (that is, "Are you likely to recommend us to your friends?"). Let's say that five clients give you a score of 10 (Promoter), ten give you a score of 9 (Promoter), three give you a score of 7 (Neutral), four give you a score of 6 (Detractor), and three give you a score of 5 (Detractor). Your NPS calculation would look like this:

15 (number of Promoters) ÷ 25 (total number of clients) × 100 = 60 percent

7 (number of Detractors) ÷ 25 (total number of clients) × 100 = 28 percent

NPS = 60 percent − 28 percent = 32

NPS scores can be interpreted as follows (Retently, 2016):

- <0 = needs improvement
- 0-30 = good
- 31-70 = great
- 71-100 = excellent

By identifying Detractors, this information allows you to ask them what you or your facility could do to get them to give you a score of 10. You may get some outlandish answers, such as "Pick me up for my workout and drop me off afterward." You will also get some actionable input, such as, "Pay more attention to me during our session (and less to the people around me)." In fact, this is a common complaint about some personal trainers. Working to resolve such issues can increase your NPS score, which translates into more people singing your praises and recommending you to others. See the accompanying sidebar regarding KPIs that are most important when you are starting up your business.

Most Important Initial KPIs

When you are starting up, the KPIs that will serve you best are the ones that address sales opportunities and sales closed. They include the following indicators.

- **Total number of members:** How do your actual membership sales compare with your projected sales?
- **Number of personal training sessions delivered per week:** How do your actual sales of personal training sessions compare with your projected sales?
- **Conversion numbers:** Are you effectively communicating the value of the solutions you offer?
- **Sales opportunities:** Are you getting enough people in front of you to have a conversation about their needs?

Reinvesting

In better businesses, it is understood that in order to retain clients or members, you need to keep improving, or at least avoid backsliding. In a fitness facility, everything wears down, from the carpets to the equipment to the paint on the walls. Even if current members become blind to the slow deterioration, new people walking through the doors will immediately see it. At one point, I belonged to a gym located in an expanded garage filled with various old pieces of equipment. The lockers were rusty and looked like old high school cast-offs. The most the owner would do to invest in the facility was to buy more grease for the weight machine guide rods. I wouldn't have worked out there if it hadn't been the only gym in town. And these days, there are enough options around that, as a business owner, you simply must maintain the upkeep of your facility and equipment. The condition of your facility reflects on your brand.

In 2013, according to the International Health, Racquet & Sportsclub Association (Rodriguez, 2014), clubs reinvested 5.4 percent of their total annual revenue, most of which was allocated to additions and improvements to the physical facility or grounds. These ongoing efforts to provide a facility and equipment that are clean, attractive, and well cared for can go a long way toward attracting and retaining members. Put simply, these investments help you keep members happy and satisfied with "their" facility, which is good both for their progress and for your financial strength.

In fact, the same report (Rodriguez, 2014) indicated that the most profitable clubs reinvested more than 17 percent of their total annual revenue—more than three times the average. Their average member-retention rate was 10 percent higher than that of the least profitable clubs, and their net membership growth was more than twice as high. Clearly, then, both current and potential members notice a club's strong commitment to its clientele—not just to making money!

More to Come

Becoming a financially profitable company depends on your ability to understand financial analyses and reports and adapt your plans accordingly. The P&L statement is the heart and soul of your finances because it tells you what is working, and what is not, over a given time period. If you don't look for these trends, it is nearly impossible to make the adjustments required for a profitable future. Another key tool is the cash flow statement, whether it is generated in a separate report or included with the

P&L. This tool helps you determine whether you can handle your day-to-day bills and maintain a reserve for unexpected expenses. Without access to cash, your company becomes vulnerable to a financial crisis.

To be able to manipulate the variables that mean the most to your financial profitability, you have to know which ones have the greatest impact. Key performance indicators (KPIs) address the variables that hold the power to change your company's future.

Finally, remember that profitable companies are not static. You need to reinvest in your company in order to keep it at the top of its game—and to keep your clients and members coming back.

Let's turn now to how you can draw in your members or clients through marketing. In order to get people to use your services, they have to know about you, like who you are and what you do, and they have to trust you. This is all part of building relationships, and building relationships is what marketing is all about.

Chapter 12

Marketing Your Services and Your Business

Getty Images/Hero Images

In order for you to get the chance to sell your products or services, people have to know that you exist. That's where marketing comes into the picture. Marketing involves creating awareness—within your target demographic—of yourself, your expertise, your company (if you own one), and your brand. It also involves engaging and moving members of that demographic to the point where they want to know more about you and, eventually, hire or buy from you.

Taking another step back, before you can market to the members of your target demographic, you have to find them. Where do they hang out? Remember that these days, you might find them both in the physical community and online. Once you do find them, you need a plan to describe who you are, what you can do, and why you do it. These details define your brand and must be articulated clearly—first to yourself and then to your target market.

Marketing has changed dramatically in the past decade, and it will continue to evolve. It is no longer confined to placing expensive ads on television and radio and in magazines and newspapers. And it certainly doesn't include getting your company's name in the phone book's "yellow pages" (perhaps I'm dating myself by even mentioning that!). Once the Internet became interactive, marketing was no longer a one-way street. This revolution allowed marketers to create relationships with their intended audiences, and those relationships brought new customers. This is not to say that traditional marketing no longer has a place, but since it can be very expensive, you need to be selective in deciding how to use it.

Even with all of these changes in the world of marketing, an in-person meeting is still the gold standard when you're seeking local consumers. Building personal connections and relationships is still the best way to promote your business. The next best thing is social media. Granted, it gives your potential clientele less information about you and your business than speaking to them in person, which, for example, allows you to read the other person's body language. But it still offers the opportunity to interact, conduct meaningful discussions, and build trust, all of which enable you to develop a following and stimulate your business.

A New Approach to Marketing

Before the rise of the Internet, companies could only send information out to their audience and hope for the desired reaction. This kind of traditional marketing has been called *interruption marketing* by entrepreneur and author Seth Godin. The term fits because traditional advertising interrupts what you're doing and tries to force you to pay attention. Think about it: Commercials interrupt your TV viewing, break up your music on the radio, and make you skip pages while reading articles in magazines and newspapers. You don't ask for this; it's just forced on you.

The Origins of Spam

The term *spam*, as applied to junk e-mail (and other interruption strategies, such as commercials and print ads), originated with the 1970s "Spam" comedy sketch by Monty Python. In the sketch, two characters are ordering breakfast at a restaurant where everything on the menu contains varying amounts of Spam (a canned meat product). Thus the character who hates Spam can't get a dish without it, and this usage of the term was applied to e-mails that nobody wants but everybody gets.

In contrast, the current style of marketing, referred to as *permission marketing*, focuses on "the privilege (not the right) of delivering anticipated, personal, and relevant messages to people who actually want to get them" (Godin, 2008). This style of marketing has been likened to getting married. You don't just meet someone and propose; you have to spend time getting to know, trust, and love someone before you pop the question. The same is true with marketing and sales. People buy from those whom they know, like, and trust. Therefore, your marketing goal is to create relationships with members of your target market and gradually build permission to sell yourself, your products, and your services to them.

Locating Your Target Market

Whatever your target market is, its members will have certain things in common that can help you find out where they spend their time. As you build a profile of your market, include as many details as possible. This approach applies whether you own a facility or work as a personal trainer. The more specific your profile, or niche, the more you can zero in on where to find your desired clientele.

Let's say that you find the most satisfaction in helping seniors. Great! That's a start. To go further, let's say that you want to work with post-rehabilitation clients and, even more specifically, post-rehabilitation clients who had joint-replacement surgery (let's also say that you're specifically trained to work with that population). Now, not only have you determined specifically who you want to work with, but also you can now figure out where to find them. For instance, you can work on creating relationships with local orthopedic surgeons and physical therapists; you might even ask to shadow a physical therapist. Other, more general options might include making connections with local senior centers (joint replacements are common among seniors). For example, you might host a workshop titled Getting the Most Out of Your New Joint.

Here's another example. I know of a personal training and group fitness studio that focuses on reaching Christians (as a religious group). As a result, its marketing materials talk about God's love and include quotations from the Psalms. Of course, that approach will not click with everyone, but it will make a connection with the studio's target audience, and, as a result, members of that market will choose this studio over others. The next step is to determine where the studio can find its people. Well, Christians can be found most anywhere, so one option is to launch a general promotion to the public. However, if the studio really wants to home in on its target market, the search should focus on local churches, Bible study groups, ministers, teachers and staff members at Christian schools, and so on.

To take another example, what if you want to work with high school athletes? You could reach out to school athletics directors, coaches, and booster clubs—all of whom are in a position to guide or make decisions involving student-athletes. In addition, it's also a good idea to use social media groups, such as those on Facebook, whose members match your target client profile. You can use such groups to start conversations that can help you build your business. Remember, you need to start by building relationships with people and groups, then gradually build permission to market to them. The process of doing so is covered later in this chapter.

Developing Your Brand

When we think of brands, we typically think of logos, but brands are not merely logos. Rather, branding involves the feelings and thoughts that come to mind when you see a

Defining your target market helps you home in on which marketing avenues will likely give you the best results.

Getty Images/Blend Images/JGI/Jamie Grill

logo or think of a specific company. Therefore, you have a brand regardless of whether you are a personal trainer working for a club, an independent contractor, or the owner of a studio or club. CrossFit's brand, for instance, is associated with no-frills "box" facilities and hard-core, high-intensity workouts. In contrast, the Curves brand is associated with unintimidating facilities where nonexercisers can get started. In another example, the personal trainers featured on the television show *The Biggest Loser*, Bob Harper and Jillian Michaels, had their own brand, which hinged on the combination of Harper being nurturing and supportive while Michaels berated her trainees.

Thus your brand consists of the feelings and thoughts that people have about you and your services—that is, their perceptions—which means that you cannot fully control it. What you *can* do is constantly work toward making sure that everything you do, say, or publicize is consistent with your brand, which in turn is based on your mission statement, your mantra, and your reason for being in this business.

Let's go back to the example of working with high school athletes. Your mission statement might be something like, "XYZ Personal Training provides the most current evidence-based training techniques to enhance high school athletes' physical performance and help them become better teammates and citizens of the world." With that as your mission statement, your mantra might be, "Building better athletes and better people."

Developing your brand, then, would involve reinforcing that stance during every face-to-face interaction, in every ad, at every event, and in every social media post. Thus you can join in and enrich conversations that address not only strength and conditioning for young athletes but also ways to help them build camaraderie, empathy, and character. Perhaps you sponsor cooperative physical challenges for teens; give presentations about eating for sport performance to parents, teens, and coaches; or simply help out with a booster club. All of these activities can help you build your brand in the eyes of your beholders!

Traditional Marketing

The traditional one-sided announcement or pitch to potential buyers is also called *outbound marketing*. I still remember the ads in the comic books that I read as a child, including the Charles Atlas bodybuilding ads with slogans such as "The Insult That

Made a Man Out of Mac" and "The Insult That Turned a 'Chump' Into a Champ." I also remember radio spots for Lay's potato chips and television commercials for cigarettes that used the slogan "Winston tastes good like a cigarette should." Whether they appeared on paper, on the radio, or on television, these ads were placed in order to reach the masses in hopes that someone would buy the product. This method offered the best way to let the largest number of people know about the product in an era of one-way contact.

Even when the Internet first came into being, it was a static, one-way marketing tool that allowed users to go to companies' websites to read about them and their products. Like advertisements in other mediums, the individual companies produced all of the content. It wasn't until the web became interactive—allowing content to be created or edited by users—that marketing really began to evolve. This user-driven environment brought with it the ability to initiate conversations and build relationships. Therefore, although traditional marketing is not dead, it is no longer the best way to bring in members of your target audience and retain them as club members or clients.

Advertising for Television, Radio, Magazines, and Newspapers

Advertising costs during Super Bowl 51 hit a record high of $5 million to $5.5 million for a 30-second commercial (Rapaport, 2017). Why would anyone pay this kind of money if traditional advertising is ineffective? Well, I for one am not sure it's worth it. In any case, before you decide to use traditional advertising, consider the price versus its effectiveness. Consider also the fact that interruption marketing is used so heavily that people become very good at ignoring it—and, in the case of TV commercials, may even use digital recorders to fast-forward right past them.

So, what's the upside? As is often the case with Super Bowl ads, creativity that grabs people's attention and educates, entertains, or inspires them makes them more likely to associate a positive feeling with the brand in question. Therefore, it is more likely to influence consumers to choose that brand. Consumers do still watch TV and read magazines and newspapers, so these media could be valuable, particularly for creating brand awareness.

If you were to run a TV ad, here are some ways to maximize your return on investment:

- Choose the shortest time segment possible. Some channels allow spots as short as 15 seconds.
- Choose a local station affiliate or local cable spot; they are not only more specific to your location but also less expensive. For example, whereas a 30-second national commercial can cost $354,000, a local affiliate spot may cost $20 to $1,000 and a local cable spot may cost only $5 to $100 (LinchpinSEO, 2017).
- Since you're using a visual medium, maximize its potential effect by showing a scenario that elicits an emotional reaction—for example, quick scenes of parents and grandparents keeping up with their kids and grandkids while playing a sport. You could tag it with a simple voiceover statement and a call to action, such as, "Life is a sport—get ready to play at Jim's Gym!"
- Indicate how people can find you. Because people won't remember all of your contact information from a short TV segment, choose the one piece of contact information that will make it as easy as possible for people to find you. It might be your phone number, website address, or physical address.
- Talk with the station's advertising department about which time slot is best for reaching your target demographic.
- Also talk with the station's ad folks about format and other guidelines.

The United States is home to many more radio stations than TV stations. Radio broadcasters range from national operations to college stations that reach only across campus. Here are some suggestions for effective radio advertising:

- Because of radio's diverse range of geographic coverage, pricing for radio ads runs the gamut. To keep costs down, choose the station with the smallest geographic reach that still covers your market area.

- Radio advertising depends on repetition. Therefore, you "need to spend a certain amount before you begin to see any worthwhile results. You can expect to spend approximately $2,000 per week in a regional market and at least $3,000 with a larger metro station" (Sugars, 2017).

- Choose the appropriate station format for your target demographic. For example, adults of ages 35 to 44 listen primarily to rock and adult contemporary (Aland, 2016). You can find your local stations and their formats at the Radio-Locator website (https://radio-locator.com).

- Because radio is an auditory medium, people are often doing other things while they partake of it. Therefore, your message should be short, sweet, and attention grabbing. To get the audience's attention, you need not only a sharp script but also music and perhaps sound effects. For instance, though it may not be the image you're trying to portray, you can imagine the sounds of people grunting and weights clanging as possible background elements in a radio ad.

- Leave time to provide your contact information and perhaps to repeat it several times. I remember a radio commercial from decades ago that repeated its phone number in a jingle, and I can still remember it: 800-325-3535. As I was writing this, I couldn't remember whose number it was, so I just looked it up. It's the customer service line for the Sheraton hotel brand. Well played, Sheraton!

- As with television ads, talk with the station's advertising department to determine the best time slot for reaching your target demographic.

- Again, as with TV ads, talk with the ad folks about any format requirements and other guidelines.

- Although radio ads are typically less expensive to produce than TV commercials (audio only versus audio and video), you still need to plan for production costs.

Free Exposure

Since cost can be such a big factor, particularly for a new business, let's take a look at how to get exposure for free.

If you're new in town, are opening a new facility, have made an achievement, or are hosting an event (particularly if it's for charity), then you have a newsworthy story. Meanwhile, news organizations—newspapers, magazines, websites, and television and radio stations—are all looking for . . . you guessed it, news. Give them what they want by sending out a media release. To maximize your chance that a news outlet will pick up your story, package the information to be as usable as possible. To that end, here are five guidelines for writing an effective media release (James, 2010):

- **Rule 1: Use the media release as a sales tool.** You can do so by communicating something about your expertise or your brand, as well as where you can be found. Keep in mind, however, that while your media release should include essential information about you and your business, it should never sound or feel like an advertisement.

- **Rule 2: Create a newsworthy story.** By definition, a news story should be newsworthy. Fortunately, people love a good story. You could tell the story of how you overcame challenges to open your business or the story of someone you have helped. For example, consider the story of Andy Zagami (http://andrewzagami.com). As a young personal trainer who had three battles with cancer, Zagami could easily have given up. Instead, he fought back, built his business, told his story in his book *Unbreakable*, and now uses his experience to help others. That's a great human interest story that most news organizations would love to cover.

- **Rule 3: Write it like a reporter would.** The more your release looks and feels like a reporter wrote it, the easier it is for a news organization to use it. Thus it should *not* have the casual feeling of a blog post. Write it in third person (no *I* or *me*) and make it grammatically correct and free of spelling mistakes. Give it an eye-grabbing headline, such as "Personal Trainer Offers Greater Quality of Life After Joint Replacement." Structure it with an intro that previews the details, then give the details themselves (that is, what you want the audience to know), and finish with a conclusion that summarizes the details.

- **Rule 4: Provide good remarks.** The media love quotes and sound bites. If you include a few that sum up the essence of your release, they may see life even after the story itself is published. For example, statements of expertise such as "According to (such-and-such expert) . . ." may show up in other articles.

- **Rule 5: Contact top outlets personally.** Do your research to identify which person in which department handles stories like yours at a given media outlet. Then send your release specifically to that person and follow up with an e-mail or phone call. If you can't find the name and contact information on the organization's website, call the office and ask for them.

And here are a few rules of my own:

- **Choose the right outlet.** Make sure that the outlet covers your kind of story *and* is connected to your target market. Imagine, for instance, sending a fitness story to a knitting journal. Your story must be a good fit in order to get covered.

- **Include high-resolution pictures.** As the saying goes, a good picture is worth a thousand words, and you should include one whenever possible. Provide the highest-resolution JPEG file you can. Do not embed it in the article as this limits how it can be used; instead, attach it separately to the e-mail.

- **Include all details.** You don't want the journalist to have to do a lot of work to use your release. Include all necessary details, as well as your contact information and a brief bio.

Another way to get free advertising is to become a resource for writers and reporters on television, radio (talk radio in particular), in print, and on the web. Many of these folks like to bring in experts to talk about the latest news. For example, when my wife, Heather, and I lived in New York City, she appeared on MSNBC a number of times to discuss various fitness topics. You could also approach local media and offer to write a column or do a news segment. Some local cable channels are constantly looking for content; some might even allow you to have your own show. To offer your services, contact the individuals in charge of the station content, news segment, column, or blog. All of these options can highlight you as an expert, thus showcasing both you and your business.

Paid Print Advertising

Now let's look at paid print advertising. One caveat: I don't address pricing here because it can vary widely. Note, however, that most periodicals offer discounts for multiple ads; for details, contact each business' advertising department. If you decide to use paid print advertising, you must develop a clear message that evokes an emotional reaction in readers. Let's say that you want to promote a group fitness class for seniors. What do you want to say about it? Think about the benefits to the participants. There are a lot of grandparents in the world, and they may live very different lives. For instance, you could draw a contrast between a grandparent who is using a walker and unable to play with grandchildren and a grandparent who is down on the floor playing with grandkids.

The copy for this ad might read, "Which grandparent do you want to be?" That grabs attention and evokes emotion. You also need to make a call to action—something that gets readers to enroll, or at least to contact you. Here's an example: "Regain lost strength and mobility. Call now to receive a free trial in our Re-Active class." Then include your name (or facility name), phone number, website address, and street address. Here again, make sure that the media outlet you choose is appropriate for what you have to offer. Most periodicals will supply you with the demographics of their readership.

Direct Marketing

Direct marketing involves advertising directly to potential consumers. It is often sent via postal service but can also be delivered by placing hangers on doors, putting flyers on vehicle windshields (I certainly used this strategy in the "old days"), or handing out leaflets on a street corner. In each of these examples, the advertisement goes directly into the hands of your target market. A direct marketing piece should follow the same guidelines as a television, radio, magazine, or newspaper advertisement. That is, it should grab the target market's attention, evoke emotion, make a call to action, and include sufficient contact information.

If you decide to send a marketing piece in the mail, you'll need to obtain a targeted mailing list. Companies exist that will compile names and addresses for you based on specific demographics, such as zip code, education level, age, sex, homeowner status, median income, interests, and more. I did a search for my demographic market using this type of service, and it came up with 5,188 contact names and addresses at a price of $290.48. That's just for the list. Add to that the costs of printing, address labels, and mailing, as well as your time, and it turns into a fairly large investment. Some direct marketing companies also provide customizable fitness ads and will print and mail the pieces for you.

The median response rate to a direct mailing in 2014 was 1 percent (Marketing Charts, 2015). Based on the 5,188 names and addresses I received, that means I could expect 51 responses to my direct mailing. That doesn't mean that 51 people will buy what I'm advertising. It does mean that I can look for 51 ad-influenced actions, which might take the form of inquiries (such as phone calls or e-mails), in-person visits by potential members or clients, or actual sales.

When considering direct mail, determine the profit margin you would need on the advertised service or product, then calculate how many respondents would have to make a purchase in order to cover the cost of the mailing. If, instead, you choose to use door hangers, vehicle flyers, or distributed leaflets, the cost is limited to the printing and the time spent in distributing them. As you consider direct mail, you should also know that the reverberating effects of effective, repeated advertising can, over time, increase the number of ad-influenced actions. The most quoted number of exposures to an ad needed to elicit action is seven. So, if you choose to advertise using direct mail and want to make the campaign as effective as possible, you should run the ad at least seven times.

Face-to-Face Marketing

For a long time, the only sales game in town was face to face, whether in the form of marketplace sellers, traveling peddlers, or door-to-door salespeople. Given this historical context, it might seem that face-to-face marketing should be grouped with traditional marketing. It differs greatly, however, from the shotgun style of advertising that sprays a message all around in hopes of hitting something.

In fact, face-to-face marketing is the easiest and best way to create a relationship and thereby help a potential member or client come to know you, like you, and trust you. Face-to-face meetings allow you to understand so much more than do other methods of marketing. Traditional ads, for instance, offer no interaction. E-mails, texts, and social media allow verbal interaction. And phone calls allow participants to hear each other's words and intonations. In contrast, face-to-face marketing provides all of these benefits by giving all parties access to each other's words, intonations, facial expressions, and body language—all of which create a quicker, deeper, two-way understanding between you and your prospective member or client. This additional information can make readily apparent whether you will be compatible with each other.

Given the power of face-to-face marketing to create relationships, you need to be proactive about getting out and creating face-to-face opportunities. This is networking! Of course, networking can also take place online, but let's discuss when and where you should work purposefully to make face-to-face connections. The *when* is easy: always! Anytime you meet new people or get to know acquaintances better, you should be aware of their level of interest in what you do. That's not to say that you should push yourself on them, but do listen for opportunities to answer their questions about health and fitness when they arise. In the meantime, get to know them better. You'll hear it from me a thousand times: People buy from people whom they know, like, and trust.

So, how do you go about meeting people? Ever since my wife and I moved to a new town and began the process of opening a new fitness studio, we have attended more meetings and social events than we ever have before. We became members of the local chamber of commerce and the Easton Business Association; performed in a local theatrical production; presented in PechaKucha Night Easton (an evening of short presentations); and attended various festivals, a masquerade ball, and a fair number of parties—all within six months after arriving!

Meeting potential clients face to face is one of the fastest ways to create connections and build relationships.

Getty Images/Hero Images

It takes conscious effort to plan this kind of schedule and to follow through by attending even when you would rather stay home. Realize, though, that networking is a part of your job even if you are employed as a personal trainer at a local gym. As you network, people will invariably ask what you do. This question starts the process of building a relationship, which can then open up an opportunity.

You can also network by locating organizations—such as church groups and athletic booster clubs—that involve or serve your target market. Find out how to get involved in them, attend meetings, get to know the members, and help them with their events. You'll soon find out that people love to talk about themselves. In talking with a person, always bring the conversation back to him or her. Often, you will be perceived as a very interesting person because you are very interested in whoever you are talking with! Down the road, after building a relationship, you can offer something that allows the person to experience some part of what you offer, such as a free fitness consultation or free trial class. Note: If you're a personal trainer who works for someone else, check with your manager to make sure that he or she approves of your offering such opportunities to potential clients.

Remember to gain permission to market to a person by taking the time to get to know him or her and by serving the person first. For example, many organizations hold fund-raising events, and donating a prize to such an event is a win-win situation. You and the organization are doing something to help the community; in exchange, you both gain exposure by letting others know who you are and what you do.

Another idea is to host your own event. For example, we held an online weight loss challenge that was free to participants. To obtain prizes to give away as part of the event, we went to local businesses for donations, which was a win-win-win situation. The participants got free fitness and weight loss information and support throughout the challenge. The businesses that donated prizes got publicity, as did we for hosting the challenge.

The downside of face-to-face networking is that it doesn't scale or work well for ever-larger audiences. It is very time consuming to meet many people in this manner. There are only so many hours in a day. If you want to reach a larger audience, you have to add other marketing methods.

Internet-Based Marketing

Even before the rise of the Internet, you could have friends all over the world whom you had never met face-to-face. They were called pen pals. Because the wait time between exchanges could easily last for weeks, these relationships were built over long periods of time. Once the Internet became interactive, it became social, which meant that people could talk to people all over the world in an instant. It's an amazing thing! Equally amazing is the speed at which you can use the Internet to develop relationships. You can use social media tools to connect with one person, one hundred people, or one thousand people at the same time. This ability creates the opportunity to show people who you are, what you do, why you do it, and that you are there to help them. Thus social media can help you become someone who is known, liked, and trusted by thousands without your ever meeting them face to face.

The Strength of Weak Ties

Our new opportunities don't lie within our circle of existing friends and family—our strong ties—but in our fringe connections: our weak ties (Granovetter, 1973). Our strong ties connect us to a tight-knit group that shares common resources and thinking. This group is unlikely to provide us with new resources or new information. For example, even if friends and family know I'm looking for a new job, we may all hear about the same two job openings. To hear about more and different opportunities, I need to turn to weak ties, such as friends of my friends, or friends of my friends' friends.

That's how social media marketing works. My friends and family already know what I do. If they wanted to hire me or join my club, they would have done so by now. However, my weak ties may not know what I do, and their friends most likely don't. So, if I post something interesting enough for my friends to share, then their friends will see it, and maybe they will post it to their circle of friends, and on and on in an ever-expanding web of networks.

This is the viral aspect of social media. LinkedIn used to prominently display your number of direct connections and also translate that number into a potential weak-tie reach, which might number a thousand times higher than your direct connections. That sounds impressive! Of course, it would take some very special content to motivate *everyone* to pass it on to their network, but it is at least theoretically possible. No matter which social media platform you use, it all works the same way: You like something and share it with your connections.

Building Your Connections

When you seek to reach deeper into your connections' networks, don't always rely on your direct connections to pass your information along. Instead, bring their networks into yours. Whenever someone who is not a direct connection likes something you post or engages you with comments, invite that person to connect directly. Building your direct connections expands your potential reach and makes it easier to create relationships with more people.

You can also strengthen your face-to-face relationships by connecting on social media. When I meet someone, I immediately find the person on Facebook (the most popular network at the time I'm writing this) and ask to connect so that I can remember the person, he or she can remember me, and we can share conversations online and build rapport and trust. I am constantly adding new friends, followers, connections, or whatever else they may be called in a specific context. I've heard many personal trainers say that they will eventually get around to building their connections. Don't wait! As the saying goes, "Dig your well before you're thirsty." It takes time to connect and build a relationship. If you wait to start, then you won't have a network when you need it.

Choosing Social Media for Marketing

In order to choose the right social media, you have to know where your target market hangs out online. My 86-year-old parents are both on Facebook, and my dad uses e-mail. They are not that different from many seniors; indeed, e-mail and perhaps Facebook are the best bets online for people over 65—Snapchat, Instagram, and Tumblr, not so much (Hoelzel, 2015).

What about your target market? Look ahead to spot trends that will affect your market—not just where they are now, but where they are heading. For example, more than one-third of Americans aged 18 to 29 have a Snapchat account, and that figure is likely to grow, according to Gary Vaynerchuk (2016), CEO of VaynerMedia. Vaynerchuk also notes that it is important to use video in your marketing and that the need for video content will only increase with time. I agree with him about video, regardless of whether you decide to use Snapchat, Instagram, Facebook, YouTube, Vimeo, or some other video tool. Be on the lookout for successful video campaigns and consider experimenting with them on your own.

As we look at various social tools, you may wonder if you have to use all of them and if they will take up too much time. Certainly, it will take some time, but less as you get more familiar with creating posts. The ideal frequency of posts depends on which platform you are using. On average, a number between one and five posts per day is recommended (Lee, 2015). I tend to try every social media platform to see where I get the best feedback, but for your own time management and sanity, you may simply want to pick two or three that are used by members of your target market. Since 71 percent of adults in the United States who go online use Facebook (Duggan, Ellison, Lampe, Lenhart, & Madden, 2015), that's probably a good place to start.

Many social media platforms offer the option of creating a page for your business, and I absolutely recommend making use of this opportunity. Among other benefits, it allows you to promote your brand with a cover photo highlighting what your business is about, obtain web traffic analytics, and create a space where people can write recommendations. Facebook even allows you to create a Book Now tab that allows people to schedule an appointment or class.

You might also benefit from using tools designed to help you make the most of your time when posting on social media. For instance, TweetDeck and Hootsuite allow you to create a post and send it to multiple social media platforms with one click. Two other tools, Buffer and Post Planner, allow you to automate the posting of items, so that you can post at opportune times without disrupting your work flow. Of course, any of these apps could change by the time you read this. To find out what's current, do an online search for social media update services and management tools.

E-mail Marketing

Though typically not viewed as a social media activity, e-mail marketing still offers you another way to connect with people via the Internet. In fact, even though people's in-boxes may be filled with spam, e-mail can still be a very effective way to obtain clients. The key is to first get the prospect's permission to connect by e-mail. The first level is simply to get the person's e-mail address. You might do so in person by simply asking the individual for it so that you can send something of interest. You might also do it as part of a "give to get" scenario on your website, blog, social media page, or anywhere else where you can exchange something of value for e-mail addresses.

The easiest, and best, thing to offer is intellectual property, whether it consists of your own information or of information that you have compiled. Such information can take many forms. Here are some examples:

- Subscription to your e-mail newsletter on health and fitness
- White paper (in-depth report) on a particular problem and its solution—but not a sales pitch or ad for your product or service (Kolowich, 2014)
- Top-10 list on a topic that will grab your target market's attention—for example, Top 10 Weight Loss Tips or Top 10 Core Exercises
- Video or audio file on a topic of interest
- E-book or other downloadable document

Many companies offer tools to capture and manage e-mail lists, as well as templates for content. Popular options include Constant Contact, MailChimp, and AWeber. Another option, KickStart Cart, will even send autoresponder e-mails and a digital delivery system for offerings. Basic-level pricing for these services ranges from free (MailChimp) to $39 per month (KickStart Cart).

Websites

Before the Internet became interactive, I designed websites using a simple software tool called Microsoft FrontPage. I didn't need to know how to write HTML code; I just created a static site that presented a few screens' worth of information. These days, of course, a successful website is updated regularly and is characterized by a large range of features, such as the following:

- Simple, clean, attractive design with a common-sense menu that links to other parts of the site
- Your story, often called About Me (or Us), which presents a clear, engaging picture of you, what you do, and why you do it
- Easy navigation that never requires more than two clicks to get to the visitor's desired information
- Video clips and associated summaries that show or describe your services and products
- Testimonials from satisfied customers (especially video testimonials)
- A free-offer link that captures e-mail addresses in exchange for something of value
- Online shopping capabilities for products such as memberships, classes, online personal training, and apparel
- Online self-scheduler tool for classes and personal training
- Links to social media sites
- Blog (ideally, integrated into the site; otherwise, accessible via an easy-to-find link)

Do you *need* a website? My gut says yes, but I have known personal trainers who run their entire business on Facebook. Moreover, I'll admit that, at one time, the only website I had was my blog site. In spite of these successes, I still recommend that you create a bona fide website. One reason to do so is that, whereas Facebook essentially owns any content you post on its platform, *you* own the content that you publish on your own website. The best-case scenario is to hire a professional to create your website, but that can be expensive. For instance, even though a designer friend just gave me a "friend discount," it still cost more than $2,000 to put together my website. But, fear not: You can also find inexpensive website-building services that allow you to do the work yourself; examples include Web.com, Wix, Weebly, and Network Solutions.

Blogs

What began as the online journal or web log—a name now shortened to *blog*—has evolved into one of the most creative and informative kinds of writing to be found. Because blogs are written in your voice, reflecting how you speak, they are fairly simple to create. They offer your commentary about . . . well, something. To use them as a business tool, stick to topics that interest your target audience and highlight your expertise, your style, and what you care about. Whether your blog posts are read directly by subscribers or included as links in e-mail messages and social media posts, they can help consumers develop a sense of trust and possibly even a sense of kinship with you. This connection can move them closer to wanting to do business with you.

Free blogging services such as WordPress, Squarespace, and Blogger make it easy to start your own blog. Just jump in and give it a try! Don't worry about how it sounds or how it's received; you really have to write one in order to get better at writing one. If you don't like how it's going, or if the style or content isn't quite the way you want, you can always delete your posts or start another blog. I've given birth to and closed down a dozen blogs over the years. Bit by bit, you get better. Some people blog daily, some weekly, and some as infrequently as once a month. Create a schedule that you can maintain, whatever it may be. As you get better at choosing a topic and writing about it, you can start to write more frequently.

Content

So, what do we write about? What should we post on the Internet for the public to read? The answer always comes back to helping people on their journey to better health and fitness by getting them to know, like, and trust us. The most effective way to do that is to become a resource by providing accurate information. In the case of social media updates, it could be as simple as providing a link to reliable information and sharing your commentary on the topic. Your comment could be as simple as, "So true!" Alternatively, you could post an article explaining why it is wrong and where readers can find better information. You could also write about challenges that members of your target market commonly experience when they try to improve their health and fitness, as well as solutions to those challenges.

If you're unsure where to find content to pass on to your connections, consider using a site that gathers information on specific topics. Examples include Reddit, Alltop, and StumbleUpon. You can personalize each of these sites to help you find the content you're looking for. You can also use this information to determine the most popular topics and then write your own blog post about them.

Although research studies can be important, people relate to, enjoy, and share *stories*. So, when you can, tell a story to get your point across. For example, people may know from research articles that exercising regularly and eating a calorically appropriate, healthful diet can help them lose weight and improve their quality of life. In and of itself, however, that information may not affect them emotionally as much as hearing about an individual—let's call her Joan Smith—whose struggle with weight and health was threatening her ability to take care of her two young children. Fortunately, Joan finally joined XYZ program, lost the weight, improved her health, and is now able to care for and play with her children. The emotional power of storytelling also explains why testimonials to you or your club can be so important in your marketing efforts.

In addition, you should disclose information about yourself. I know some personal trainers who keep their website, blog, and social media postings limited to business. Boring! That approach relays nothing about who you are, yet personal details are crucial when you're trying to forge new relationships. If I happen to mention that my sons are swimmers, someone will invariably think to themselves, "My boys are swimmers too," and now we have something in common. That said, you need to realize that everything you post will be scrutinized. Never post anything that contradicts the brand image you are trying to build. My Facebook page is viewable by everyone, and it offers a combination of my professional views and personal details. Thus I am very thoughtful about the content I post. Nothing slips by that is not appropriate for my brand or my audiences.

Keys to Interaction and Relationship Building

Whether in regard to a blog post, a status update, or your website, it's common for people to comment on some aspect of your content. In many cases, they make a knee-jerk reaction; that is, they read and then comment immediately. This is what we hope for: interacting with the people who consume our content. To encourage this interaction, you can go beyond choosing content that's interesting to your target market. You can also prompt readers to respond. For example, you can end a post with a question: "Do you have a similar issue?" "What strategies do you use to overcome this challenge?" "What are your thoughts?" Anything you can do to initiate direct interaction can foster a relationship. You can also tag or mention people (but only those who like being tagged or mentioned—be sure of this ahead of time) to get them involved in the conversation. Just seeing a conversation take place between you and someone else (or even between two other commenting parties) can get others more interested in a post.

At this point, you may be thinking, "All of this advice deals with sharing content and building relationships, but when can I ask people to join my club or sign up for personal training?" The answer depends on the dynamics between you and the individuals you're talking about. As soon as someone asks you a direct question about your products and services, you can have that conversation. As for determining your mix of information and promotion, the marketing platform Rallyverse suggests the following proportions: 30 percent owned (that is, original content), 60 percent curated (that is, information taken from other sources), and 10 percent promotional with an offer (Lee, 2014).

According to this formula, then, one in 10 posts can be promotional. However, the tone should still be light. Here's an example of a social media post promoting a boot camp: "Planning out the 5:30 p.m. boot camp for tomorrow. The playlist is rocking, but before I finalize the exercises I'm hoping to get some input from you. What boot camp exercise would you like to see in class?" This post indicates what and when the class is and asks for readers' input while also helping them picture themselves in the class.

Choosing Your Media

Beyond choosing which social media platforms to use, you also need to decide how to deliver your content. As mentioned earlier, Gary Vaynerchuk believes that video is the future. If done well, it grabs and holds people's attention. Your video could present any of various possibilities: an exercise demonstration, a snippet from a lecture, highlights from an event, or a video blog or webcast. This is not to say that other media don't work. Plain text can work, but, again, a picture can be worth a lot of words. And if pictures get attention, videos get even more. In addition to traditional live-action videos, you can also create animated videos that add a different creative spin. Options for making quick-and-easy animated videos include Moovly, GoAnimate, and Nawmal.

Podcasts, or audio-only recordings, are also very popular, and, like radio programs, they can be listened to while doing other tasks. I like to listen to them while driving, cooking, painting, or doing any number of other things when I can't be visually distracted. Podcasting tools include SoundCloud, PodOmatic, and Podbean. Like blogs, podcasts can be heard either by individuals who subscribe directly to your channel or by people who follow a link that you share through e-mail or social media. In the beginning, try making some audio recordings without worrying about sharing them. Check the recordings for sound quality and clarity of content. When you're confident in the quality, start sharing your recordings. Content quality is more important than length, so you might start by uploading a minute-long segment offering tips and, if you find yourself getting positive feedback, build from there.

Creating a Marketing Schedule

Some marketing happens every day, whether you are out in public or online. Other forms of marketing need to be planned for. If you run the same ad or video too much, or if you often promote the same thing, then people may become blind to it. Instead, maximize the effect of your marketing by creating an overall plan with a purposeful schedule that emphasizes delivering a variety of messages.

One simple way to begin is to focus on national holidays, which make for easy tie-ins; for example, I run a Zombie Boot Camp for Halloween. Next, check your community's activity calendar for meetings and events that you can use as opportunities for face-to-face networking. A community calendar can also help you avoid scheduling an event at the same time as another event—or help you purposefully piggyback your event on another one. For example, you might plan a Hog Wild Boot Camp before the start of the local BaconFest.

Another marketing approach based on external events is to tie in with National Health Observances; for example, February is American Heart Month as promoted by the American Heart Association. Each observance has its own website, and many provide promotional materials that you can use in conjunction with your own marketing plan. In fact, the American Heart Association offers a Workplace Health Playbook (http://playbook.heart.org/) that provides ideas and materials for use in promoting healthier living. For instance, you could host a heart-health lecture series or run a Share Your Heart campaign in which you post an inspirational or meaningful heart picture or video (perhaps with a small logo representing your business) that you ask your followers to share with someone they love.

On top of these marketing opportunities, think about what you have to offer in terms of services and products. Focus on one possibility during each quarter or season and stage an event, such as an open house, for which the central theme addresses your chosen focus. For example, let's say that you offer a weight loss program that includes nutritional coaching and personal training. For January, February, and March, you could run a weight loss challenge that culminates in an open house where the winners are honored, prizes are given away, and healthy snacks are served. You could also have people sign up to receive a weekly e-mail newsletter containing weight loss tips.

Whether you use a paper calendar, a computer spreadsheet, or a smartphone app, map out each year as fully as you can so that you have time to plan and to allocate funds to cover the expenses you will incur. You may have heard the saying, "Failing to plan is planning to fail," and it really does apply to your marketing schedule. A well-planned schedule can keep a constant flow of new members or clients coming into your business.

More to Come

The goal of marketing is to create public awareness of you, your services, and your company (or the place where you work). Begin by making sure that you are clear about your brand and the message you want to send to potential members or clients. Then engage the members of your target market by building relationships with them. Gradually, you will receive permission from people to make offers about your products and services, and with these offerings comes a promise of helping people achieve their goals.

Initially, you may create the desired public awareness through traditional marketing on television and radio, in periodicals, or through direct marketing mailings or flyers. The most effective marketing, however, involves building relationships, which happens only through interaction. This interaction can come in the form of face-to-face networking, e-mail, or social media exchanges.

Before you can market to potential members or clients, you have to know where to reach them. Are they at the local church, the chamber of commerce, the high school? Or perhaps the best way to reach them is through social media platforms. Choose the avenues that get you closest to your target audience so that you are better able to get to know them. As you contemplate the various aspects of marketing to your potential members or clients, develop a plan that lays out how and when you will use your marketing tools. Creating a schedule can keep you on track and ready to connect at the optimal times.

Be aware that online resources and social media platforms can change in a heartbeat. However, though some may be different by the time you read this book, the principles will remain the same. People buy from people whom they know, like, and trust. With this in mind, start building relationships!

Marketing and creating relationships is the initial part of securing individuals as your members or clients. Then comes the actual point of making the sale. This is a stumbling block for so many personal trainers because the terms *selling* and *salespeople* come with the connotation of being shady and underhanded. In chapter 13, Learning the Art of Selling, you'll discover that the act of selling can be a very positive thing for all parties involved.

Chapter 13

Learning the Art of Selling

Getty Images/andresr

If you are in business, then you must sell. That's how you stay in business and make a living. It's a necessity that, sadly, few people understand. Let's begin our look at the art of selling by considering the misunderstandings and misconceptions that most people hold about sales and salespeople. Then we'll look at when and where sales opportunities present themselves, either on their own or through your marketing efforts. None of this much matters, however, unless you become skilled at taking potential members or clients through the sales process to the point where they happily buy from you.

The Misunderstanding of Selling

My own sales history put in place a disdain for sales (and anything to do with it) that stayed with me for more than a decade. I was a young, idealistic exercise professional who had just moved to Boston after three years of working in the Human Performance Center at the University of Maine. I used a strong understanding of exercise science to help people change their lives through exercise, and I was ready to save the world. When I got a job as a personal trainer at a club, I soon became the fitness director because I knew more about exercise than most of the staff and was eager to move up in the business. Being a good student, I watched and learned from the other managers. Within the first six months, the sales manager and general manager positions opened up, and I figured that I could do those jobs as well. After presenting my case to the owner, I was offered and then accepted all three positions.

To go along my sales manager position, I was sent to a "sales training" course. In the eyes of the sales consultant who led the course, all that mattered were sales numbers—hard sales—not the health and wellness, or even the satisfaction, of members. Just grab the credit card and charge as much as you can. She explained how to set up elaborate trips and gifts to be awarded to the salespeople with the highest numbers. Then she hit us with the game plan: Oversell the club by pushing one- to three-year memberships until we were too crowded, then hope members didn't show up. Wow! This was not why I had gotten into the health and fitness business.

When I found out later that the consultant had praised one of our salespeople for selling a membership to someone looking for a mime class—which we didn't even offer—I knew I had to resign. From that point on, anything to do with "sales" turned my stomach. Many fitness professionals feel the same way; for them, the mere terms *sales* and *selling* bring to mind images of unscrupulous infomercials and telemarketers. The concept and the process seem shady and insincere.

My enlightenment about sales came while I was working as curriculum coordinator at what was then the third-largest health club chain in the United States. As part of that job, I wrote the in-house training manuals for the chain's 1,700 personal trainers. At one point, my boss asked me to add a section on sales training. I felt sick about it and told her about my distaste for anything related to sales. She told me that I was being ridiculous and that I was one of the best salespeople she knew. She explained that my confidence, enthusiasm, and desire to help others are exactly what selling is all about. What a foreign concept! Her words marked the start of my personal redefinition of sales. Selling is not evil, and neither are salespeople (or at least they don't have to be!).

In fact, we are all salespeople in one way or another. According to one study, one in nine people in the U.S. workforce holds traditional sales positions, and the other eight spend 40 percent of their workday "persuading, influencing, and convincing others" (Pink, 2012, p. 21)—in essence, selling. Our personal lives are also filled with sales-influenced situations: "Come see this movie." "Try this restaurant." "Vote for this candidate." These statements, and many others, constitute attempts to persuade others.

In the business world, debate exists over the semantics of sales. According to sales icon Jeffrey Gitomer (2004), "People don't like being sold, but they love to buy" (p. 5).

You could think of it like this: "Selling" is something that you are doing to potential members or clients, whereas "buying" is something they do for themselves. I disagree with this viewpoint, which, once again, tries make "sales" the bad guy. In reality, the rap on sales comes from millennia of people selling purely to benefit the seller, not the buyer. But it doesn't have to be that way.

In other words, the quality of the sales experience for both the seller and the buyer really boils down to intent. Sales should focus on helping the buyer solve a problem by using a solution provided by the seller. In fact, if you believe that a potential client's best chance to achieve his or her goals for fitness or health involves working with you, then wouldn't you be doing a disservice if you *didn't* try to persuade that person?

Why People Buy

Early in my career, I learned that people buy based on their wants and not their needs. Wants are emotional, and emotions drive purchases. One theory suggests that people buy either to move toward pleasure or to move away from pain (Carroll, 2015). That makes some sense to me. In the fitness world, people may want to work out to reach a new physical level that helps them feel better about themselves, perhaps by looking better, being stronger, or being faster—in other words, moving toward pleasure. They may also want to work out to recover from injury, get healthier, or keep illness at bay—that is, to avoid pain.

Other discussions focus on factors that help individuals buy. For instance, in a list of elements that contribute to buying, Gitomer (2004) includes six that relate directly to how consumers feel about the salesperson. Among others, these factors include liking, trusting, and being comfortable with the salesperson. Other elements included in Gitomer's list are more "classic" wants in that they relate to how the product serves the consumer's needs and how fairly it is priced for the value. Gitomer's list illustrates precisely what is preached by many books on sales and marketing: Consumers buy from people whom they like and trust.

Recognizing Sales Opportunities

For fitness professionals, a sales opportunity is a chance to help others achieve their goals. Marketing is about creating sales opportunities, but that's not the only way those opportunities can arise. In fact, they are all around us, all the time. When they appear, we have one main goal: to get the potential member or client to sit down with us and discuss his or her wants and needs. Sure, we can provide guidance on the fly, but if we seek to give our best personalized recommendations, then we need to have a confidential, one-on-one consultation to discuss the person's health history, lifestyle questionnaire, and goals.

Even if a person is simply looking for a club membership in order to work out, you still need to make sure that he or she is healthy enough to start (or continue). You also need to determine whether your facility offers what the person is looking for. This question relates not only to equipment but also to the look and feel of your space. Therefore, you should encourage the person to tour the facility and make sure it's the right place.

What if someone comes in and wants to sign up for a personal training program right then and there? Many would say, "Take the money now!" because the person could change his or her mind. I disagree, and here's why: You don't know enough about the person to recommend the best type of program. If you sign up the person for a program now and it turns out not to be the right thing, then you have to backtrack and either return the person's money or resell with the correct membership or program. Either scenario leaves the potential member or client feeling less taken care of and thinking less of your capabilities. You can minimize your risk for these outcomes by persuading the individual to come in and talk with you in person.

The sales opportunities described in the following subsections include chance encounters in the community (such as meeting someone at a party, a community event, or a grocery store) as well as encounters with members or guests at the club (whether you are on duty or just there working out).

Chance Encounters

Picture the last time you met someone at a party or other gathering. The person finds out you're a personal trainer and immediately asks how to build their chest, get six-pack abs, or lift their butt. What did you do? You should first recognize that this encounter gives you an opportunity to help someone, then work toward persuading the person to meet you for a consultation.

To begin that process, listen to the person's question and give it your complete focus. Then ask a *couple* (not a lot) of open-ended questions to get the person to provide more detail about his or her goals. These questions not only elicit more information for you but also show the other person that you're listening and that you care to know more. Again, however, this isn't the time to get into an in-depth conversation. For one thing, either or both of you may not have the time at the moment; in addition, you should have the more substantial talk in a private setting where you can ask personal questions. Until then, you can't make specific recommendations, because you don't yet have the full picture.

At this point, if you think you can help the person, say, "I'd love to sit down sometime to really talk this through so I could make a personalized recommendation for you. Is that something you'd be willing to do?" If the person says no, then he or she is likely not ready to commit to a lifestyle change or exercise program anyway. If, on the other hand, the person says yes and has access to his or her schedule, arrange the consultation by saying, "When would be a convenient time for you to meet? Are mornings or evenings better for you? Would _____ work for you?" Then set the appointment and

New clients can be the result of unexpected meetings and casual discussions.

Getty Images/Cecilie_Arcurs

say, "Great!" Next, exchange contact information by asking, "May I have your phone number so I can confirm with you the day before?" Also, in case the person needs to reschedule later, say, "Here is my contact information."

If the person is interested but doesn't have access to his or her schedule at the moment, request his or her contact information and ask if it's okay for you to get in touch later to set up a consultation. You can say, "May I have your phone number so I can give you a call to set up a convenient time and date for us to meet?"

Do not—I repeat, do *not*—simply give the person your business card and ask for a call to set up the consultation. The person may lose your card, forget about calling, or choose some other fitness club or personal trainer, and there you are, left by the phone, waiting for a call. In contrast, if you get the person's contact information, then you can be proactive and make the call to schedule an appointment.

In the Club and On Duty

This section and the one that follows involve not just sales but also marketing, because they address situations in which you're working to create a sales opportunity in an unplanned face-to-face interaction. Therefore, they *become* sales opportunities.

Let's say you're working in a club, in uniform, and a member is coming in to take your class, or working out on the training floor, or using a cardio machine. You know that he's interested in fitness because he's already working out. Your natural inclination should be to find out how he's doing at reaching his fitness goals. After all, we want everyone to succeed, right?

The first step is to find an appropriate time to approach the member—not, for example, while he's in the middle of a set of squats. Introduce yourself (unless he already knows you) and give him a compliment, even if he's doing something wrong. For instance, you might say, "You're really working hard over here!" or "You're becoming a regular here. Good for you—that's a real commitment!" Then ask about his goals: "May I ask what you're training to achieve?" After he answers, ask him to describe his plan for reaching his goals. (Most people are winging it.) Follow that up by asking about his progress. If he has a reasonable plan, is making headway, and is happy with it, then don't press for a longer conversation. Compliment him once again and leave an opening to check in again at a later date: "Great, glad to hear things are going well. Keep up the good work! If it's okay with you, I'll check back with you in a couple weeks to make sure you're still progressing. Would that be okay?" He should be fine with that; you haven't pushed sales or done anything awkward, so the contact with a staff person and a future opportunity to ask questions are all positive.

What if he doesn't have a reasonable plan? Maybe he's just doing a little of this and a little of that, or perhaps he's trying to use the latest workout idea in some magazine but is still happy with his progress. Again, if he's happy, don't press, but you can make a suggestion: "Great, glad to hear things are going well. But if you were doing a program created specifically to meet your needs, you could be doing even better. We could schedule a time to sit down and talk about your program to see what we could do to make it even more effective. Does that sound like something that would interest you?" If he says yes, book it. If he says no, then assure him that's okay and end by asking permission to check in with him in a couple of weeks. Always make sure you leave the member feeling good about the interaction so that any future encounters are friendly and comfortable.

In the Club and Off Duty

When you're in the club and off duty, you may experience a couple of scenarios. For one, you could go in uniform and use that "official" presence to engage members.

Before doing so, however, check with your club to make sure that you are allowed to work while off the clock. In my last long-term job as a fitness director, the club did not have floor hours (see chapter 2), and I encouraged personal trainers to come in during the hours they devoted to building their business in order to "work the floor" as if they were being paid to do so. Although they did not get paid for their time, they put in this work to help build their client base. In this scenario, they engaged members as if they were on duty.

The other scenario occurs each time you do your own workout at the club. Doing so creates a casual opportunity for members to approach you, and you should capitalize on it. Members will get a chance to see a "pro" in action. They may ask you questions about how and why you do certain exercises. Although these conversations may slow down your workout, you must weigh that cost against the opportunity to gain new clients. Because of this benefit, I always encourage personal trainers to work out at their own club. Once you answer the person's initial question, such interactions should proceed in the same way as when you are on duty in the club: "I like doing this exercise because . . ." or "How about you? What are you training for? How are things going with that?" If you decide to take this approach to your own workout, do not wear headphones—they send the message that you are unavailable.

ABC: Always Be Curious

The ABCs of sales have often been associated with the phrase "always be closing," which was popularized in the 1992 film *Glengarry Glen Ross* (New Line Cinema). I'd like to shift the meaning of the ABC acronym to "always be curious." Your sincere curiosity about how members are doing creates more opportunities than you can imagine.

In fact, I was explaining this concept to an intern one day when a member who had recently undergone knee surgery limped by. I asked her how she was feeling and how the physical therapy was going. She said that she had finished physical therapy but still had a long way to go in order to feel comfortable restarting her previous activities. The next question I asked is a great one for cutting to the chase, and I highly recommend that you add it to your repertoire: "So, what's your plan?" Once the question was asked, she recognized the reality and replied, "I don't have one. I guess we should sit down and come up with one." It was a perfect illustration for the intern of how always being curious can open up opportunities to help people. The members of your club have great potential for becoming new clients. Don't let the chances pass you by.

The Sales Process

Whether you sell memberships, classes, programs, or personal training, the sales process starts with your first meeting with a potential member or client. In unplanned encounters such as those addressed in the preceding section, the first few seconds of meeting someone can set the course for a future relationship. This section addresses how to make a good first impression on a potential member or client. It also walks through the additional steps that make up the sales process: establishing rapport and trust, performing a cooperative review of the person's health history and lifestyle questionnaire, clarifying the person's goals, summarizing the resulting challenges, recommending a course of action, and, finally, obtaining a commitment from the prospective client.

Making a Positive First Impression

Although first impressions can be formed very quickly (in as little as two seconds), they are formulated by processing a great many bits of information (Gladwell, 2007,

p. 13). As a result, *everything* matters. For a quick list of key points that add up to a positive first impression, see the checklist in the sidebar.

First Impression Checklist

- **Be on time.** Nothing throws up a red flag like showing up late for a first (or any) meeting. Don't do it. It tells the other person, "I don't care about you. Your time is not important." If, for some unavoidable reason, you are late, don't make excuses. Whoever you are meeting doesn't care. Just apologize sincerely and assure him or her that it won't happen again.

- **Wear clean, professional attire.** Whether your role is owner, manager, or personal trainer, look the part. That may mean slacks and a dress shirt or the personal trainer uniform. Whatever the details, you should look like you care how you look.

- **Be well groomed.** Your hair should be combed or brushed, your hands and nails clean, and your face clean shaven. If you are trying to grow a beard or other facial hair, trim around it so that it looks like a conscious effort as opposed to forgetting to shave after a weekend in the woods.

- **Don't smell.** This one may seem obvious, and in fact it should be obvious that you need to avoid body odor. In addition, however, steer clear of perfume, cologne, and aftershave. You may like how it smells, but it could still be a real turnoff to the person you're meeting. If you still decide to wear a scent, keep it very light.

- **Smile genuinely.** People want you to be happy to see them, and nothing expresses that feeling like a warm, sincere smile. Many people can tell the difference between a fake smile and an honest one that reaches your eyes (Maples, 2011). You should be glad to meet this person. Show it!

- **Make eye contact.** It's very hard to feel that someone is listening to you and connecting with you if he or she doesn't make eye contact. In addition, if you don't make eye contact, you may miss subtle cues from the other person.

- **Greet the person by name with a warm voice and enunciate clearly.** People love hearing their own name. Greeting a person warmly by name while offering a sincere smile and direct eye contact can be very welcoming and initiate rapport.

- **Offer a firm handshake that matches the other person's level of pressure.** Handshakes that are too limp ("dead fish") or too firm ("I'm strong and powerful and you're not!") can quickly turn people off. To strike the right balance, offer a stiff hand that matches the pressure exerted on your hand by the other person (but don't go floppy even if there is very little pressure).

- **Use confident, open body language.** Much has been said about how body language leaves an impression. In addition to implementing the points discussed earlier, stand tall (but not rigid) in order to show confidence. Square your body to the other person so that she knows you're with her and there for her. At the same time, keep your body open—not blocked, for instance, by crossed arms—to show that you're making yourself vulnerable to her.

- **Be positive and enthusiastic.** Your enthusiasm can be contagious, and you want your potential member or client to share your excitement.

- **Be yourself.** "We live in a society where raw and real is valued because it is so rare" (Robbins, 2015). Sincerity and honesty are attractive. If you are not sincere and honest, potential members and clients will either sense it now or find out later. Either way, it will negatively affect how they feel about you.

Establishing Rapport and Trust

Why does building rapport and trust matter? "People do business with the people they know, like, and trust" (Carmody, 2014). Or, as sales guru Zig Ziglar (n.d.) put it, "If people like you, they'll listen to you, but if they trust you, they'll do business with you." So, you want people to like you and trust you.

After you create a good first impression, the keys to building rapport and trust can be boiled down to a few additional notes. As you bring a potential member or client to the designated space for your private meeting or consultation, start a casual conversation. You could talk about the weather, ask if the person is new in town, or compliment him or her on an article of clothing—anything you can do to help the person begin to feel comfortable. Continue in this manner for a short while as you both sit down and get settled. While listening, match the person's language. If he or she uses simple words and phrases, do the same. Speaking in words and terms that are uncommon to the person creates a barrier that will hinder your effort to build rapport.

As the conversation proceeds, ask open-ended questions that give the person a chance to tell his or her story. You should really want to get to know this person, and this meeting or consultation gives you that chance. Lean in slightly and listen intently to the person's responses. Note things that you have in common—for example, "My boys were in Boy Scouts too." Similar experiences help create a bond. Remember, however, that this time is about your guest; therefore, you should do much more listening than talking. As the Greek philosopher Epictetus said, "We have two ears and one mouth so that we can listen twice as much as we speak." Use active listening techniques by giving quick affirmations such as, "Yes," and "Oh, wow," as well as repeating, paraphrasing, and clarifying to let the person know that you are listening and that you understand. Continue the open-ended questions and active listening throughout the meeting or consultation.

Cooperatively Reviewing the Health History and Lifestyle Questionnaire

Of course, the information provided on a health history and lifestyle questionnaire is important when you are creating an individualized program for a client. However, this information is just the kickoff for a full interview that can give you much greater insight into the person. Together, the two of you will elaborate on and clarify what is important in creating a plan to help the client reach his or her goals.

In fact, almost every question included in a health history and lifestyle questionnaire can be the subject of a full discussion. For example, if the health history reveals that the person recently underwent a knee replacement but has been cleared to work out, you should ask for more details: "Can you tell me more about when it bothers you and whether it prevents you from doing things you want to do?" The answer to that two-part question may even spur another question as you try to get to the heart of the issue, which involves not only any applicable exercise or activity limitations but also how the person *feels* about them.

Clarifying Goals

Often, when individuals state their goals, they speak in a general way, such as, "I want to lose weight" or "I want to get toned." Therefore, you need to help them articulate in specific terms both their vision and how they would feel upon achieving it. To put it another way, goals have layers, and you need to help people peel back the layers to find out what really matters.

For example, one of my clients said that he wanted to get into "better cardiovascular condition." When I asked what that term meant to him, he said, "So I can run faster." I then asked, "Why is it important to run faster?" "So I can compete in a road race." "Any race in particular?" "Every year, my family runs in a 10K race, and I always come in last. I want to improve my running speed so I can beat them this year." Aha! Now we have a specific goal, which allows us to formulate specific recommendations for achieving it. I then asked, "How would it feel to beat your family?" His reply was, "I would be on top of the world!" Now we have also identified an emotional motivation, which is far more meaningful than getting into "better cardiovascular condition."

Summarizing Challenges

At this point, you and your potential member or client have covered, in considerable depth, the relevant health and lifestyle circumstances. You have also weighed them against clearly defined goals. Now, you can identify the challenges that he or she will face in pursuing those goals. Present a summary of these challenges and ask if they are accurate. If not, ask the prospective client to clarify the goals, then give him or her a revised summary of challenges. Take your time with this process; the better you understand the person's goals, the better you can summarize the challenges. And that's what leads you to the next step, which is central to the art of selling.

Recommending a Course of Action

You can now recommend a course of action—your solution for the potential member or client: "With that in mind, my recommendation is . . ." Lay out a specific course of action, whether it involves joining the club, purchasing a certain package of personal training, or participating in a certain program. Explain, point by point, how the solution will help the person overcome the impending challenges. This description should include maximizing the results, minimizing the risks, and enabling the person to experience the specific feeling that he or she seeks—for instance, in the case of the family runner, being "on top of the world."

The manner in which you present your recommendation is crucial. That manner, along with your interactions with the person up to this point, establish the perceived value of your recommendation. Some people suggest offering two or three recommendations,

Sales can be as simple as making an honest recommendation.

thereby giving the prospective member or client a choice. Do not, however, offer more than three. Having too many choices can leave a person unable to make a decision (a state often referred to as "analysis paralysis"). As long as you avoid this pitfall, giving the potential member or client a choice—even though *you* determine the packages or programs offered—helps the person commit more strongly to following through on whichever option he or she chooses. For example, you might recommend that the person choose one of two personal training options that you believe will provide the best results.

Getting a Commitment

Once you make your recommendation, it's time to ask for a commitment. Often referred to as "closing," this part of the process is the most difficult step for most people. Yes, you are going to ask for money, but that's the wrong way to think about it. What you're really asking is whether the person accepts the plan you've laid out. "How does that sound to you?" "Does that sound like something you'd like to do?" In the case of offering two options, you might ask, "Which of these two do you feel would work better for you?" You might also want to ask, "When would you like to start?"

If things go well, the person then says something like, "Good" or "Yes," followed by "The first one sounds better" or "Next week would be good." You can then respond matter-of-factly with an appropriate statement, such as, "Great! Let's take care of the payment, and you can start your membership right away" (or, "Great! Let's take care of the payment and get you booked for your first session").

Objections

In some cases, the person will not be ready to commit. Even if you feel that you covered all of your bases, the person may raise objections. Of course, objections are less likely to pop up now if you were thorough during the information-gathering stage of the consultation. In any case, the majority of objections are really questions that have yet to be answered. Therefore, most objections can be resolved by informing the person about offsetting benefits or by providing clarification statements.

When you discuss offsetting benefits, you acknowledge a challenge and compare it with potential benefits: "Yes, it can be difficult to change your habits, but won't it be worth it when you're finally able to run that road race you've been dreaming about?" Clarification statements, on the other hand, let the person know that he or she is wrong (in a nice way) and then provide the truth of the matter (that is, they clarify): "Many people still believe that doing cardio training with lower intensity and longer duration is the best way to lose weight. But research now shows that high-intensity interval training can be more effective in getting you leaner than just doing a classic cardio workout."

Here are some typical objections stated by people who are concerned about fitting exercise into their lives:

- "I don't have enough time to exercise."
- "Exercise is too boring."
- "I'm too old to start exercising."
- "I'm injured."
- "I'm too sick."
- "I just can't seem to get motivated."
- "I don't know where to start."
- "I'm too tired to exercise."
- "I don't have the support I need at home."
- "I can't afford the gym (or personal training)."

When you hear one of these objections, ask, "What makes you say that?" Then let the person explain his or her objection in more detail. Hearing this explanation will help you catch what you may have missed earlier or learn more about how the person feels. This additional information will help you address the objection specifically, whether through offsetting benefits, clarification statements, or both.

Realize, too, that this potential member or client did come to this first meeting or consultation. That is, he or she left the comfort of home or took a break from work in order to join you in this meeting. Therefore, the person must have an interest in joining the club or starting personal training. Why else would he or she have come? Now, the person needs your help to make the decision to start.

For example, let's say that the voiced objection is that the person feels too old to start exercising. One good reply would be, "You aren't the first one to think that!" This statement tells her that it's okay to feel the way she does. You might add, "In fact, it used to be thought that as we age we will just continue to lose strength, flexibility, and stamina and there really isn't anything we can do about it." This statement offers more support for her feelings. "But, in recent years, a great deal of research has shown that we don't have to lose these abilities. In fact, we can start exercising at any age and *improve* our strength, flexibility, and stamina. The result is that you will be able to continue doing things you want to do and maintain your independence." This clarification statement assures her that she can indeed reach her goals!

Ideally, you prepare generally framed offsetting benefits and clarification statements for each possible objection. You can then frame them more specifically in the moment to relate to the particular individual with whom you are talking.

Now, let's talk about what most people view as the biggest objection to joining a club or participating in personal training: the price. Yes, in truth, there are some people who cannot afford club membership or personal training. Most often, however, price comes up as an objection because the value of what you are offering hasn't been shown clearly enough. In fact, when that value is sufficiently established, price may not even come up until the person has agreed to your recommendation.

If, on the other hand, price truly poses a challenge for your prospective member or client, work with the person—if you can or are allowed to—by chipping the offering down to a point where it fits the person's budget. For example, let's say that you recommend three, one-hour personal training sessions per week for eight weeks as the best way for the person to reach his or her goal. The price, however, is too high for the person to afford. You might find that the person's budget could afford the price of three *half-hour* sessions with you per week or the price of a *single* one-hour session per week with you and two sessions that the person performs on his or her own. Another option might be to do three one-hour personal training sessions per week for the first two weeks, then do one session every other week thereafter.

It's up to you and the potential member or client to figure out something that fits the budget. The silver lining here is that once the person starts working with you, he or she often comes to see the value of your services and steps up the program to something closer to your original recommendation.

If you have ever wondered why service companies are reluctant to give prices over the phone, it's because without the opportunity to demonstrate value, price is the only factor that the consumer has to compare. In that case, the cheapest price wins. Therefore, price should be the last thing addressed so that you have time to build rapport, trust, and value.

Fear of Rejection

Sometimes personal trainers hesitate in asking for a commitment because they fear rejection. What if the prospective client or member says no even after you discuss the offsetting benefits and use clarification statements? You have to understand that this is not a personal rejection, but a rejection of the recommendation that you made. Perhaps you didn't demonstrate the value well enough, or perhaps the person truly can't afford it, or perhaps the person really believes that he or she can proceed without your help. Unless you're an annoying person, it's not about you.

When they do say no, recognize their concerns, reassure them, and *give them more*: "Okay, I understand your financial concerns. If you're going to do this on your own, these are the things that you need to focus on . . ." Then detail the plan, along with the person's responsibilities, and ask, "Do you have any questions?" Once you've answered any current questions, say, "If you have any questions later, or if you don't seem to be getting the results you'd hoped for, please feel free to call or e-mail me." Follow that by asking permission to check in at a later date: "Would it be okay if I give you a call in a couple weeks to see how you're doing?"

Most people expect that once they say no, that's the end of your help. By offering more assistance, you leave them feeling great about you, and if they change their mind or need help in the future, they will come back to you. And even if they don't ever use your services, they're likely to speak highly of you to their friends and perhaps refer them to you.

More to Come

Making sales is a major part of building a successful business. Unfortunately, it has acquired a bad reputation through its misuse and abuse by salespeople who had only their own welfare in mind, not the welfare of those to whom they were selling. The process of selling gives us the chance to help people achieve their health and fitness goals. As fitness professionals, we should look forward to that opportunity. To make good use of it, we need to recognize when sales opportunities happen—which is all of the time, whether out in the community, in the club while on duty, or even when you are just working out.

However, you can't offer a plan of action without knowing the details. Therefore, you must gain the chance to have a private meeting or consultation with the potential member or client in order to learn enough to make a personalized recommendation. Furthermore, knowing that people buy from people whom they like and trust, you need to make every effort to create a good first impression, then build rapport and trust through a sincere desire to know more about a person in order to help him or her achieve identified goals. When you learn about the person's obstacles and challenges—and help the person clarify his or her goals—then you can make an informed recommendation about the best path forward.

If the prospective client or member raises any objections, they can most likely be resolved through offsetting benefits or clarification statements. If the objection is price, then you may not have sufficiently built up the value of your recommendation. In some cases, however, price may in fact be a problem. If so, consider alternative offerings to see if you can work out something that fits the person's budget.

Above all, the biggest fear in sales is that of rejection. Realize that it's not personal; the person is rejecting not you but the offer. When the sale cannot be made, help the individual by providing guidelines for succeeding on his or her own. If you do so, the person will leave feeling surprised, happy, and ready to refer others to you. If you can learn to look forward to and enjoy selling the gift of health and fitness, then you're on your way to creating a successful business and a successful career in our industry.

In previous chapters, we have discussed building relationships with your target market, other businesses, and with your community. Relationships, particularly ones that you want to be long-term, depend on effective communication. It's important to note that not all people communicate the same way. To assure clear understanding between yourself and others, you want to know and be able use various styles of communication. The next chapter will explain these styles and how to use them.

Chapter 14

Communicating With Clients, Businesses, and the Community

Getty Images/Hero Images

If I were to ask if you know how to communicate with others, you might roll your eyes and say, "Of course I do." And you may very well be good at it. However, sometimes we settle for good when we have the opportunity to become great. Communication is critical to the success of our clients and our businesses; therefore, any improvement we make in this area is well worth the time it requires.

People use various styles of communicating and learning, and this variation can affect your efforts not only to acquire new members and clients but also to retain them. These styles also affect your interactions with co-workers and employees, businesses with whom you might partner, and the community in which you live and work. Therefore, as you strengthen your communication skills, you increase your opportunities to understand others and be understood by them. Greater understanding brings greater empathy, as well as the chance to develop deeper relationships as we build rapport and trust.

Styles of Communication

Communication styles have been classified in many ways. Some models have been used for many years, such as Carl Jung's categories of *thinking, feeling, sensation*, and *intuition*; this model was used as the basis for the Myers-Briggs personality test. Among other examples, the Hartman Personality Profile classifies individuals according to personality types referred to as *red, blue, white*, and *yellow*. Sally Hogshead's Fascination Advantages uses categories labeled *innovation, passion, power, prestige, trust, mystique*, and *alert*. And DISC theory categorizes individuals according to *dominance, influence, steadiness*, and *compliance*.

The goal of all of these methods is to understand how people process and react to a variety of information. If we understand our natural tendencies in dealing with diverse situations—as well as how others may react—then we can present our point of view, provide information, and introduce a product or program in the ways that will be best received by others. To get an idea of how, let's take a deeper look at the DISC method.

DISC Method

The groundwork for DISC theory was laid by psychologist William Moulton Marston in his book *Emotions of Normal People*, originally published in 1928 and recently republished in a number of editions. Marston was disillusioned with psychology's seeming inability (perhaps due to lack of interest) to describe "normal" behavior. Therefore, he worked to define how people's personal sense of power can affect their personality and behavior. (Side note: Marston also created the first polygraph test, as well as the comic book heroine Wonder Woman!)

Although Marston never developed an assessment tool, many others have used his personality descriptions to create questionnaires aimed at categorizing individuals. Some companies that offer online assessments based on this model include Discus (www.axiomsoftware.com), Your Life's Path (www.thediscpersonalitytest.com), and Online DISC Profile (www.onlinediscprofile.com).

In order to appreciate how the DISC approach can help us understand ourselves and communicate effectively with others, we need to discuss the styles themselves in some depth (DISC Insights, n.d.). As shown in figure 14.1, the styles are represented in a circle with a vertical line splitting the left and right halves and a horizontal line splitting the top and bottom halves. The left side represents task-oriented personalities, whereas the right side represents people-oriented personalities. Similarly, the top half represents individuals who are outgoing, whereas the bottom half represents those who are reserved.

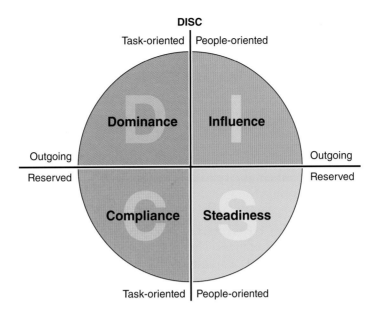

Figure 14.1 DISC styles.

Of course, these two lines—the vertical and the horizontal—also create four segments, or quarters, that each have two traits. The top left quadrant, referred to as *dominance* (D), represents outgoing and task oriented. The top right quadrant, *influence* (I), represents outgoing and people oriented. The bottom right quadrant, *steadiness* (S), represents reserved and people oriented. And the bottom left quadrant, *compliance* (C), represents reserved and task oriented. Each of these DISC personality styles is associated with additional traits, needs, and optimal ways of communicating. Let's take a closer look at each quadrant.

Dominance

The dominance (D) personality type is outgoing and task oriented. People who fit this category like to take control, lead the charge, and get things done. D's thrive on challenge and need to have a sense of control. Because they are outgoing, self-assured, and focused on the task at hand, they often take on leadership roles. They can get themselves in trouble, however, because they tend to care little about others' feelings. Thus they may be sarcastic, blunt, and uncaring. To work with and get what you need from D's, do the following:

- Put them in charge of projects.
- Allow them to work autonomously (whenever possible).
- Keep discussions short and to the point.
- Indicate what you need in the form of a choice: "I need to have that proposal by Friday. What's the soonest you can get it to me?"
- Help them get better at showing patience, sensitivity, and willingness to listen to and work with others.

Influence

The influence (I) personality type is outgoing and people oriented. People who fit this category like to be with people and be in the limelight. They are charismatic, social, and genuinely caring. They also want others to think highly of them; in fact, they are ego driven. I's can be impulsive and may lose interest in something if they believe that the grass is greener on the other side. In spite of being adventurous, they also fear being laughed at or ignored. To work with and get what you need from I's, do the following:

- Give them opportunities to be in the public eye by doing presentations or leading groups in activities.
- Publicly praise them for doing things well.
- Always allow them to save face; never criticize them in public.
- Help them develop their ability to stay focused and stick with projects.

Steadiness

The steadiness (S) personality type is reserved and people oriented. People who fit this category are nurturers and caretakers. They don't want the spotlight, and they don't like change; they do like routine. S's hate conflict and are eager to cooperate. This combination can be problematic, because they can easily get walked over and taken advantage of. It may also lead them to act as enablers by avoiding conflict and seeking to please others. S's need to feel secure and know that you are there for them. To work with and get what you need from them, do the following:

- Show them appreciation, and they will give you their loyalty.
- Give them roles in which they can support others.
- Help them become more assertive and able to promote themselves.
- Help them through big changes.
- Teach them how best to confront others.

Compliances

The compliance (C) personality type is reserved and task oriented. People who fit this category value quality and accuracy. They are detail driven and like getting things done. In addition, C's like being correct and are willing to do the research to assure it; they can also be perfectionists. They tend to be very organized and (more than D's, I's, and S's) will put in the time to see that a project gets done well. C's value personal growth but can be negative, critical, and unsociable. To work with and get what you need from C's, do the following:

- Give them opportunities to learn and grow.
- Allow them to work on their own.
- Help them listen to and interact with others.
- Focus on facts and details of the task at hand; they won't need you to cheer them on.

As we analyze the various personality styles, we must realize that no one falls strictly within a given DISC quadrant. We are each a mixture; one quadrant may represent our dominant style, but others will also come into play. For instance, I took a version of the DISC assessment, and the results showed that I was C dominant, lower (but virtually even) in D and S, and lowest in I. So, one interpretation would be that I am task oriented (D and C), focused on details and accuracy, and able to work well alone (C). I also have the capability to take charge and lead (D) and can be social and nurturing (S) but have less desire to be a "star."

That's pretty accurate. I am very concerned with "getting it right," and I do a great deal of my research and writing in relative solitude (C). Armed with knowledge, I then happily lead others in projects and do not hesitate to take to the stage and present

Getty Images/Maskot

Understanding personality types can enhance the relationships you have with your clients.

that information (D). At the same time, I'm a nurturer and want to help take care of others (S), but I'm unlikely to showboat simply for the sake of being in the limelight (I). I may do it, though, if I think it will entertain others.

The Importance of Understanding Personality Styles

Understanding personality styles can help us communicate more effectively with others in at least two ways. First, if we understand our own style, then we can recognize the filter through which we view others. For instance, we might often wonder, "If I can do this, why can't others?" The answer, of course, is that others are not wired like we are. Ideally, self-awareness gives us the ability to pull back and see others and ourselves as we truly are. Second, when we understand someone else's hierarchy of traits, what makes up their personality style, then we can approach that person in the ways that are most meaningful to him or her. This ability brings down any biases or walls (real or perceived) that might otherwise stand between us. These benefits apply when working with clients, co-workers, and employees.

"We hire people for their technical skills and fire them for their behavior" (Belchamber, 2013). In my experience, this statement is dead on. In fact, I can't remember needing to fire someone for a lack of technical skills; instead, the problem involves behavior or their ability to communicate effectively.

Does this mean that we need to formally test everyone in order to communicate effectively? Well, spending $30 to $40+ to administer an online assessment to a potential hire (someone with whom you have had previous interactions) may be well worth it. Think of how much time is spent with new hires! And many companies nowadays do use personality assessments as part of their hiring process. Please note, however, that because everyone includes a mix of personality factors, we can, to some extent, coach people up (or down) on traits that we'd like to see more (or less) of. Therefore, hiring strictly for personality type as indicated by testing could cause you to miss out on a good candidate.

For everyone else (existing employees, other business owners, or members of community organizations), it is neither necessary nor feasible to test them. If we understand the characteristics associated with various personality traits, then we can figure out a person's dominant style by observing his or her behavior.

Styles of Listening

Nothing—yes, I used an absolute, and I'm willing to repeat it—nothing is more important in building relationships than being able to really listen to others. Without this ability, you cannot fully understand how best to serve that person, either as a professional or as a friend. Throughout the day, we may find ourselves listening in many ways. In one model (Hardman, 2012), those various ways are categorized into eight styles.

- **Inactive:** Inactive listening involves hearing the other person speak without really understanding or retaining what is being said or engaging with the speaker. You may do this kind of listening when you get stuck at a party "talking" with the boring friend of a friend. You may also do it when a topic goes over your head and you feel like you're hearing an adult drone on and on in a Charlie Brown television special: "Wah wa-wah wa-wah wah wah . . ."

- **Passive:** Passive listening can be characterized as hearing but not listening—for example, having music on in the background while you attend to something else. In conversation, it differs from inactive listening in that passive listening involves no attempt to focus on what is being said.

- **Selective:** Selective listening, also known as selective hearing, is something we're all familiar with. It's what we do when we're hearing only what we want to hear. My wife, Heather, and I learned early on in raising our sons that they could tune us out. So, if we wanted their attention, we would include words such as *Legos* and *Toys "R" Us* in the middle of a sentence. When we did that, the boys' heads would snap around to find out what we were talking about.

- **Competitive:** Competitive listening occurs when someone listens just enough to jump in and talk about himself or herself. In other words, it's a status challenge in which the person tries to seem more important. We've all met folks like this—people who, no matter what accomplishment you may have achieved, they have done something better and will jump at the chance to tell you about it. I've even overheard personal trainers (not good ones, mind you) do this with clients: "Oh, doing a 5K is nice, but when I ran the marathon last year . . ." For a humorous example, do a web search for the old Monty Python sketch titled "Four Yorkshiremen," in which each man tries to top the others' stories of how hard they had it growing up.

- **Combative:** Though similar to competitive listening in its attempt to feel better about oneself, combative listening seeks to diminish others by attacking their thoughts or abilities. If you ever find yourself in a brainstorming session with a group that hasn't been coached on the concept that all ideas are valid, then you'll probably hear someone offer an idea that draws a retort such as, "That will never work!" or "That's a stupid idea!" Maybe the idea would in fact never work, but the act of saying so is an attempt to assert superiority.

- **Attentive:** Attentive listening involves taking an interest in understanding what is being said. Unlike active listening, however, this style does not involve giving purposeful feedback to the speaker. For example, as a member of an audience, you might listen attentively to a speaker giving a lecture. Because this communication is one sided—you do not interact with the speaker—the information you receive and your understanding of it are limited to the face value of the speaker's monologue.

- **Active:** Active listening occurs when you really connect with what an individual is saying and purposely convey that connection to the speaker. You might do so through repetition, asking open-ended questions (such as "How?" or "Can you tell me about . . ."), or paraphrasing back to the speaker what he or she has said. This sort of listening may also involve using short phrases to signal acknowledgment, such as, "Right" or "I understand" or "Wow, that must have been difficult."

- **Reflective:** Very similar to active listening, reflective listening involves connecting with the speaker but with the added goal of helping the speaker think through and solve issues or challenges. In other words, you act as a facilitator by helping the speaker flesh out ideas and possible solutions. Here's an example: "You've said that getting healthier is very important to you and that you know a fitness program needs to be part of the solution. At the same time, I hear you saying that you never seem to have time in the day to work out. What are some ways that you could fit exercise into your schedule?"

Clearly, some of these listening styles are completely inappropriate when trying to connect with others. The three styles that we should work to use are the last three: attentive, active, and reflective. Attentive listening sets us up to learn and understand from the speaker; in other words, we do it more for our own benefit. Active listening allows us not only to learn and understand but also to let the speaker know that we hear and understand. The effect can be profound: "Making someone 'feel felt' simply means putting yourself in the other person's shoes. When you succeed, you can change the dynamics of a relationship in a heartbeat" (Goulston, 2010, p. 48).

Reflective listening, however, is the technique that we really need to be accustomed to using, because, as fitness professionals, we will be approached by others who seek (or feel that they need) to change. These people may be employees, co-workers, or members or clients. They need to be heard, to "feel felt," and to be guided toward finding their own solutions. Remember that when people play a role in coming up with a solution, they buy in to a greater extent and are more likely to stick with it and succeed.

Sometimes the need is not only for you to listen to someone else; you may also need that person to listen to you. For many years, I have heard presenters explain sales systems that include asking consumers a series of questions to which they will say yes. In this way, according to these presenters, consumers get into the habit of saying yes and will continue to do so when you ask them to buy. I've personally never subscribed to this approach; in fact, it strikes me as false and manipulative.

In contrast, I recently came across a different way to help people get to yes. This model, referred to as the "persuasion cycle," is addressed by Mark Goulston in his

Clients want to know that you understand and care about them.

book *Just Listen* (2010). It was inspired by the transtheoretical model of intentional change and the concept of motivational interviewing. Goulston has taught this model to the FBI and to hostage negotiators.

The persuasion cycle attempts to move a person from

- resisting to listening,
- listening to considering,
- considering to willingness,
- willingness to doing, and
- doing to being glad they did and continuing to do.

For me, what's new here are the steps that involve moving from resisting to listening and from listening to considering. Of course, resistance exists in the example of hostage negotiations, but it can also exist in everyday situations such as persuading employees to buy into a new policy, addressing jealousy between co-workers, and selling personal training packages. Potential members or clients often fear being "sold" something that they don't want. For instance, I've had new club members begin their free fitness consultation with the opening line, "I'm not going to do any personal training, so don't try to push that on me."

In such situations, if you use active and reflective listening techniques—restating what the individual is expressing and asking if you have it right—they will say yes. You can then follow up by saying, "What I'm hearing is that you feel like . . . Is that correct?" By restating the person's position, you catch his or her attention. As a result, the person starts to listen instead of blocking out what you're saying. With each additional *yes*, the person's walls come down a little more, which moves him or her from resisting to listening and from listening to considering. These yeses, however, are not uttered as part of a mindless pattern but as responses to the fact that the person "feels felt" by you. *That* is a connection—and the start of a relationship.

Styles of Learning

Beyond styles of behavior, presentation, discussion, and listening, communication also hinges on how we teach our employees, co-workers, and clients. Not everyone learns best in the same way, so if we want to teach others so that they understand and use the information we share, then we need to use the approaches that are most meaningful to them. Various schools of thought exist in regard to styles of learning, and the ones I find most helpful are the VAK and VARK models.

VAK and VARK Models of Learning

Our learning can be deeply associated with the senses that we rely on most. The VAK and VARK models are identical in their sensory classifications of learning, with one exception. VAK, developed first by psychologists in the 1920s, stands for *visual, auditory*, and *kinesthetic*. VARK, developed by Neil Fleming, adapts VAK by adding the element (represented by the *R*) of *reading and writing* (VARK Learn Limited, 2016). An argument could be made that reading is visual and that writing combines visual and kinesthetic, but Fleming thought them significant enough to include as a distinct element.

As we look at sensory learning styles, we need to realize that, as with the DISC communication model, a person is not wholly characterized by one learning style. Each person may have a most effective style of learning, a least effective one, and shades of gray in between. This combination of styles is why it is so important that we use multisensory methods when teaching others.

Examples of Communication in Personal Training

At this point, you have developed some understanding of the various styles of communication but may not know just how to apply them in your day-to-day business interactions. Implementing that knowledge can seem challenging. Some practical applications are provided in the following examples.

Communication With Clients

By using active listening techniques in an initial interview with a client, you discover that she is the mother of three young children and cares for her aging mother. In terms of personality, she is a caretaker, a nurturer, and an S (that is, characterized by steadiness). This analysis also suggests that she is reserved, doesn't like public attention, tries to please others, and dislikes conflict. Thus it may be very difficult for her to put herself first and commit to making time to work out. However, if you praise her for coming to the interview and talk about how taking care of herself will benefit others in her life, then you will have her ear. Then explain that you can work with her in a less populated corner of the gym where she will not be "on display" and thus will be more comfortable. Tell her that you can even teach her some exercises that she can take home and teach to her mother. This way, you appeal both to her need to take care of herself and to her inclination to take care of others.

Communication With Businesses

A local business is thinking about adding a corporate wellness program. In a meeting with the human resources director, you use reflective listening to help him clarify his vision for the program. He is curt and, having done his research, quickly lays out what he's looking for. He is C dominant (that is, oriented toward compliance). His plan is based on outdated information, but you know that C's dislike being wrong. Therefore, you praise him for his research, then use current research to suggest an approach that would work better. Next, you give him a bulleted list of the best corporate wellness initiatives, and then, having listened and understood what he is looking for, recommend the program that best suits his company's needs and his vision. You back up your recommendation with facts. He may decide to do more research on his own, but you have set yourself up as a front-runner in his search for a wellness program provider.

Communication With Your Community

To promote a new senior exercise program that you've developed, you want to create an open house event. You want the event to help people learn what it would be like to take part in this program. To accomplish this goal, you want people at the open house to see, hear and read about, and feel the program. You choose to set up a video of the program that loops during the open house and to play the program's music throughout the event. You also prepare visually enticing flyers that describe the details of the program and place them strategically throughout the club. To top it off, you decide to give a lecture and demonstration so that attendees can get a visceral sense of what the senior exercise program is all about. This full sensory experience will create the best opportunity to gain participants for the program.

The following list provides brief descriptions of each learning style represented in the VARK model.

- **Visual:** Visual learners respond well to pictures, images, color, diagrams, mind maps, and, of course, visualization. They may find visual demonstrations or handouts with photos very helpful for understanding concepts and exercises.
- **Auditory:** Auditory learners prefer to receive information by hearing it. Specific options include lectures, group discussions, phone conversations and conference calls, and other

audio programming (for instance, I listen to audio books). Thus verbal explanation is a great way to get information across to auditory learners. They may also respond well to rhythm and music.

- **Reading and writing:** People with this preference understand and retain information better when it is presented via the written word, whether they are reading it or writing it down themselves. In addition, research has shown that taking handwritten notes improves memory and understanding more than is the case with taking notes on a laptop (Mueller & Oppenheimer, 2014). Therefore, when addressing learners in this group, allow time for them to take notes in longhand.

- **Kinesthetic:** Kinesthetic learners learn by doing and prefer hands-on approaches. They like to try out whatever task is being taught in order to better understand it. To meet this need, include participation as an integral part of their education, particularly when teaching physical movement. For example, after demonstrating a new resistance training exercise, let a kinesthetic learner try it out (rather than merely instructing the person to watch you do it).

Tell, Show, Do, Apply

To review, because people learn in different ways, we should structure our teaching to match their needs. In addition, although a given person may have a dominant learning style, there is also a mixture that works best for him or her. Therefore, we can maximize people's chances of learning something well by using multisensory VARK teaching.

Two great ways to integrate multiple mediums are the "tell, show, do" and the "tell, show, do, apply" approaches (Gardner, 2013). *Tell* refers to the auditory message, such as explaining an exercise. *Show* refer to the visual element of demonstration by the instructor. *Do* indicates kinesthetic hands-on elements in which the student attempts the activity. And you can also add *apply* when you want the individual to use the concept in a different situation. This element might be viewed as combining the visual and the kinesthetic as learners try to do something that they visualize. You can also add the reading and writing facet by having learners take longhand notes during *tell* and *show* elements.

More to Come

Knowing yourself and recognizing the filters through which you see others allows you to free yourself to see people as they truly are and really hear what they are saying. This combination of understanding yourself and others sets the groundwork for effective communication. So, how do we recognize those filters in the first place? One answer is to use the DISC model of personality styles—*dominance, influence, steadiness,* and *compliance*—which can help us recognize our own filters as well as those of others, such as potential (and current) members and clients. Before we can determine an individual's personality style, we need to hear what he or she is saying. We do that by using active and reflective listening techniques that help the person "feel felt" and allow him or her to open up to us.

People also learn in different ways, including visual, auditory, reading and writing, and kinesthetic (VARK for short). Therefore, we need to interact, guide, and instruct people in various ways. Doing so helps them understand and enables us to set tasks, present ideas, teach new concepts and movements, and offer solutions in a way that maximizes their potential. Win-win!

Maybe by this point you have come to realize that you are going to be one busy camper. With all of the skills needed and the time required to run a business, you will undoubtedly reach a point where you will need to outsource some of those tasks. Chapter 15 will help you start to identify those things that you don't have the time to do, don't have the skills to do, or just don't want to do and give some options for places to turn for help.

Chapter 15

Identifying Options for Outsourcing Your Tasks

Getty Images/sturti

Whether you are a staff member at a fitness facility, a self-employed personal trainer working at a club, or a personal trainer and owner of a facility, there will be times when you wish you could find someone else to help you out or do a task for you—especially when you start to get busy (and successful!).

There are three main reasons to outsource a task. First, you don't have time to do it; you're so booked with clients or have so many things to do that you cannot possibly get to them all. Second, you don't have the knowledge or skills to do a given task. Even if you've been in the industry for a while and have acquired a lot of the needed skills, there will still be specialty areas that you should hand over to the relevant pro. In addition, being multiskilled can lead you to try to do everything yourself, which is rarely the best use of your time. Remember, the mere fact that you *can* do something doesn't necessarily mean that you *should* do it. The third reason for outsourcing is that you just don't want to do a certain task. You may think this sounds a bit whiny, but if the task stresses you out or makes you unhappy, why not get someone else to do it? Life is too short.

One personal trainer who worked for me asked if I would hire her an assistant to help with her weekly administrative duties. I didn't, but my suggestion to her was to hire one! If she paid someone $10 per hour to do an hour's worth of work per week, then she could use that hour to do personal training, for which she was paid $35 per hour. As a result, she would earn $25 for that hour and be freed from the task she didn't want to do. Sounds worth it to me! As this chapter goes along, we'll look at some of the tasks that *you* might delegate or outsource.

Delegating or Outsourcing

Delegating and outsourcing both involve getting someone else to do something for you. They differ in that delegating involves assigning a task to an employee, whereas outsourcing involves hiring an outside specialist (Brassfield, 2013).

You can delegate tasks to an employee if you have one. Honestly, I have never been very good at this because in order to be confident that the job will get done right, I need to spend time training the employee to do it right. But I tend to feel too busy doing everything myself to have time to train someone else. For help in countering this tendency, see the 70 percent rule discussed in the sidebar on effective delegation. I've also been a sucker for taking on too much. Someone would ask, "Mark, do you think you could do _____ for me?" Invariably, I'd say yes, which would leave me with every bit of my own work and then some. The resulting stress led me to resign from more than one job.

This sort of difficulty with delegating is part of the reason for setting up systems and training materials that allow people to learn quickly and efficiently how to do certain tasks. Hindsight is a wonderful thing, but learn from my experience and set up those systems sooner rather than later in order to enable effective delegation.

If you don't know how to do something or don't have enough skill to do it well, then you need to outsource that task to someone else or find a product that can do it. People to whom you outsource a task generally require little or no training; in fact, they may teach you something.

Solutions for Hire: Tasks You May Want to Outsource

The decision about whether to outsource depends on your specific needs, wants, and abilities. As you lay out what you want to accomplish—whether as a club or studio

Keys to Effective Delegation

1. Don't delegate tasks that can be eliminated. If an employee can do the task at least 70 percent as well as you can, then delegate it (Schleckser, 2014).
2. When delegating a task, state the objectives clearly.
3. Provide all necessary information and resources.
4. Grant the authority needed to accomplish the task.
5. Establish a time line for the task.
6. Check on progress and answer any questions, but do not micromanage.
7. Review the completed task and provide feedback.
8. Thank the employee.
9. Delegation creates stronger, more capable teams by giving team members the trust and authority to do tasks that you might otherwise reserve for yourself.

owner or as a personal trainer (either working for a club or as an independent contractor)—ask yourself which jobs you really need to do yourself and which ones you don't. Perhaps someone else can offer better quality, speed, cost, or benefit to your business—or simply save you from the hassle of doing it yourself (Senger, 2012). Whatever your reason, two criteria for outsourcing a task are that it should be "both time consuming and well defined" (Ferriss, 2007, p. 123).

So much goes into managing your business, and outsourcing may be the answer to handling some of those tasks. If so, it may take the form of a person, a company, or a licensed product or program.

Billing and Collection

Asking for money tends to present a challenge for personal trainers, and that challenge may persist if you take on a management or ownership role. One solution is to use a daily or monthly automatic billing system arranged through your bank or merchant account. However, there are always cases of late payment, insufficient funds, and credit card kickbacks (due to expired, canceled, or replaced cards). Collecting this lost income can be awkward, uncomfortable, and time consuming. One way to handle this task is to use a collection agency. If you choose this option, make sure that the agency is accredited by the Better Business Bureau (BBB); a couple of examples are Advanced Billing & Consulting and Financial Network Recovery. Of course, you can also do your own search on the BBB website.

Payroll and Accounting

Withholdings, filings, and record keeping require a specialized skill set. Therefore, unless you work at a large company, payroll and accounting are usually outsourced rather than handled by a staff member. You may choose to work with a local firm to enable face-to-face meetings; alternatively, you can use an online system, such as ASAP Accounting & Payroll or Business Accounting Services.

Information Technology (IT)

IT jobs include setting up and maintaining your computer system. In addition, although online programs are available to help you build and maintain a website (for example,

As a business owner, it's important to know that you can't do it all. At some point, you will need to outsource some tasks.

Getty Images/iStockphoto/Dutko

Network Solutions, Weebly, and GoDaddy), you may want to hire a website development company to build you a site that is attractive, user friendly, and smartphone friendly. This company is unlikely to be the same one that sets up your computer system. I specify *company* rather than *person* for the website because I have seen IT-related people be unresponsive and leave clients hanging around waiting for updates. With a company, there should be more than one person who can step up and help you with any issue.

It is also helpful to personal trainers and fitness facilities to have a smartphone app. Apps can be used for everything from seeing a class schedule to booking a class or session and paying for it—all through one's phone. You may find that this task can be handled by the company that builds your website. Another option is to use third-party software that can be integrated into your website by subscription. At Jiva Fitness, we use MINDBODY software for online scheduling and payment of personal training sessions and group fitness classes. The company also offers an app that allows your clients or members to go directly to your scheduling and payment site. Another option for this service is Zen Planner.

Legal

Unless you're a lawyer who is familiar with your state's requirements, managing the legal aspects of your business is definitely a task to outsource. Your lawyer will help you with corporate agreements, member and employee contracts, and forms that need to be worded correctly in order to be legally binding. Although I would suggest creating a relationship with a local lawyer, you can also find some legal assistance online from companies such as LegalZoom and LegalShield.

Licensed Programs

Creating well-constructed programs can be a very time-consuming process. Outsourcing this job to a reputable company for licensed group fitness classes can provide you with a consistent participant experience that includes set music and choreography, as well as specific instructor training and certification. For those reasons, at Jiva Fitness, we use MOSSA for many of our classes. Other providers include Les Mills, Zumba, and SilverSneakers.

Small-group training programs can offer similar challenges, and companies are also available to help with this programming. Examples include MOSSA, TRIBE Team

Training, and IMPACT. Another programming area that you may choose to outsource is that of nutrition and weight loss. Some companies offer fully systemized turnkey nutrition programs that include everything from marketing to nutritional prescriptions; examples include DietMaster Pro, dotFIT, and Biometrics Nutrition & Fitness. All of these licensed program options can save you time on research, development, and staff training.

Continuing Education

Given my deep experience in the industry, I have plenty to teach personal trainers, group fitness instructors, managers, and owners. Even so, there's still plenty I don't know. In addition, even the information I do possess is sometimes received better when it comes from an outside source. (Have you ever tried to teach something to a family member? Too close to home to listen!).

To find outside expertise, you could take your team to a clinic or conference, which, depending on where you live, may be easily accessible. Check with various fitness organizations to find out where and when they are holding events. Good possibilities include the American College of Sports Medicine, the National Strength and Conditioning Association (which offers clinics in every state), and IDEA. You might also choose to have someone come to your facility to provide an educational session—perhaps a presenter you have seen before or a local professional. You can also host special trainings by groups such as TRX and Kettlebell Concepts. Another option is to offer your team access to online courses and articles from providers such as ClubConnect and PTontheNet.

Emergency Training

You should establish a written emergency procedure that all personnel know about and practice at least annually. In addition, every employee should be CPR and AED certified. At our current facility, as well as one where I worked previously, I wrote the emergency procedures after researching the latest guidelines. Because that previous facility had more than 50 staff members, I got certified to teach CPR and AED use in order to ensure that all staff members maintained their certifications. That solution may not be feasible for you. Fortunately, companies exist that can evaluate your facility, create your emergency procedures, and certify you and your staff in CPR and AED use. One example is ClubSafe. You can also find CPR and AED training classes by contacting your local chapter of the American Heart Association or the American Red Cross.

Janitorial Services

A clean, tidy space or club is essential to the comfort of your clients or members (it also helps you meet both local and national health and safety laws). In the start-up phase of a business, you may find yourself doing all of these things yourself. As the traffic increases, however, you will of course get busier and will likely need to find help. If you hire a janitorial service, make sure that it is insured in case of breaking something or spilling chemicals that stain your carpets.

Equipment Maintenance

With almost 40 years in the industry, I can handle many day-to-day repairs. But should I? When you repair your own equipment, you may violate the warranty agreement, which means that you may be left uncovered by the warranty if something goes wrong with the equipment. Damaged or incorrectly repaired equipment can also put you in danger of a lawsuit if someone gets injured using it. If you want to avoid these risks, you can retain an equipment repair and maintenance company that is approved by the manufacturer to work on its equipment. Doing so can help protect you and your company from lost warranty coverage and liability from nonapproved equipment repair. It can also minimize downtime (members don't like to see their favorite piece of equipment out of order!). The company you retain should be insured in case something goes wrong during or after the repairs. Ask your equipment manufacturers if they can recommend a company near you.

Landscaping

If you have any land surrounding your facility, make it as attractive as possible. Prospective members' first impression of you and your business begins forming as soon as they approach your facility. A well-groomed, well-designed yard or entry shows that you are a professional who takes aesthetics seriously. Find a talented local landscaper to help you make the most of your facility's exterior.

Snow Removal

The need for this job depends, of course, on where you are located. When I lived in Maine, snow removal was a very important factor! We would have employees shovel and salt the steps and sidewalks, but plowing was definitely an outsourced task. The equipment (plows and backloaders and such) was specialized and very expensive, and the service was always on call.

Fitness Sales Systems

If the sales process still eludes you, or you need help putting together a consistent sales training program for your team, you can seek an outside company to provide a system for personal training and program sales. Examples include Pro Fitness Program and Close Clients.

Newsletters

Fitness e-newsletters add value for clients and members, and, in my opinion, you should offer one. You can do it yourself by using a service such as Constant Contact, AWeber, or MailChimp. Or you can use a service that custom-brands a newsletter for you with prepared health and fitness content and e-mails it to your contact list. Examples include Fitpro, Fitness Newsletter Solution 3.0, and Customized Nutrition Newsletters.

Marketing and Social Media

No one knows your brand (whether personal or company) like you do. Even so, you may find yourself needing help to get your message out to your target market. Larger companies maintain a whole department devoted to marketing, but smaller ones may find it more economical to outsource at least part of this task. If you outsource either your marketing in general or your social media marketing in particular, make sure that you approve or at least monitor everything *before* it goes out to the public. This micromanagement may seem to defeat the purpose of hiring out the work, but, at least in the beginning, you need to make sure that the person or company you hire is putting out the right message for your brand. Once they build your trust, you can give them freer rein.

In hiring someone to do your marketing or social media marketing, look first at people or companies that are familiar with you. They are more likely to know where you're coming from and less likely to misrepresent you. Typically, this would mean hiring local. However, if there are no clear candidates locally, you could look to national companies. Good companies will spend time getting to know you and your company so they can represent you as authentically as possible. Examples of national social media marketing companies include LYFE Marketing, Viral In Nature, and Friendemic.

Answering Services and Virtual Receptionists

In these days of high-tech solutions, if we don't have a receptionist we tend to go "old school" and use an answering machine to manage our phone calls. However, you can do better than simple automation. Live answering services not only enhance the member experience but also filter calls to separate those you want to take from those you don't. Examples include Ruby Receptionists, VoiceNation, and Answering Service Care.

Independent-Contractor Fitness Personnel

If you want more personal training capacity but don't want to deal with adding an employee, then hiring a personal trainer who works as an independent contractor (IC) may be the right solution for you. Before you hire one, screen thoroughly, check references, and remember that you have limited control over how ICs perform their work.

Group fitness instructors are another option for IC hires, particularly because they tend to work so few hours. This option may be especially appealing if the instructor is certified to teach a package provided by a group fitness organization such as MOSSA or Les Mills; with that certification, unless the instructor has an awful personality, he or she will deliver a great class. In contrast, instructors for Zumba, Spinning, and SilverSneakers may not be quite as assured, because, though they have specific training, they can also put together their own class. Finally, freestyle classes are the least consistent because they consist of whatever the instructor chooses, which makes for highly variable quality. As a result, I am far less likely to hire a freestyle instructor as an IC.

Professional Guidance

If we want to be at the top of our game, we must keep learning. We can learn from books, articles, conferences, clinics, webinars, peers, and, if we are smart or lucky, a

Outsourcing tasks, such as cleaning, can help free up time you need to manage your business.

Getty Images/sturti

mentor. Some of these learning opportunities cost money, whereas others are free. If you are not getting the professional guidance that you need in order to build and promote your business, seek out a mentor. That person may come in the form of a consultant, a business coach, or a more experienced colleague. Whoever it is, you should feel that he or she is the right fit for you in terms of personality and skill set.

Resources for Outsourcing

Billing and Collection

- Advanced Billing & Consulting (www.advancedbillingandconsulting.com)
- Financial Network Recovery (http://fnetrecovery.com)
- Better Business Bureau list of collection agencies (www.bbb.org/sdoc/accredited-business-directory/collection-agencies)

Payroll and Accounting

- ASAP Accounting & Payroll (www.businessasap.com)
- Business Accounting Services (businessaccounting.com)

Website Development

- Network Solutions (www.networksolutions.com)
- Weebly (www.weebly.com)
- GoDaddy (www.godaddy.com)

Online Scheduling and Payment

- MINDBODY (www.mindbodyonline.com)
- Zen Planner (https://zenplanner.com)

Legal Matters

- LegalZoom (www.legalzoom.com)
- LegalShield (www.legalshield.com)

Licensed Programs for Group Fitness

- MOSSA (http://mossa.net)
- Les Mills (www.lesmills.com)
- Zumba (www.zumba.com)
- SilverSneakers (www.silversneakers.com)
- Spinning (www.spinning.com)

Licensed Programs for Small-Group Training

- MOSSA (https://mossa.net/group-fitness/vipr-workout)
- TRIBE Team Training (www.tribeteamtraining.com/clubs)
- IMPACT (www.nestacertified.com/impact-group-fitness-business-system)

Licensed Programs for Nutrition and Weight Loss

- DietMaster Pro (www.dietmastersoftware.com/products/professional-nutrition-software/dietmaster-professional)
- dotFIT (www.dotfit.com/licenseoptions)
- Biometrics Nutrition & Fitness (www.biometricshealth.com/benefits.htm)

Cost Versus Benefit

For everything we do in business, we should look at the return on investment (ROI). That is, we should analyze both what it costs and the return (or benefit) that it creates in order to determine whether the expense is worth it. Before diving into the details,

Continuing Education—General
- ACSM (www.acsm.org/attend-a-meeting/upcoming-meetings)
- NSCA (www.nsca.com/events)
- NSCA local events (www.nsca.com/Events/State-and-Regional-Events)
- IDEA (www.ideafit.com/fitness-conferences)

Continuing Education—Specialty Training
- TRX (www.trxtraining.com/course-schedule)
- Kettlebell Concepts (www.kettlebellconcepts.com/index.php/fitness-facilities)

Continuing Education—Online Courses and Articles
- ClubConnect (www.clubconnect.com)
- PTontheNet (www.ptonthenet.com)

Emergency Procedure Training
- ClubSafe (clubsafe.com)
- CPR/AED training American Heart Association (www.heart.org)
- American Red Cross (www.redcross.org)

Fitness Sales Systems
- Pro Fitness Program (profitnessprogram.com)
- Close Clients (closeclients.com)

Newsletter—Self-Produced
- Constant Contact (www.constantcontact.com)
- AWeber (www.aweber.com)
- MailChimp (mailchimp.com)

Newsletter—Packaged
- Fitpro (fitpronewsletter.com)
- Fitness Newsletter Solution 3.0 (fitnessnewslettersolution.com)
- Nutrition Newsletters (customizednutritionnewsletters.com)

Marketing and Social Media
- Lyfe Marketing (www.lyfemarketing.com)
- Viral In Nature (http://viralinnature.com)
- Friendemic (www.friendemic.com)

Answering Services and Virtual Receptionists
- Ruby Receptionists (www.callruby.com)
- VoiceNation (www.qualityansweringservice.com)
- Answering Service Care (www.answeringservicecare.net)

let's put things in perspective by revisiting the reasons you would contemplate outsourcing in the first place:

- You don't have time to do the task.
- You don't have the necessary skills to do the task.
- You don't want to do the task.

In some cases, you could push through and do a task that you don't want to do, but it will get tedious and that's not why you started your own business, right? And remember, even if you work for someone else, if outsourcing would make your life better or give you more time to make more money, then you can—and should—still hire help. So, either way, if the need is there, you really should get help.

Next, consider the ROI. If the issue is lack of time or not wanting to do a given task, then one simple way to begin your analysis is to make an educated guess about how long it would take you to do the job if you did have the time and wanted to do it. One note from my own experience: It almost always takes longer than you think it will, so multiply your guess by 1.5. Then multiply that number of hours by your usual hourly income. The result gives you a baseline cost for the task. Can you outsource it for the same amount or less? If so, then do it! Even if it costs more, if you think the quality of the outsourced work is better than what you could produce and therefore worth a bit more than your estimated baseline, you may still choose to outsource it.

If you're thinking about outsourcing a task for which you lack the skill set, does it really need to be done now or could it wait until you're more able to afford it? For example, you might decide to print some very simple business cards to get you by for a while rather than paying a graphic designer to create them. If the task must be done now—for example, securing a lawyer to help write or approve your waivers or informed consents—then shop around and ask others for recommendations. Look for attorneys who are familiar with your state's relevant laws, then obtain price quotes for the job, and may the best lawyer win! Remember that the ROI consists of the value you receive, not the price that you pay. Thus it might consist of money, additional time to do what you need to do, peace of mind, or simply more joy when you do less of a task that you dislike.

More to Come

Delegating and outsourcing can provide solutions when you don't have the time, the skill, or the desire to do a particular task. Legal services are necessary, whereas other services are optional. For instance, depending on your needs and ability to pay, you might outsource financial aspects of your business, such as billing, collection, payroll, and accounting. If time is a concern, you might license turnkey programs for group fitness, small-group training, or nutritional guidance rather than creating and implementing them from scratch. You can outsource management of the physical facility to janitorial, equipment maintenance, landscaping, and snow removal companies. In addition, you can hire an outside source to help you with sales systems, marketing, social media, and customizable e-newsletters to build your business.

Bottom line, you can have many services done by someone else if your time and effort will be better spent elsewhere. Don't hesitate to delegate when you can or outsource when you must.

At this point in the book, we've covered most of the business basics. The last chapter dives into the never-ending job of growing your business. From working on member and client retention to creating intellectual property, we'll look at many of the ways you can continue to help more people and, consequently, do better financially yourself.

Chapter 16

Growing Your Business

Getty Images/iStockphoto/bowdenimages

In the preceding chapters, we've discussed what is needed in order to start and build your business: As a personal trainer on staff, you build your clientele and your position at the club. As an independent contractor, you build your brand and expand your reach. And as a personal trainer, manager, and owner of your own facility, you are responsible for all facets of a thriving company and may even oversee construction of the building itself.

Once you're up and running, the work *really* begins. It involves a never-ending effort to build your client or member base, increase your offerings, obtain greater commitment (and greater success) from each client or member, and seek additional sources of income to increase your net profit. In this final chapter, we'll cover several new topics and revisit some that are important to emphasize as you strive to grow your business. Specifically, we'll cover retention; referrals, recommendations, and rewards; networking; new programs and services; upselling; and intellectual property.

Retention

Retention refers to keeping clients or members, whereas *attrition* refers to losing them. Why is it important to know your retention rate? Well, if you have a retention rate of 100 percent, then you're doing great at keeping your clients happy. In fact, they're so happy that they never leave you. Therefore, you need to focus now on marketing to drive *new* business. On the other hand, if your retention rate is 40 percent—in other words, 60 percent of your clients or members are jumping ship—then you need to focus more on keeping your clients than on gaining new ones.

It is more cost effective to retain clients and members than to acquire new ones. Although I see different numbers regarding the cost of gaining a new client, you can figure a ballpark cost simply by totaling your monthly marketing expenses (for ads, flyers, newsletters, social media updates, paid sales commissions, and so on) and dividing the result by the number of new clients or members acquired that month. Whatever that number turns out to be, it's less expensive to work at retaining current clients and members. In addition, they're more likely to reach their goals if they continue working out with you—and that makes everyone happier!

Retention Standards

It's hard to find meaningful retention standards by which to measure your success, but one goal to aspire to is the bar set by the clubs and fitness facilities of IHRSA, the International Health, Racquet & Sportsclub Association. Membership in IHRSA is purely voluntary (there is an annual fee), and fitness facilities are not required to join IHRSA. As a result, there are only about 10,000 IHRSA member clubs worldwide, and only a fraction of the 36,180 health clubs in the United States are IHRSA members (International Health, Racquet & Sportsclub Association, 2016b). However, IHRSA clubs have an average retention rate of 72.4 percent (International Health, Racquet & Sportsclub Association, 2016b). That rate may sound amazing, but it is not surprising since IHRSA clubs are dedicated to caring for their members and improving their performance in accordance with IHRSA's mission statement: to "grow, protect and promote the health and fitness industry, and to provide its members with benefits that will help them be more successful" (International Health, Racquet & Sportsclub Association, 2016a). Those should be the goals of every club!

The average retention rate for fitness studios has been reported as 76 percent (Association of Fitness Studios [AFS], 2016, p. 31). I believe this standard is realistic for fitness studios because many of the retention strategies (such as more personal attention) that can be used for clubs are already more inherent in the nature of a smaller facility. Granted, joining a studio is likely to cost more per month (if it offers monthly memberships)—on average, $104 per month for unlimited group fitness at a studio versus $58 per month at a larger club (Statistic Brain, 2016). However, studios are also more likely to know and connect with individual participants, help them set realistic goals, and guide them in what to do and how to do it. This engagement tends to keep people coming in and using their membership.

Here's another factor to consider: Clubs with higher joining fees and higher monthly fees are perceived to offer greater value. In fact, "within the industry, there is and has always been a correlation between price and attrition: the higher the price, the lower the attrition; the lower the price, the higher the attrition" (Ekstrom, 2004). Of course, the client's commitment is equally important—the more a person is willing to pay, the more deeply he or she is committed (Ekstrom).

This phenomenon should factor into your decision about the right pricing and packaging for your club, studio, or service. However, before you decide to raise your prices to improve retention by creating greater perceived value, understand that perceived value comes with expectations. If I'm paying $150 per month for a membership, I expect a clean, attractive facility with great service. In contrast, if I'm paying $10 per month, I'm expecting equipment that works (at least most of the time), and that's about it. If the value you deliver is not in line with, or better than, your price, then people will recognize that gap and look for another option.

As for commitment, you can imagine the thought process: "I'm not so sure about this gym thing. I may not like it. Let me just try the cheap one." If the person then goes unsupervised, following no real program, then he or she is unlikely to succeed and therefore very likely to stop coming.

Causes and Solutions of Member Drop-Out

How long, on average, does a new member keep coming back to a club? The answer may surprise you: Of members that go to the health club less than four times per month, 41 percent of them will have dropped out by month three and 44 percent by month six. Even of those attended more than 12 times per month, 13 percent will have dropped out by month six (PTDirect, n.d.).

Why does someone who paid to be a member decide to drop out? And what can you do about it? Here are some reasons for which people leave and some strategies for retaining them.

- **Found it too expensive.** While it's true that in some cases the cost of membership doesn't fit an individual's budget, for many people it's simply a matter of not seeing the value in being a member. As a personal trainer, you may find that you can reduce the economic burden by offering small-group training or group fitness classes as alternatives to one-on-one training. If you oversee a club's programming, you might offer non-prime-time memberships at a reduced rate, memberships for group fitness only, or group-fitness punch cards (which are often offered digitally).

- **Didn't feel like they belonged.** Nobody likes to feel alone, especially when others are present. One of the most highly referred to quotes when talking about member connection and engagement comes from the theme song for the television sitcom *Cheers*—the one about everybody knowing your name and always being glad you came. Similarly, you want clients and members to feel that they belong, that they matter, and that you care about them. Always smile at your clients and members, greet them by name, ask about them, take a sincere interest in what they have to say, and, yes, be glad they came! I tell personal trainers that the members who are most likely to need their help are not the gregarious, outgoing ones but those who are quiet, off to the side, and often noticeably uncomfortable. These are the folks at risk of not returning.

- **Had unrealistic expectations.** "I wanted to lose 10 pounds in two weeks and didn't. I'm not coming anymore." That may sound silly to us, but people sometimes get it in their head that change should happen fast; then when it doesn't, they feel disheartened and give up. The problem is, they don't know what they don't know. For this reason, it is crucial to meet with all new members within the first couple of days to discuss their goals. This advice also applies to personal trainers, who should set expectations as a part of the initial consultation. If the club cannot arrange a separate meeting with a new member to cover expectations, then, at a minimum, it should be addressed in discussion and possibly in printed material when the member joins.
- **Didn't know what to do.** If a person doesn't know what to do, then he or she will not succeed. Fortunately, as with unrealistic expectations, this problem can be corrected by going through an initial consultation with a personal trainer. After the meeting, the individual may come away wanting to participate in personal training, small-group training, or group fitness in order to receive additional education and guidance.
- **Didn't really use their membership.** Of course, people who don't use their memberships are wasting their own money. The key for you is to engage members who have not come to the club for a while. For help with this task, you can use club check-in software. Many such applications can be set to alert you about members who have not checked in for a set period of time. Invite these individuals to a new class offering, a lecture, or anything that may entice them to get started again.

Referrals, Recommendations, and Rewards

One of the best ways to build your business is to get current clients or members to refer family, friends, and others to you. Such referrals allow you to speed up or even skip the process of helping prospects come to know, like, and trust you, because someone they already know, like, and trust has vouched for you. Fortunately, people want to give referrals. It gives them a good feeling and a sort of cachet, or social capital, with the people they refer.

We all know this to be true. For instance, someone asks you to recommend a restaurant or movie, and you excitedly provide your choice and then wait to find out whether his or her experience was as good as yours. When it was, you feel great and have a sense of pride in your referral. You may also feel that your social standing with the person has gone up a notch or two.

So, how do you get people to make a referral? Some answers are provided in the following subsections.

Being Remarkable

"*Remarkable* is a really cool word, because we think it just means 'neat.' But it also means 'worth making a remark about'" (Godin, 2003). In other words, we throw words around without really thinking about their true meaning. Here are two other examples: *outstanding* and *exceptional*. These words mean, respectively, that we stand out in a crowd and that we stand as an exception to the norm. *Average*, on the other hand, doesn't fire people up or leave them wanting to pass your name on to others.

Getty Images/iStockphoto/Jacob Ammentorp Lund

When clients find you and your services remarkable, they are likely to tell other people about you.

You can be remarkable in various ways, not all of which are desirable. If you were really bad at your job, people would talk about you, but they certainly wouldn't refer others to you. You could also be the most knowledgeable fitness professional around and help your clients achieve great results. Or you could be remarkably caring and, through that caring, help clients to care more for themselves and thereby enjoy great results. You could also be the most entertaining, helping clients enjoy their workouts, put more effort into them, and achieve great results. Or you could be a combination of any or all of these things and get great results.

Creating Client or Member Evangelists

Beyond merely providing referrals, an evangelist actively seeks to convert others. Creating an evangelist requires being remarkable, but that alone is not enough. For more, see the sidebar on optimizing evangelists for your business.

Asking for the Referral

Sadly, evangelists tend to make up a small portion of our clientele. The majority of our clients and members don't run out to tell the world about you, even if you are remarkable. Perhaps they simply don't think about referring, or perhaps they are introverted or shy and a little uncomfortable speaking up about your business. The best time to ask for a referral is when the client or member talks about a success or expresses pleasure with you or your company. You can respond by saying something like, "I'm so happy to hear that, Janet. Do you know anyone else who might be interested in getting the same results?"

If the answer is yes, offer the person a free trial class, free consultation, or other gift to give to the friend. The item will not only remind the referrer to follow through but also provide extra incentive for the potential guest. Remember, if the referral works out, it will raise the client's or member's status in the eyes of the guest. If the person feels uncomfortable making the referral, offer to invite the individual yourself on the person's behalf. If the person does offer to make the referral himself or herself, don't be afraid to follow up: "So, John, did you get a chance to invite your friend in for a class?"

How to Optimize Evangelists for Your Business

Evangelists tend to possess seven traits that we can focus on in order to maximize our chance of creating evangelists (McConnell, 2007):

- **They passionately recommend you.** Passion is the key here, and it comes from the ways in which you make yourself stand out, such as your ability to connect with them or the quality of your offerings.
- **They believe in your company and its people.** You've got to share your story, your company's story, and your employees' stories. These stories should be clear, authentic statements about why you do what you do, where you came from, and what your mission is. The more your story drives you, the more likely people are to climb aboard to share the ride with you.
- **They purchase your products or services as gifts.** Make it easy for them to share a piece of you or your business. For example, you might offer gift certificates, branded apparel, or other products that support your business.
- **They give unsolicited praise and suggestions.** Always, always, always be appreciative of the person's input. To follow up, extend the unsolicited feedback by asking the person's opinion on another matter.
- **They forgive you when you make an occasional mistake.** Like friends and family, evangelists forgive you for almost anything if you claim ownership of the mistake, apologize, and don't let it happen again.
- **They don't want to be paid.** Evangelists look to convert others, not to get paid, because they believe in you and your business. Paying them for referrals or giving kickbacks may even insult them. On the other hand, a handwritten thank-you note can be very meaningful to them.
- **They feel part of something bigger.** We all want to be part of something bigger, something meaningful. Invite potential evangelists to play a larger role by seeking their help. You might, for instance, ask them to serve on an advisory board or event committee.

Asking for the Recommendation

Although a referral is a kind of recommendation, let's define *recommendation* for our purposes here as a public endorsement. Thanks to social media, there are now many opportunities to give a thumbs-up to a business or service. This public praise, though not targeting an individual, can be very important because people will consume any information about you or your business. When people see a recommendation on your website or social media account, it brings them one step closer to knowing, liking, and trusting you—and therefore one step closer to becoming a new client or member. When a client or member has had a good experience, ask him or her to write a review or to rate you on a social media platform of choice.

Offering Rewards for Referrals

Many personal trainers and clubs offer rewards for giving referrals. The reward may be a free session, a free month's membership, a free t-shirt, or some other service or product. There is nothing wrong with that, but I'm not inclined to set up an ongoing "exchange" for referrals. I don't like the idea of creating the expectation. I'd rather surprise someone who has sent referrals with a reward; for example, you might give one reward to the person who made a referral *and* one to the person who was referred to you.

Another idea is to conduct a campaign or initiative to gain referrals. The key here is to hold it for a relatively short time (from one week to one month) and to mark it clearly with a kickoff and a closing event. Make it a big deal—a celebration, in fact—and focus it on getting friends, loved ones, and others more active in improving their health and fitness. If you like, give a prize to the person who refers the most people, but also be sure to recognize everyone who refers *anyone* to you. To contribute to the party atmosphere, provide healthy food and drinks, music, decorations, and even some kind of physical game.

To succeed with such an event, you must plan ahead, make sure that everyone knows about it, and create a buzz through face-to-face interactions, social media, and e-mails. Also, make sure that the closing event is *really* fun, because it will leave a lasting impression on everyone who participates (and even on those who just "hear all about it").

Increasing Your Reach Through Networking

You may have heard the old saying, "It's not what you know but *who* you know." Let's revise that to clarify the real point: "It's not who you know but who knows you." Networking involves creating opportunities to build relationships with others, getting to know them, and, in turn, having them get to know you. Of course, networking is a kind of marketing and is therefore addressed in chapter 12, which focuses on marketing in general. But networking is such an important part of growing your business that it's worth revisiting here.

Your network is made up of other professionals to whom you can refer clients or members, such as massage therapists, chiropractors, orthopedic surgeons, or even car mechanics. Clients and members appreciate good professional referrals, and each referral you make helps you gain a little social capital. By referring people to other high-quality professionals, you also gain appreciation from those professionals, which increases the chance that they will refer some of their patients, clients, or customers to you.

My wife, Heather, and I are fortunate that our new hometown of Easton, Pennsylvania, offers so many opportunities to get out and meet people. Last weekend, I went to an art gallery's opening. This weekend, I'm taking my sons to a rock concert featuring local bands to benefit the city's theater. When you get out in the community, you will bump into people you know, they'll introduce you to their friends, and you'll do the same. As a result, your network gets a little bigger. There are always local events that you can attend and get involved with. Here are a few ways to find them: go to your community's website and look for a calendar of events; do a web search for local business networking opportunities; check with the local chamber of commerce for events; and ask people what events are coming up or where you can find out about them.

Enter these networking opportunities into your social media calendar (they are social, after all) and go to them with a plan for what you want to accomplish. For example, the benefit concert this weekend features three bands. The lead singer, songwriter, and guitarist for one of the bands is one of my clients. My goal is to meet the rest of his band, connect with the lead singer of another band that I have met but don't know well, and meet the lead performer of the third band. After the benefit, I'll follow up by sending each of them a message via Facebook saying what a pleasure it was to meet them (assuming it turns out to be!) and ask if we can connect on Facebook. If they agree, then I will start to follow their posts, "like" things that I do in fact like (always be authentic and sincere), comment when I have something to add to the conversation, and help promote their events whenever I can.

Tips for Networking

Here are some keys to networking effectively:

- Choose your events and opportunities based on the likelihood of attendance of your target market.
- Go to the event with a plan specifying whom you want to meet and what you want to accomplish.
- Be authentic and open—the real you. Never pretend to be something or someone you're not.
- Start by mingling with people you know, but always look to meet new people. If you don't push yourself to interact with others, then you won't get to know anyone new.
- If you're sitting, sit with people you don't know. Doing so will help you strike up conversations with people outside of your circle.
- Ask open-ended questions that will give you insight into people, such as, "What's your greatest passion?" or, if you want to keep things simpler, "What do you hope to achieve at these events?"
- Steer the conversation so that it focuses on the other person, not on you. Take a sincere interest in what the person is saying.
- Don't try to sell. This is an opportunity to begin a relationship. Your future business comes from established relationships, and it takes time to build them.
- Be a connector—someone who connects others. If you meet someone who doesn't know anyone else, or who knows very few others, introduce that person to everyone you know. He or she will be indebted to you. I've benefited from some great connectors who took me under their wing and introduced me to others. I will always be thankful to them.
- Part with a phrase such as, "Can't wait to talk again." Set the expectation that you will see the person again: "I look forward to talking with you again at the _____ meeting next week." Or, "I'd love to continue this conversation. Do you have any time next week to meet for coffee?"
- Follow up. If you said you would get in touch, then do so; otherwise, your word begins to mean less. Even if you didn't arrange a follow-up, at least connect on social media and express that you enjoyed meeting the person.

You can do these types of things too! It just boils down to being purposeful in your efforts. I guarantee that the people you connect with will be happy to have your support. In addition, your interest, authenticity, and enthusiasm will pique their interest, and they will want to know more about you.

If there aren't any (or enough) events near you, you can create your own—anything from a large-scale benefit to a simple dinner. In Keith Ferrazzi's book *Never Eat Alone* (2014), he discusses how he hosted dinner parties that become a great networking tool. He suggests that your mission should be to find out someone else's passion and the story that goes with it. For example, if your passion is your family, I might ask you to tell me about one of your favorite family adventures. You're probably going to love talking about it, and hearing about it will give me real insight into who you are.

Offering New Programs and Services

Whether offered to current clients or members or to prospective ones, new programs and services may help you build your business. The big three services to offer are personal training, small-group training, and group fitness. These are the most common services offered, and, for personal trainers who are starting a business, they most likely constitute a simple expansion of what you have already been doing.

As you contemplate expanding what you offer, consider how the potential new offering would affect your brand. For instance, when a luxury car manufacturer decides to make an economy vehicle, it waters down the brand (or at least the *perception* or *reputation* of the brand), thereby making it less special. Similarly, if you are known for specializing in hardcore powerlifting and you add a cardio dance class to your offerings, your powerlifting clients or members may feel a little less at home, a little less like your place is their place. There are, however, many programs and services that could fit your clientele and your philosophy.

In chapter 9, we discussed programs and bundling. Putting multiple services together in a time-limited package to meet a specific goal can be a great way to create a new source of income. You may also be able to offer pieces of these programs as stand-alone products. Let's say that you start your business by offering personal training and group fitness. You could add nutritional coaching, group support meetings, lectures, workshops, meal preparation classes, or various groups or "clubs" (such as running, obstacle course, and parkour). Really, you can add *anything* as long as it meets the purpose and enhances the community of your business.

When you create a new program or add a new service, go through the full process of determining the appropriate pricing and marketing for the product. Here's a review of factors that affect pricing:

- What are your operating expenses? This category includes items such as materials, equipment, and marketing costs.

- How much can your target market afford to pay? The answer may depend in part on whether the new program is intended as an add-on for current members and clients or as a way to draw in new people.

- How many participants can you expect based on the demographics? Here again, the size of your market may depend in part on whether the new offering is intended as an add-on for current clientele or a way to draw in new people.

- Does your competition offer a similar program or service? This question is less important if you are creating the new product for current clientele, since you have already gained their trust and loyalty. If it's for a new market, however, you need to know whether your competition offers a similar program and, if so, what the price is.

- If the new program targets a new market, what is your unique selling proposition? How are you different from your competition?

- What is the perceived value of the new offering among your target market?

- What do *you* believe the new offering is worth? Why do you believe that?

- What is your time worth? Consider both the time required to create the program (all hours spent getting it ready to deliver) and the time required to deliver it.

The answers to these questions will help you determine whether the program is worth delivering. If you can't charge enough to cover all expenses, don't offer it, unless you're doing so as a form of charity.

Upselling: Selling More to Current Clients

"Would you like to supersize that?" The term *upselling* typically refers to suggesting an upgraded sale or additional purchase. Many clubs try to upsell memberships: "You can add unlimited racquetball for only $15 more per month." Or the pitch might address towel service, locker rental, a monthly massage, or—well, you get the idea.

Although this is a common practice, the customer may feel nickeled-and-dimed to death if you keep adding layers to the sale. Therefore, my suggestion about upselling is to keep it to one or two items—and only ones that will enhance the individual's experience and likelihood of success. For example, say that a client has difficulty with getting up in the morning to get to the gym. If you like, you could suggest adding a wake-up service to the program. Or perhaps a client needs extra accountability to follow a food plan. You might suggest adding a weekly session of nutrition coaching (if you're trained to do that). Upselling with these kinds of services can help your clients succeed while also bringing in more revenue for you.

Additional services can also be sold at times other than the initial point of sale. For instance, current clients or members may discover—or you may discover while working with them—that they have additional needs. Even though you might suggest the same additional services to a potential client or member, it is easier to sell them to a current client or member, who already knows, likes, and trusts you. Because the person has experienced your value, he or she trusts that you would not offer something unless it provides a benefit.

Intellectual Property Products

Most of what we do as personal trainers and instructors is limited by the number of hours in a day. We can take steps to maximize our hourly wage, such as offering small-group training or a group fitness class. Still, we can work only so many hours, which puts a ceiling on our ability to build our business. Of course, if you are a business owner, you can hire others to help you make more income. And one thing we can all do, regardless of whether we work for a club or own one, is to offer and sell intellectual property.

Upselling can increase your clients' success and help you grow your business.

Getty Images/iStockphoto/bowdenimages

Intellectual property is a creation of the mind and can consist of written, visual, or auditory work. Once created, such property can serve as an ongoing source of passive income—passive in the sense that all of the research and development is completed and the only work going forward is to market and sell the product. The following lists give some examples of intellectual property (along with possibilities for passive income) that you can develop for your colleagues and clients.

Written

- **Books:** You can easily create short, informational books printed locally or sold online as e-books.
- **Articles:** These are usually used to establish (that is, demonstrate) your expertise, but you can also turn them into a subscription-based product.
- **White papers:** Like articles, these are usually used to establish your expertise. But they can also serve as great marketing tools as people that would like to receive them can be asked to supply their e-mail address in return (which adds to your e-mail marketing list).
- **Workout journals:** These items mostly contain blank pages for writing down dates, exercises, sets, reps, and workout comments. However, you can add some motivational quotes and personal branding to create a salable product.
- **Exercise diagrams:** These might appear in a book, article, or workout journal, but they can also be used in other items such as informational workout charts and exercise cards.

Visual

- **Recorded lectures:** Anything you present live should be recorded and considered for use as a passive income source.
- **Exercise or educational recordings:** DVDs are easy to create and can be reproduced as needed for sale at your facility or online.
- **Online courses:** The needed technology is now readily available for creating an online educational course through e-learning sites such as Udemy, Teachable, and Pathwright. The potential topics are countless—for example, Yoga for Busy Moms and The Science of Brain Fitness.
- **Video podcast:** You can produce subscription-based, episodic presentations of any length on a wide range of topics. Most are offered free of charge, but you can also charge a fee.

Auditory

- **Recorded lectures:** As with the visual category, any presentation you make should be recorded, and you can pull the audio portion out for sale as a separate product.
- **Podcasts:** As with recorded lectures, you can offer an audio-only version of a video podcast.
- **Workout motivation or instruction:** I've heard various musical playlists with voice overlays in which an instructor coaches the listener (usually for running) in warming up, increasing intensity, sprinting, backing off, and so on. Be careful of copyright laws applicable to music.

When you produce intellectual property, you need to protect it so that others cannot claim it as their own. According to the U.S. Copyright Office (2012), the Copyright Act generally gives the owner of copyright the exclusive right to reproduce, distribute, perform, or display the work publicly or to authorize others to do so. Copyright is secured automatically upon creation of the work; in other words, no formal copyright application is necessary.

Still, though publishing the work (in whatever form) is no longer required, doing so provides another layer of protection by giving you a way to prove that the work is yours. Publication simply means distributing copies of the work, either by sale, lease, or loan. When you publish, it is advisable to actively claim your copyright by including three items: the word *copyright* (or the symbol ©), the initial date of publication, and the owner's name. Here's an example: "© 2019 Human Kinetics." You can still go through the formal process of registering for a final layer of protection, but that is not necessary.

Conclusion

Opening your doors, hanging your shingle, and saying that you are ready to take in business is only the beginning. Establishing and building your business will take time and a great deal of effort. Once you gain clients or members, you need to keep them coming back. Most will keep coming if they are set up for success from the beginning. You can do so by enabling them to feel like they belong at your facility, helping them develop realistic expectations, teaching them what to do (or assuring that they have the right ongoing guidance), and keeping them accountable for getting in their workouts. When these elements are in place, the fees you charge will be worth the value received.

When your clients or members are happy with what you offer, they can help you build your business through referrals and recommendations. Although some people who believe in you will turn themselves into evangelists for you and your business, most people will need you to ask them to tell others about you. If they agree, they can spread the word either by directly connecting with others or by giving online recommendations that reach the masses.

Either way, don't just sit by and expect others to bring in all of your new business. Instead, get out into the community and network. Find community events, go with a plan to meet certain individuals, or simply get to know local residents whom you have yet to meet. Be curious about others and make it your mission to get to know what inspires them. Afterward, follow up and offer an opportunity to interact again. Gaining new business through networking rarely happens right away. Meeting someone is only an opportunity to *start* building a relationship.

Beyond selling memberships and personal training sessions, you can also build your business by increasing your revenue per client or member. You can do so by upselling additional services, either at the start of a new membership or class or as you continue to work and interact with established clients or members. If people are prepared to buy one service or offering to help them reach their goals, then it may not be a huge leap for them to add another that can help them even more.

Finally, by adding intellectual property products to your offerings, you can create a stream of passive income that can enhance your bottom line. These offerings can take the form of written, visual, or auditory products addressing various topics that can help your clients or members succeed in their quest to improve their health and fitness.

Taken together, these opportunities can help your business grow and prosper. Start planning now how you will implement them, and your business will (continue to) grow!

Appendix A
Business Plan Templates

As you start to plan your business, you need to look at all the various aspects that are important to its success. Writing a business plan is a great tool in doing that. The templates provided in Appendix A are meant to help you with that planning process, whether you are seeking outside financing or not. As with all templates, these forms are a starting point and, while you could just fill in the blanks, you should also feel free to adapt them as you see appropriate. If you get stumped while filling any out, refer back to chapter 5 for fleshed-out examples.

The templates included in this appendix include:

- Cover letter template. While not actually part of the business plan, it is meant to introduce the plan to potential investors.
- Business plan templates:
  - › Executive summary. While this is the first part of the business plan, remember to write it last—after you have all of the details of the plan written out.
  - › Business or company description
  - › Market analysis and demographics
  - › Competitive analysis
  - › Management plan
  - › Financial plan
  - › Capital required template
  - › Marketing plan template

▊ Cover Letter

(Your name)
(Your company's name)
(Your company's address)
(Your company's city, state, and zip code)
(Your company's phone number)
(Your e-mail address)

(Contact name)
(Position, if known)
(Lending organization's name)
(Lending organization's address)
(Lending organization's city, state, and zip code)

Dear Mr. or Ms. *(Choose one.)* _____,

   (Mention your relationship or establish how you heard about the lending organization; here are three possible starters.)

   As we discussed in our recent phone conversation *(or meeting)* . . .

   I was referred to you by _____.

   I read about you and your company in _____.

   I'm submitting our business plan for *(your company's name)* in hopes of securing funding of $_____ from your _____ *(bank or other type of institution)* to provide for _____. *(State your case here in the form of your elevator speech or abbreviated version of your executive summary.)*

   Thank you for your time and consideration in reviewing our business plan. I would be happy to hear any feedback and answer any questions that you might have concerning *(your company's name)*.

Sincerely,

_____

(Your signature)

_____

(Your printed name)

From M.A. Nutting, 2019, *The business of personal training* (Champaign, IL: Human Kinetics).

(Even though the executive summary is the second item in the business plan and the first item to be presented, you should write it after the other sections are finished so that you can give an accurate description. Limit the executive summary to three pages at most. This is your chance to give an overview of your business plan and highlight the key points of your company's future success.)

Executive Summary

Our Company

(Describe the basics of your company and what you want to accomplish.)

_____

_____

_____

_____

Our Services

(List the services and, if applicable, the products that you will be providing.)

_____

_____

_____

_____

Our Market

(Specifically describe your ideal clientele and the demographics of your geographic area in order to show that you have a market for your services.)

_____

_____

_____

_____

Our Competition

(List any other clubs or businesses in your geographic area that could potentially capture your market; briefly describe them as compared with your company.)

_____

_____

_____

_____

Our Advantages

(Why will your target market choose you over the competition? What makes you stand out?)

_____

_____

_____

_____

(continued)

From M.A. Nutting, 2019, *The business of personal training* (Champaign, IL: Human Kinetics).

(continued)

What differentiates (*your company's name*) from our competition are (*aspect 1*), (*aspect 2*), and (*aspect 3*).

_____
_____
_____
_____

(*State aspect 1 in full and give the necessary details to be convincing.*)

_____
_____
_____
_____

(*State aspect 2 in full and give the necessary details to be convincing.*)

_____
_____
_____
_____

(*State aspect 3 in full and give the necessary details to be convincing.*)

_____
_____
_____

Financial Summary

(*This summary should provide not a detailed financial report but a quick overview. Address revenues, expenses, and net profit or loss for the first three years; also include start-up costs, predicted accrued debt to break-even point, and needed capital.*)

	Year 1	Year 2	Year 3
Revenue	$_____	$_____	$_____
Expenses	$_____	$_____	$_____
Net	$_____	$_____	$_____
Start-up costs for (*your company's name*):			$_____
Accrued debt through break-even point:			$_____
Capital needed:			$_____

Marketing

(*What methods will you use to attract your target market? Where can your market be found?*)

_____
_____
_____
_____

From M.A. Nutting, 2019, *The business of personal training* (Champaign, IL: Human Kinetics).

■ Business or Company Description

(*Describe in detail what problems your company seeks to solve and for whom.*)

_____
_____
_____
_____
_____
_____
_____

(*How will you solve your clients' problems? What are your solutions?*)

_____
_____
_____
_____
_____
_____
_____

(*Your company name*)'s Mission:

_____
_____
_____
_____
_____
_____
_____

(*Your company name*)'s Mantra:

_____
_____
_____
_____
_____
_____

■ Market Analysis and Demographics

(Define your target market in as much detail as possible.)

Age _____

Gender _____

Income _____

Racial or cultural characteristics _____

Exercise experience level _____

Location in relation to your business _____

(Discuss your target market as it relates to the demographics of your area. Show that you will be able to find and acquire enough clients in your chosen business location.)

_____

_____

_____

_____

_____

_____

_____

_____

_____

_____

_____

_____

_____

_____

_____

_____

_____

_____

_____

_____

From M.A. Nutting, 2019, *The business of personal training* (Champaign, IL: Human Kinetics).

■ Competitive Analysis

(*List all competitors in your area, their distance from your location, and their specific target markets.*)

_____

_____

(*List all primary services and attributes that are important to research about your competitors, then compare their offerings and descriptors with those of your company. You can illustrate your findings clearly by using a comparison table.*)

_____

_____

(*Describe your company's strengths, weaknesses, opportunities, and threats.*)

Strengths _____

_____

_____

_____

Weaknesses _____

_____

_____

_____

Opportunities _____

_____

_____

_____

Threats _____

_____

_____

_____

From M.A. Nutting, 2019, *The business of personal training* (Champaign, IL: Human Kinetics).

225

■ Management Plan

Management Team

(*List your company's key people and positions, the strengths of the key people, and the primary duties of the positions. If your company has a management hierarchy, describe it as well. In addition, indicate how you will handle accounting, payroll, and facility maintenance.*)

_____

_____

_____

(*Your management hierarchy, if there is one, can be presented in an organizational chart.*)

Person

Position _____

Strengths _____

Primary duties _____

Person

Position _____

Strengths _____

Primary duties _____

Person

Position _____

Strengths _____

Primary duties _____

Person

Position _____

Strengths _____

Primary duties _____

Person

Position _____

Strengths _____

Primary duties _____

From M.A. Nutting, 2019, *The business of personal training* (Champaign, IL: Human Kinetics).

◼ Financial Plan

Start-Up Costs

(Map all of your financial information in as much detail as possible. Categorize or group similar expenses or fees.)

ONE-TIME FEES (NOT TO BE PAID AGAIN)	$

Equipment costs

Facility setup

ANNUAL FEES (FIRST YEAR)	

Total for start-up

Monthly Expenses and Revenue

(List your monthly expenses and revenue for at least the first three months.)

Budget items	Month 1	Month 2	Month 3	Continue?
MONTHLY EXPENSES				
Facility and operations				

(continued)

From M.A. Nutting, 2019, *The business of personal training* (Champaign, IL: Human Kinetics).

227

(continued)

Budget items	Month 1	Month 2	Month 3	Continue?
MONTHLY EXPENSES				
Payroll				
Total monthly expenses				
MONTHLY REVENUE				
Membership income				
Personal training income				
Total monthly revenue				
Total net monthly revenue (revenue − expenses)				

(Describe assumptions related to variables such as growth in the number of personal training sessions provided each month, as well as your projected break-even point.)

Break-Even Point

(Estimate your break-even point, defined as the number of personal training sessions or memberships needed to bring in enough revenue to meet expenses. In what month do you reach this point?)

Fixed monthly costs: _____

Price of one unit (*session or membership*): _____

Variable costs (*such as a percentage paid to a personal trainer*): _____

Break-even point = *fixed monthly costs ÷ (price of one unit [session or membership] − variable costs [such as a percentage paid to a personal trainer])*

From M.A. Nutting, 2019, *The business of personal training* (Champaign, IL: Human Kinetics).

■ Capital Required

(You have calculated your start-up costs. Now show the monthly debt [net loss] and the total accrued debt. That, plus start-up costs, equals the amount of capital needed.)

Month	Net loss ($)
1	
2	
3	
4	
5	
6	
7	
8	
9	
Continue?	

Total for indicated months

Capital required = start-up costs + accrued debt

Start-up costs: _____

Accrued debt: _____

Capital required: _____

From M.A. Nutting, 2019, *The business of personal training* (Champaign, IL: Human Kinetics).

229

▪ Marketing Plan

(Indicate specifically how you will reach your target market. What media will you use, when, and with what frequency? This information can be provided in the form of a list or a yearlong calendar. Consider the following avenues.)

Social media

Facebook _____

Twitter _____

YouTube _____

Instagram _____

LinkedIn _____

Pinterest _____

Tumblr _____

Your company website

Print media, articles, press releases, and/or ads

Flyers _____

Brochures _____

Business cards _____

Ads in local newspapers or other publications _____

Television ads
Radio ads
Participation in community activities

5K runs _____

Health and fitness fairs _____

Farmers' markets _____

Interviews or regular educational spots for local publications and radio or television stations

_____

_____

_____

_____

_____

From M.A. Nutting, 2019, *The business of personal training* (Champaign, IL: Human Kinetics); Source: Electronic Physical Activity Readiness Medical Examination (ePARmed-X+). Available: http://eparmedx.com<http://eparmedx.com/>. Reprinted with permission of the PAR-Q+ Collaboration.

Appendix B

Personal Trainer–Client Forms

2017 PAR-Q+

The Physical Activity Readiness Questionnaire for Everyone

The health benefits of regular physical activity are clear; more people should engage in physical activity every day of the week. Participating in physical activity is very safe for MOST people. This questionnaire will tell you whether it is necessary for you to seek further advice from your doctor OR a qualified exercise professional before becoming more physically active.

GENERAL HEALTH QUESTIONS

Please read the 7 questions below carefully and answer each one honestly: check YES or NO.	YES	NO
1) Has your doctor ever said that you have a heart condition ☐ OR high blood pressure ☐?	☐	☐
2) Do you feel pain in your chest at rest, during your daily activities of living, **OR** when you do physical activity?	☐	☐
3) Do you lose balance because of dizziness **OR** have you lost consciousness in the last 12 months? Please answer **NO** if your dizziness was associated with over-breathing (including during vigorous exercise).	☐	☐
4) Have you ever been diagnosed with another chronic medical condition (other than heart disease or high blood pressure)? **PLEASE LIST CONDITION(S) HERE:** _____	☐	☐
5) Are you currently taking prescribed medications for a chronic medical condition? **PLEASE LIST CONDITION(S) AND MEDICATIONS HERE:** _____	☐	☐
6) Do you currently have (or have had within the past 12 months) a bone, joint, or soft tissue (muscle, ligament, or tendon) problem that could be made worse by becoming more physically active? Please answer **NO** if you had a problem in the past, but it *does not limit your current ability* to be physically active. **PLEASE LIST CONDITION(S) HERE:** _____	☐	☐
7) Has your doctor ever said that you should only do medically supervised physical activity?	☐	☐

☑ **If you answered NO to all of the questions above, you are cleared for physical activity.**
Go to Page 4 to sign the PARTICIPANT DECLARATION. You do not need to complete Pages 2 and 3.

- ▶ Start becoming much more physically active – start slowly and build up gradually.
- ▶ Follow International Physical Activity Guidelines for your age (www.who.int/dietphysicalactivity/en/).
- ▶ You may take part in a health and fitness appraisal.
- ▶ If you are over the age of 45 yr and **NOT** accustomed to regular vigorous to maximal effort exercise, consult a qualified exercise professional before engaging in this intensity of exercise.
- ▶ If you have any further questions, contact a qualified exercise professional.

⬤ **If you answered YES to one or more of the questions above, COMPLETE PAGES 2 AND 3.**

⚠ **Delay becoming more active if:**
- ✔ You have a temporary illness such as a cold or fever; it is best to wait until you feel better.
- ✔ You are pregnant - talk to your health care practitioner, your physician, a qualified exercise professional, and/or complete the ePARmed-X+ at **www.eparmedx.com** before becoming more physically active.
- ✔ Your health changes - answer the questions on Pages 2 and 3 of this document and/or talk to your doctor or a qualified exercise professional before continuing with any physical activity program.

✝ OSHF
Ontario Society for Health and Fitness

Copyright © 2017 PAR-Q+ Collaboration   1 / 4
01-01-2017

From M.A. Nutting, 2019, *The business of personal training* (Champaign, IL: Human Kinetics); Source: Electronic Physical Activity Readiness Medical Examination (ePARmed-X+). Available: http://eparmedx.com<http://eparmedx.com/>. Reprinted with permission of the PAR-Q+ Collaboration.

2017 PAR-Q+

FOLLOW-UP QUESTIONS ABOUT YOUR MEDICAL CONDITION(S)

1. Do you have Arthritis, Osteoporosis, or Back Problems?

If the above condition(s) is/are present, answer questions 1a-1c   If **NO** ☐ go to question 2

1a. Do you have difficulty controlling your condition with medications or other physician-prescribed therapies? (Answer **NO** if you are not currently taking medications or other treatments)   YES☐ NO☐

1b. Do you have joint problems causing pain, a recent fracture or fracture caused by osteoporosis or cancer, displaced vertebra (e.g., spondylolisthesis), and/or spondylolysis/pars defect (a crack in the bony ring on the back of the spinal column)?   YES☐ NO☐

1c. Have you had steroid injections or taken steroid tablets regularly for more than 3 months?   YES☐ NO☐

2. Do you currently have Cancer of any kind?

If the above condition(s) is/are present, answer questions 2a-2b   If **NO** ☐ go to question 3

2a. Does your cancer diagnosis include any of the following types: lung/bronchogenic, multiple myeloma (cancer of plasma cells), head, and/or neck?   YES☐ NO☐

2b. Are you currently receiving cancer therapy (such as chemotherapy or radiotherapy)?   YES☐ NO☐

3. Do you have a Heart or Cardiovascular Condition? *This includes Coronary Artery Disease, Heart Failure, Diagnosed Abnormality of Heart Rhythm*

If the above condition(s) is/are present, answer questions 3a-3d   If **NO** ☐ go to question 4

3a. Do you have difficulty controlling your condition with medications or other physician-prescribed therapies? (Answer **NO** if you are not currently taking medications or other treatments)   YES☐ NO☐

3b. Do you have an irregular heart beat that requires medical management? (e.g., atrial fibrillation, premature ventricular contraction)   YES☐ NO☐

3c. Do you have chronic heart failure?   YES☐ NO☐

3d. Do you have diagnosed coronary artery (cardiovascular) disease and have not participated in regular physical activity in the last 2 months?   YES☐ NO☐

4. Do you have High Blood Pressure?

If the above condition(s) is/are present, answer questions 4a-4b   If **NO** ☐ go to question 5

4a. Do you have difficulty controlling your condition with medications or other physician-prescribed therapies? (Answer **NO** if you are not currently taking medications or other treatments)   YES☐ NO☐

4b. Do you have a resting blood pressure equal to or greater than 160/90 mmHg with or without medication? (Answer **YES** if you do not know your resting blood pressure)   YES☐ NO☐

5. Do you have any Metabolic Conditions? *This includes Type 1 Diabetes, Type 2 Diabetes, Pre-Diabetes*

If the above condition(s) is/are present, answer questions 5a-5e   If **NO** ☐ go to question 6

5a. Do you often have difficulty controlling your blood sugar levels with foods, medications, or other physician-prescribed therapies?   YES☐ NO☐

5b. Do you often suffer from signs and symptoms of low blood sugar (hypoglycemia) following exercise and/or during activities of daily living? Signs of hypoglycemia may include shakiness, nervousness, unusual irritability, abnormal sweating, dizziness or light-headedness, mental confusion, difficulty speaking, weakness, or sleepiness.   YES☐ NO☐

5c. Do you have any signs or symptoms of diabetes complications such as heart or vascular disease and/or complications affecting your eyes, kidneys, **OR** the sensation in your toes and feet?   YES☐ NO☐

5d. Do you have other metabolic conditions (such as current pregnancy-related diabetes, chronic kidney disease, or liver problems)?   YES☐ NO☐

5e. Are you planning to engage in what for you is unusually high (or vigorous) intensity exercise in the near future?   YES☐ NO☐

OSHF
Ontario Society for Health and Fitness

Copyright © 2017 PAR-Q+ Collaboration   2 / 4
01-01-2017

From M.A. Nutting, 2019, *The business of personal training* (Champaign, IL: Human Kinetics); Source: Electronic Physical Activity Readiness Medical Examination (ePARmed-X+). Available: http://eparmedx.com<http://eparmedx.com/>. Reprinted with permission of the PAR-Q+ Collaboration.

2017 PAR-Q+

6. **Do you have any Mental Health Problems or Learning Difficulties?** *This includes Alzheimer's, Dementia, Depression, Anxiety Disorder, Eating Disorder, Psychotic Disorder, Intellectual Disability, Down Syndrome*

If the above condition(s) is/are present, answer questions 6a-6b   If **NO** ☐ go to question 7

6a.	Do you have difficulty controlling your condition with medications or other physician-prescribed therapies? (Answer **NO** if you are not currently taking medications or other treatments)	YES ☐ NO ☐
6b.	Do you have Down Syndrome **AND** back problems affecting nerves or muscles?	YES ☐ NO ☐

7. **Do you have a Respiratory Disease?** *This includes Chronic Obstructive Pulmonary Disease, Asthma, Pulmonary High Blood Pressure*

If the above condition(s) is/are present, answer questions 7a-7d   If **NO** ☐ go to question 8

7a.	Do you have difficulty controlling your condition with medications or other physician-prescribed therapies? (Answer **NO** if you are not currently taking medications or other treatments)	YES ☐ NO ☐
7b.	Has your doctor ever said your blood oxygen level is low at rest or during exercise and/or that you require supplemental oxygen therapy?	YES ☐ NO ☐
7c.	If asthmatic, do you currently have symptoms of chest tightness, wheezing, laboured breathing, consistent cough (more than 2 days/week), or have you used your rescue medication more than twice in the last week?	YES ☐ NO ☐
7d.	Has your doctor ever said you have high blood pressure in the blood vessels of your lungs?	YES ☐ NO ☐

8. **Do you have a Spinal Cord Injury?** *This includes Tetraplegia and Paraplegia*

If the above condition(s) is/are present, answer questions 8a-8c   If **NO** ☐ go to question 9

8a.	Do you have difficulty controlling your condition with medications or other physician-prescribed therapies? (Answer **NO** if you are not currently taking medications or other treatments)	YES ☐ NO ☐
8b.	Do you commonly exhibit low resting blood pressure significant enough to cause dizziness, light-headedness, and/or fainting?	YES ☐ NO ☐
8c.	Has your physician indicated that you exhibit sudden bouts of high blood pressure (known as Autonomic Dysreflexia)?	YES ☐ NO ☐

9. **Have you had a Stroke?** *This includes Transient Ischemic Attack (TIA) or Cerebrovascular Event*

If the above condition(s) is/are present, answer questions 9a-9c   If **NO** ☐ go to question 10

9a.	Do you have difficulty controlling your condition with medications or other physician-prescribed therapies? (Answer **NO** if you are not currently taking medications or other treatments)	YES ☐ NO ☐
9b.	Do you have any impairment in walking or mobility?	YES ☐ NO ☐
9c.	Have you experienced a stroke or impairment in nerves or muscles in the past 6 months?	YES ☐ NO ☐

10. **Do you have any other medical condition not listed above or do you have two or more medical conditions?**

If you have other medical conditions, answer questions 10a-10c   If **NO** ☐ read the Page 4 recommendations

10a.	Have you experienced a blackout, fainted, or lost consciousness as a result of a head injury within the last 12 months **OR** have you had a diagnosed concussion within the last 12 months?	YES ☐ NO ☐
10b.	Do you have a medical condition that is not listed (such as epilepsy, neurological conditions, kidney problems)?	YES ☐ NO ☐
10c.	Do you currently live with two or more medical conditions?	YES ☐ NO ☐

PLEASE LIST YOUR MEDICAL CONDITION(S) AND ANY RELATED MEDICATIONS HERE: _____

_____

GO to Page 4 for recommendations about your current medical condition(s) and sign the PARTICIPANT DECLARATION.

 OSHF
Ontario Society for Health and Fitness

From M.A. Nutting, 2019, *The business of personal training* (Champaign, IL: Human Kinetics); Source: Electronic Physical Activity Readiness Medical Examination (ePARmed-X+). Available: http://eparmedx.com<http://eparmedx.com/>. Reprinted with permission of the PAR-Q+ Collaboration.

2017 PAR-Q+

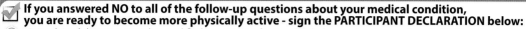

☑ If you answered NO to all of the follow-up questions about your medical condition, you are ready to become more physically active - sign the PARTICIPANT DECLARATION below:

▶ It is advised that you consult a qualified exercise professional to help you develop a safe and effective physical activity plan to meet your health needs.

▶ You are encouraged to start slowly and build up gradually - 20 to 60 minutes of low to moderate intensity exercise, 3-5 days per week including aerobic and muscle strengthening exercises.

▶ As you progress, you should aim to accumulate 150 minutes or more of moderate intensity physical activity per week.

▶ If you are over the age of 45 yr and **NOT** accustomed to regular vigorous to maximal effort exercise, consult a qualified exercise professional before engaging in this intensity of exercise.

⬤ If you answered YES to one or more of the follow-up questions about your medical condition:

You should seek further information before becoming more physically active or engaging in a fitness appraisal. You should complete the specially designed online screening and exercise recommendations program - the **ePARmed-X+ at www.eparmedx.com** and/or visit a qualified exercise professional to work through the ePARmed-X+ and for further information.

⚠ Delay becoming more active if:

✓ You have a temporary illness such as a cold or fever; it is best to wait until you feel better.

✓ You are pregnant - talk to your health care practitioner, your physician, a qualified exercise professional, and/or complete the ePARmed-X+ **at www.eparmedx.com** before becoming more physically active.

✓ Your health changes - talk to your doctor or qualified exercise professional before continuing with any physical activity program.

- ⬤ You are encouraged to photocopy the PAR-Q+. You must use the entire questionnaire and NO changes are permitted.
- ⬤ The authors, the PAR-Q+ Collaboration, partner organizations, and their agents assume no liability for persons who undertake physical activity and/or make use of the PAR-Q+ or ePARmed-X+. If in doubt after completing the questionnaire, consult your doctor prior to physical activity.

PARTICIPANT DECLARATION

- ⬤ All persons who have completed the PAR-Q+ please read and sign the declaration below.

- ⬤ If you are less than the legal age required for consent or require the assent of a care provider, your parent, guardian or care provider must also sign this form.

I, the undersigned, have read, understood to my full satisfaction and completed this questionnaire. I acknowledge that this physical activity clearance is valid for a maximum of 12 months from the date it is completed and becomes invalid if my condition changes. I also acknowledge that a Trustee (such as my employer, community/fitness centre, health care provider, or other designate) may retain a copy of this form for their records. In these instances, the Trustee will be required to adhere to local, national, and international guidelines regarding the storage of personal health information ensuring that the Trustee maintains the privacy of the information and does not misuse or wrongfully disclose such information.

NAME _____   DATE _____

SIGNATURE _____   WITNESS _____

SIGNATURE OF PARENT/GUARDIAN/CARE PROVIDER _____

——— For more information, please contact ———
www.eparmedx.com
Email: eparmedx@gmail.com

Citation for PAR-Q+
Warburton DER, Jamnik VK, Bredin SSD, and Gledhill N on behalf of the PAR-Q+ Collaboration. The Physical Activity Readiness Questionnaire for Everyone (PAR-Q+) and Electronic Physical Activity Readiness Medical Examination (ePARmed-X+). Health & Fitness Journal of Canada 4(2):3-23, 2011.

Key References
1. Jamnik VK, Warburton DER, Makarski J, McKenzie DC, Shephard RJ, Stone J, and Gledhill N. Enhancing the effectiveness of clearance for physical activity participation; background and overall process. APNM 36(S1):S3-S13, 2011.
2. Warburton DER, Gledhill N, Jamnik VK, Bredin SSD, McKenzie DC, Stone J, Charlesworth S, and Shephard RJ. Evidence-based risk assessment and recommendations for physical activity clearance; Consensus Document. APNM 36(S1):S266-s298, 2011.
3. Chisholm DM, Collis ML, Kulak LL, Davenport W, and Gruber N. Physical activity readiness. British Columbia Medical Journal. 1975;17:375-378.
4. Thomas S, Reading J, and Shephard RJ. Revision of the Physical Activity Readiness Questionnaire (PAR-Q). Canadian Journal of Sport Science 1992;17:4 338-345.

The PAR-Q+ was created using the evidence-based AGREE process (1) by the PAR-Q+ Collaboration chaired by Dr. Darren E. R. Warburton with Dr. Norman Gledhill, Dr. Veronica Jamnik, and Dr. Donald C. McKenzie (2). Production of this document has been made possible through financial contributions from the Public Health Agency of Canada and the BC Ministry of Health Services. The views expressed herein do not necessarily represent the views of the Public Health Agency of Canada or the BC Ministry of Health Services.

⸸ OSHF
Ontario Society for Health and Fitness

Copyright © 2017 PAR-Q+ Collaboration   4 /4
01-01-2017

From M.A. Nutting, 2019, *The business of personal training* (Champaign, IL: Human Kinetics); Source: Electronic Physical Activity Readiness Medical Examination (ePARmed-X+). Available: http://eparmedx.com<http://eparmedx.com/>. Reprinted with permission of the PAR-Q+ Collaboration.

Personal Wellness Profile

Name: _____ Date: _____

Phone (home): _____ (work): _____ (mobile): _____

E-mail address: _____ Date of birth: _____ Age: _____

Gender: _____ Height: _____ Weight: _____ Occupation: _____

In case of emergency, whom may we contact?

Name: _____ Relationship: _____

Phone (home): _____ (work): _____ (mobile): _____

Primary physician (name): _____ (phone): _____ (fax): _____

Date of your last physical examination: _____

STATUS AND HISTORY

Have you had or do you presently have any of the following conditions? (*Check if yes.*)

—— Cancer

—— Rheumatic fever

—— Recent operation

—— Edema (swelling of ankles)

—— High blood pressure

—— Low blood pressure

—— Seizures

—— Lung disease

—— Heart attack

—— Fainting or dizziness (with or without physical exertion)

—— Diabetes

—— High cholesterol (total): _____ (HDL): _____ (LDL): _____

—— High blood sugar (glucose)

—— Orthopnea (the need to sit up in order to breathe comfortably) or paroxysmal nocturnal dyspnea (sudden, unexpected shortness of breath at night)

—— Shortness of breath at rest or with mild exertion

—— Chest pains

—— Palpitations or tachycardia (unusually strong or rapid heartbeat)

—— Intermittent claudication (calf cramping)

—— Pain or discomfort in the chest, neck, jaw, arm, or other area (with or without physical exertion)

—— Known heart murmur

—— Unusual fatigue or shortness of breath with usual activities

—— Temporary loss of visual acuity or speech or short-term numbness or weakness in one side, arm, or leg of your body

—— Other: _____

From M.A. Nutting, 2019, *The business of personal training* (Champaign, IL: Human Kinetics).

Adapted, with permission, from NSCA, 2012, Client consultation and health appraisal, by T.K. Evetovich and K.R. Hinnerichs. In *NSCA's Essentials of personal training,* 2nd ed., edited by J. Coburn and M. Malek (Champaign, IL: Human Kinetics), 171-172.

____ Orthopedic issues (problems with any of the following):

☐ foot   ☐ ankle   ☐ knee   ☐ hip   ☐ back   ☐ neck

☐ shoulder   ☐ elbow   ☐ wrist   ☐ hand

____ If taking medications, please list:

_____

_____

Do you have any (or any other) conditions that may interfere with exercising?

☐ Yes   ☐ No

If yes, please describe briefly:

_____

_____

Do you smoke?   ☐ Yes   ☐ No

If yes, how much per day, and what was your age when you started?

How much per day: _____ Age: _____

FAMILY HISTORY

Have any of your first-degree relatives (i.e., parent, sibling, or child) experienced any of the following conditions? (Check if yes and indicate the age at which the condition occurred.)

____ Heart arrhythmia

____ Heart attack

____ Heart operation

____ Congenital heart disease

____ Premature death (before age 50)

____ Significant disability secondary to a heart condition

____ Marfan syndrome

____ High blood pressure

____ High cholesterol

____ Diabetes

____ Other major illness _____

Explain checked items:

_____

_____

_____

_____

(continued)

From M.A. Nutting, 2019, *The business of personal training* (Champaign, IL: Human Kinetics).

Adapted, with permission, from NSCA, 2012, Client consultation and health appraisal, by T.K. Evetovich and K.R. Hinnerichs. In *NSCA's Essentials of personal training*, 2nd ed., edited by J. Coburn and M. Malek (Champaign, IL: Human Kinetics), 171-172.

(continued)

ACTIVITY HISTORY

1. What is your current level of physical activity?

   ☐ Sedentary   ☐ Active lifestyle
   ☐ Currently exercising   ☐ Competitive athlete

2. Do you currently participate in a regular exercise program?

   ☐ Yes   ☐ No   If yes, describe briefly:

   _____

   _____

3. What is your body weight now? _____ What was it one year ago? _____ At age 21? _____

4. Do you feel that you are overweight?   ☐ Yes   ☐ No

   If so, by how much? _____

5. Do you follow, or have you recently followed, any specific dietary intake plan, and in general how do you feel about your nutritional habits?

   _____

6. Have you ever performed cardiorespiratory (aerobic) training exercise?
   ☐ Yes   ☐ No

7. Have you ever performed resistance training exercise?   ☐ Yes   ☐ No

8. List, in the order of importance to you, your personal health and fitness objectives.

   a. _____

   b. _____

   c. _____

9. Have you ever worked with a personal trainer?   ☐ Yes   ☐ No

From M.A. Nutting, 2019, *The business of personal training* (Champaign, IL: Human Kinetics).

Adapted, with permission, from NSCA, 2012, Client consultation and health appraisal, by T.K. Evetovich and K.R. Hinnerichs. In *NSCA's Essentials of personal training*, 2nd ed., edited by J. Coburn and M. Malek (Champaign, IL: Human Kinetics), 171-172.

Physician's Clearance

Individual information requested for (patient's name): _____

Physician's name: _____

Physician's telephone: _____

Physician's fax: _____

Please indicate your recommendation for your patient regarding commencement of increased physical activity.

1. _____ My patient may participate in any activities without restrictions.

2. _____ My patient may participate in any activities with the following restrictions:

_____

_____

_____

3. _____ I do not recommend that my patient participates in any activities at this time.

Physician's signature: _____ Date signed: _____

Return form to: _____

Phone: _____ Fax: _____

From M.A. Nutting, 2019, *The business of personal training* (Champaign, IL: Human Kinetics).

Informed Consent and Release

I desire to voluntarily participate in a personal training program as designed, recommended, and supervised by _____ (personal trainer's name or facility's name).

I understand that any recommended aerobic, weight training, conditioning, or testing session(s) are designed to place an increasing workload on my body's systems, including, but not limited to, the cardiorespiratory, muscular, skeletal, tendinous, and ligamentous systems. The reactions of these systems to aerobic, weight training, conditioning, or testing session(s) cannot be predicted with complete accuracy. There is a risk of certain changes occurring during and/or following each session. These changes could include some or all of the following: muscle tears or soreness, joint pain or soreness, abnormalities of blood pressure or heart rate, ineffective heart functioning, and, possibly, heart attack and/or death. Also, risks may be encountered related to improper use of exercise equipment or by negligence of other individuals.

I further understand that not all risks can be described or included in this informed consent and release form; despite that, I still desire to voluntarily participate.

In signing this informed consent and release form, I acknowledge that I have read about and understand the risks involved; that any questions I may have have been answered to my satisfaction; that every reasonable effort has been made to ensure my safety and health; that I enter into this program willingly and understand that I may withdraw at any time; and that I shall and hereby do release and hold _____ (personal trainer's name, facility's name, or both) harmless from and against any and all loss, cost, damage, injury, liability, or expense, or claims thereof to or with respect to any injury to myself or damage or loss of my property during my participation in this program.

Furthermore, I agree to contact and see my personal health care professional for all personal medical care.

I, (print name) _____ , have read the preceding information and give consent and release for the duration of my participation in this program.

Date: _____

Signed: _____

Signature of parent or guardian if participant is less than 18 years old:

_____

Witness:

_____

The law varies from state to state. No form should be adopted or used without individualized legal advice.

240   From M.A. Nutting, 2019, *The business of personal training* (Champaign, IL: Human Kinetics).

Assessment Recording Form

Check one: ☐ Pretest ☐ Posttest

Client's name: _____

Age: _____

Goals:

_____

_____

_____

_____

Preparticipation screening notes:

_____

_____

_____

_____

Assessment dates:

_____

_____

_____

_____

Comments:

_____

_____

_____

_____

(continued)

From M.A. Nutting, 2019, *The business of personal training* (Champaign, IL: Human Kinetics).

Adapted, with permission, from NSCA, 2012, Fitness assessment selection and administration, by S. Rana and J.B. White. In *NSCA's Essentials of personal training,* 2nd ed., edited by J. Coburn and M. Malek (Champaign, IL: Human Kinetics), 188.

(continued)

Test	Score or result	Classification
Vital signs		
Resting blood pressure		
Resting heart rate		
Body composition measures		
Height		
Weight		
Body mass index (BMI)		
Waist circumference		
Hip circumference		
Waist-to-hip ratio		
Percent body fat (method:_____)		
Fitness tests		
Cardiorespiratory endurance (method:_____)		
Muscular endurance (method:_____)		
Muscular strength (method:_____)		
Flexibility (method:_____)		
Other tests (method:_____)		

From M.A. Nutting, 2019, *The business of personal training* (Champaign, IL: Human Kinetics).

Adapted, with permission, from NSCA, 2012, Fitness assessment selection and administration, by S. Rana and J.B. White. In *NSCA's Essentials of personal training,* 2nd ed., edited by J. Coburn and M. Malek (Champaign, IL: Human Kinetics), 188.

Cleaning Checklist for Floors, Walls, and Ceilings

FLOORS

☐ Check for large cracks and standing dirt or grime.

☐ Check for splintering and breaking on platforms.

☐ Check any bolts or screws that go into the floor.

☐ Ensure that no glue is extruding from the floor.

☐ Ensure that the floor is sturdy and locked in place.

☐ Check carpeting for mold, mildew, and tears.

WALLS

☐ Check walls for dirt buildup.

☐ Replace mirrors if cracked.

☐ Clean mirrors of smudges at least once weekly.

☐ Clean windows of smudges at least once weekly.

☐ Dust windowsills and any shelving weekly.

CEILINGS

☐ Ensure that lights work properly.

☐ Clear any dust or cobweb buildup.

☐ Ensure that nothing attached to the ceiling is loose.

☐ Replace ceiling tiles as soon as possible when needed.

From M.A. Nutting, 2019, *The business of personal training* (Champaign, IL: Human Kinetics).

Adapted, by permission, from NSCA, 2016, Facility design, layout, and organization, by A. Hudy. In *NSCA's essentials of strength training and conditioning*, 4th ed., edited by G. Haff and T. Triplett (Champaign, IL: Human Kinetics), 636.

Facility and Equipment Maintenance Log

EXERCISE FACILITY

Floor

☐ Inspected and cleaned daily

☐ Wooden flooring free of splinters, holes, protruding nails, and loose screws

☐ Tile flooring resistant to slipping; no moisture or chalk accumulation

☐ Rubber flooring free of cuts, slits, and large gaps between pieces

☐ Interlocking mats secure and arranged with no protruding tabs

☐ Nonabsorbent carpet free of tears; wear areas protected by throw mats

☐ Area swept and vacuumed or mopped on a regular basis

☐ Flooring glued or fastened down properly

Walls

☐ Wall surfaces cleaned two or three times per week (or more often if needed)

☐ Walls in high-activity areas free of protruding appliances, equipment, and wall hangings

☐ Mirrors and shelves securely fixed to walls

☐ Mirrors and windows cleaned regularly (especially in high-activity areas, such as around drinking fountains and in doorways)

☐ Mirrors placed at least 20 inches (50 centimeters) off the floor in all areas

☐ Mirrors not cracked or distorted (and replaced immediately if damaged)

Ceiling

☐ All ceiling fixtures and attachments dusted regularly

☐ Ceiling tile kept clean

☐ Damaged or missing ceiling tiles replaced as needed

☐ Open ceilings with exposed pipes and ducts cleaned as needed

EXERCISE EQUIPMENT

Stretching and Body-Weight Exercise Area

☐ Mat area free of weight benches and equipment

☐ Mats and bench upholstery free of cracks and tears

From M.A. Nutting, 2019, *The business of personal training* (Champaign, IL: Human Kinetics).

Adapted, with permission, from NSCA, 2012, Facility and equipment layout and maintenance, by S. Takahashi. In *NSCA's Essentials of personal training* 2nd ed., edited by J. Coburn and M. Malek (Champaign, IL: Human Kinetics), 620-622.

- ☐ No large gaps between stretching mats

- ☐ Area swept and disinfected daily

- ☐ Equipment properly stored after use

- ☐ Elastic cords secured to base with safety knot and checked for wear

- ☐ Surfaces that contact skin treated with antifungal and antibacterial agents daily

- ☐ Nonslip material present and intact on top surface and bottom or base of plyometric boxes

- ☐ Ceiling height sufficient for overhead exercises (at least 12 feet [3.7 meters]) and free of low-hanging items (such as beams, pipes, lighting, and signs)

Resistance Training Machine Area

- ☐ Easy access to each station: at least 2 feet (0.6 meter) between machines; optimally 3 feet (0.9 meter)

- ☐ Area free of loose bolts, screws, cables, and chains

- ☐ Proper selectorized pins used

- ☐ Securing straps functional

- ☐ Parts and surfaces properly lubricated and cleaned

- ☐ Protective padding free of cracks and tears

- ☐ Surfaces that contact skin treated with antifungal and antibacterial agents daily

- ☐ No protruding screws or parts that need tightening or removal

- ☐ Belts, chains, and cables aligned with machine parts

- ☐ No worn parts (such as frayed cables, loose chains, worn bolts, and cracked joints)

Resistance Training Free-Weight Area

- ☐ Easy access to each bench or area: at least 2 feet (0.6 meter) between machines; optimally 3 feet (0.9 meter)

- ☐ Olympic bars spaced properly: 3 feet (0.9 meter) between ends

- ☐ All equipment returned after use to avoid obstruction of pathways

(continued)

From M.A. Nutting, 2019, *The business of personal training* (Champaign, IL: Human Kinetics).

Adapted, with permission, from NSCA, 2012, Facility and equipment layout and maintenance, by S. Takahashi. In *NSCA's Essentials of personal training* 2nd ed., edited by J. Coburn and M. Malek (Champaign, IL: Human Kinetics), 620-622.

(continued)

☐ Safety equipment (such as belts, collars, and safety bars) properly used and returned

☐ Protective padding free of cracks and tears

☐ Surfaces that contact skin treated with antifungal and antibacterial agents daily

☐ Securing bolts and apparatus parts (such as collars, curl bars) tightly fastened

☐ Nonslip mats on squat-rack floor area

☐ Olympic bars able to turn properly; also properly lubricated and tightened

☐ Benches, weight racks, standards, and the like secured to the floor or wall

☐ Nonfunctional or broken equipment removed from area or locked out of service

☐ Ceiling height sufficient for overhead exercises (at least 12 feet [3.7 meters]) and free of low-hanging items (such as beams, pipes, lighting, and signs)

Weightlifting Area

☐ Olympic bars properly spaced: 3 feet (0.9 meter) between ends

☐ All equipment returned after use to avoid obstruction of lifting area

☐ Olympic bars able to rotate properly; also properly lubricated and tightened

☐ Bent Olympic bars replaced; knurling clear of debris

☐ Collars functioning

☐ Sufficient chalk available

☐ Wrist straps, belts, and knee wraps available, functioning, and stored properly

☐ Benches, chairs, boxes kept at a distance from lifting area

☐ Mats free of gaps, cuts, slits, and splinters

☐ Area properly swept and mopped to remove splinters and chalk

☐ Ceiling height sufficient for overhead exercises (at least 12 feet [3.7 meters]) and free of low-hanging items (such as beams, pipes, lighting, and signs)

Cardiorespiratory Exercise Area

☐ Easy access to each station: at least 2 feet (0.6 meter) between machines; optimally 3 feet (0.9 meter)

☐ Bolts and screws tight

From M.A. Nutting, 2019, *The business of personal training* (Champaign, IL: Human Kinetics).

Adapted, with permission, from NSCA, 2012, Facility and equipment layout and maintenance, by S. Takahashi. In *NSCA's Essentials of personal training* 2nd ed., edited by J. Coburn and M. Malek (Champaign, IL: Human Kinetics), 620-622.

- ☐ Functioning parts easily adjustable

- ☐ Parts and surfaces properly lubricated and cleaned

- ☐ Foot and body straps secure and not ripped

- ☐ Measurement devices for tension, time, and revolutions per minute properly functioning

- ☐ Surfaces that contact skin treated with antifungal and antibacterial agents daily

FREQUENCY OF MAINTENANCE AND CLEANING TASKS

Daily

- ☐ Inspect all flooring for damage and wear.

- ☐ Clean (sweep, vacuum, or mop) and disinfect all flooring.

- ☐ Clean and disinfect upholstery.

- ☐ Clean and disinfect drinking fountain.

- ☐ Inspect connection of all fixed equipment with floor.

- ☐ Clean and disinfect equipment surfaces that contact skin.

- ☐ Clean mirrors.

- ☐ Clean windows.

- ☐ Inspect mirrors for damage.

- ☐ Inspect all equipment for damage; wear; loose or protruding belts, screws, cables, or chains; insecure or nonfunctioning foot and body straps; and improper functioning or signs of improper use of attachments, pins, or other devices.

- ☐ Clean and lubricate moving parts of equipment.

- ☐ Inspect all protective padding for cracks and tears.

- ☐ Inspect nonslip material and mats for proper placement, as well as damage and wear.

- ☐ Remove trash and garbage.

- ☐ Clean light covers, fans, air vents, clocks, and speakers.

- ☐ Ensure that equipment is properly returned and stored after use.

(continued)

From M.A. Nutting, 2019, *The business of personal training* (Champaign, IL: Human Kinetics).

Adapted, with permission, from NSCA, 2012, Facility and equipment layout and maintenance, by S. Takahashi. In *NSCA's Essentials of personal training* 2nd ed., edited by J. Coburn and M. Malek (Champaign, IL: Human Kinetics), 620-622.

(continued)

Two or Three Times per Week

☐ Clean and lubricate cardiorespiratory machines, as well as guide rods on selectorized resistance training machines.

Once per Week

☐ Clean (dust) ceiling fixtures and attachments.

☐ Clean ceiling tiles.

As Needed

☐ Replace light bulbs.

☐ Clean walls.

☐ Replace damaged or missing ceiling tiles.

☐ Clean open ceilings that have exposed pipes or ducts.

☐ Remove (or place a sign on) broken equipment.

☐ Fill chalk boxes.

☐ Clean bar knurling.

☐ Clean rust from floor, plates, bars, and equipment with rust-removing solution.

From M.A. Nutting, 2019, *The business of personal training* (Champaign, IL: Human Kinetics).

Adapted, with permission, from NSCA, 2012, Facility and equipment layout and maintenance, by S. Takahashi. In *NSCA's Essentials of personal training* 2nd ed., edited by J. Coburn and M. Malek (Champaign, IL: Human Kinetics), 620-622.

Appendix C
Business Resources

Resources in the Fitness Industry

Club Solutions **Magazine**

http://clubsolutionsmagazine.com/category/blog/

This industry-specific business magazine addresses the newest trends and discusses common issues in health clubs around the United States.

International Health, Racquet and Sportsclub Association (IHRSA)

www.ihrsa.org/blog

IHRSA is the world's leading organization for health club management and offers great research on health club business trends. Some of its information is open to the public, some is provided to members only, and some can be bought in the form of in-depth reports.

Member Solutions

www.membersolutions.com/blog

This organization is primarily a membership billing service, but its blog also offers very good business information.

The Business of Personal Training

https://marknutting.com

Yes, I have a blog too, where I can continue providing you with business ideas and solutions.

The Personal Trainer Development Center

www.theptdc.com/articles/

Founder Jonathan Goodman has gathered some of the best fitness professionals to write articles on topics of interest to more than just club-based fitness entrepreneurs. Topics range from marketing to niche populations to online personal training.

Thomas Plummer

https://thomasplummer.blog

Thomas Plummer is a widely sought presenter who has worked in the fitness industry for more than 30 years and authored several books on club sales and management.

General Business Resources

Most business principles are universal—in other words, they are relevant to any industry—and some of the freshest ideas come from outside the fitness business. In fact, most of what I have learned about business has come from outside of our industry.

SCORE

www.score.org

This nonprofit business-mentoring organization is supported by the governmental agency known as the U.S. Small Business Administration. It provides mentoring at little or no cost through its volunteer staff, many of whom are retired business professionals.

Small Business Administration

www.sba.com

This site should be one of your first stops when starting a business because it offers a wealth of all-topic business information. *Note*: This is a private entity, not to be confused with the governmental agency known as the U.S. Small Business Administration.

General Business Periodicals

Although these resources are subscriber-based magazines (whether hard copy or digital), their sites offer great business articles for free.

Entrepreneur

www.entrepreneur.com

FastCompany

www.fastcompany.com

Harvard Business Review

https://hbr.org

Inc.

www.inc.com

Business Bloggers

Rich Brooks

www.takeflyte.com/blog

Rich is a tech and social media guru whom I pestered in my early days of using social media. He was one of the key people in helping me learn how to use social media for business. In addition to the blog noted here, his posts can be found on many top business sites.

Seth Godin

http://sethgodin.typepad.com

Author of 18 books (many of which I have read), Seth is a force in the world of marketing and management. One of his newest projects is a four-week online business intensive called altMBA (altmba.com).

Guy Kawasaki

https://guykawasaki.com/blog/

Guy Kawasaki came to public notice as one of the key figures responsible for marketing the Macintosh computer line back in 1984. A venture capitalist, he is currently the chief evangelist for Canva, an online graphic design tool that I use constantly and recommend highly. He has also authored more than 10 business books.

Gary Vaynerchuk

https://www.garyvaynerchuk.com

"Gary Vee" is most impressive for his vision of how social media can be used to drive business and, frankly, his own personal drive in building his father's liquor-store business via Wine Library TV into his own full-service digital media company, VaynerMedia. Gary is also a venture capitalist and author of four best-selling books, as well host of the online Q&A show *#AskGaryVee*.

Additional Helpful Sites

The following sites are ones that I have used to find specific kinds of information; some of them are general business sites, whereas others focus on social media. The key is to understand that great online resources are available for you to use as you continue building your business. Always continue learning.

All Business

www.allbusiness.com

A Smart Bear (Startups + Marketing + Geekery)

https://blog.asmartbear.com

Business Insider (Small Business Section)

www.businessinsider.com/warroom/small-business

Business Owners' Idea Café

www.businessownersideacafe.com

Freelancers Union

https://blog.freelancersunion.org

HubSpot

https://blog.hubspot.com

Huffington Post Business Section

www.huffingtonpost.com/section/business

Mashable Business

http://mashable.com/business/?utm_cid=mash-prod-nav-ch

Small Business Trends

https://smallbiztrends.com

***Smart Hustle* Magazine**

www.smarthustle.com

Social Media Examiner

www.socialmediaexaminer.com

StartupNation

https://startupnation.com

TheSelfEmployed.com

www.theselfemployed.com

Under 30 CEO

http://under30ceo.com

References

CHAPTER 1 Discovering Your Purpose and the Scope of What You Can Do

American Council on Exercise (ACE). (2013). *Salary report for health and fitness professionals.* www.acefitness.org/salary/docs/ACE_SalarySurvey.pdf

Bureau of Labor Statistics, U.S. Department of Labor. (2016). *Fitness trainers and instructors.* www.bls.gov/ooh/personal-care-and-service/fitness-trainers-and-instructors.htm

International Health, Racquet & Sportsclub Association (IHRSA). (2014). *The IHRSA health club consumer report: 2014 health club activity, usage, trends and analysis.* Boston, MA: Author.

Janot, J. (2004, June 1). Do you know your scope of practice? *IDEA Fitness Journal, 1*(1).

Kawasaki, G. (2015). *The art of the start 2.0: The time-tested, battle-hardened guide for anyone starting anything.* New York, NY: Portfolio.

Malek, M.H., Nalbone, D.P., Berger, D.E., & Coburn, J.W. (2002). Importance of health science education for personal fitness trainers. *Journal of Strength and Conditioning Research, 16*(1), 19-24.

Maslow, A. (1966). *The psychology of science: A reconnaissance.* New York: Harper & Row.

Schroeder, J. (2015, October). 2015 IDEA fitness industry compensation trends report. *IDEA Fitness Journal, 12*(10), 42-53.

Sinek, S. (2011). *Start with why: How great leaders inspire everyone to take action.* New York, NY: Penguin.

U.S. Department of Agriculture. (2017, April 19). *MyPlate.* www.choosemyplate.gov/MyPlate.

U.S. Department of Health and Human Services. (2017, July 12). *Dietary guidelines.* https://health.gov/dietaryguidelines

CHAPTER 2 Choosing to Be a Personal Trainer for a Fitness Facility

Association of Fitness Studios. (2015). *2015 Association of Fitness Studios operating & financial report* (p. 43).

American Council on Exercise (ACE). (2013). *Salary report for health and fitness professionals.* www.acefitness.org/salary/docs/ACE_SalarySurvey.pdf

Baicker, K., Cutler, D., and Song, Z. (2010, February). Workplace wellness programs can generate savings. *Health Affairs, 29*(2), 304-311. http://content.healthaffairs.org/content/29/2/304.full

Easton Park and Recreation. (2017). *Mission statement.* www.eastonrec.com/info/dept/details.aspx?DeptInfoID=999

IDEA Health & Fitness Association. (2015, September). IDEA fitness industry compensation trends report. *IDEA Fitness Journal, 12*(9), 47-49.

International Health, Racquet & Sportsclub Association (IHRSA). (2012). *The future is bright: U.S. health club employment outlook.* Boston, MA: Author.

International Health, Racquet & Sportsclub Association (IHRSA). (2014). *IHRSA health club consumer report: 2014 health club activity, usage, trends, and analysis.* Boston, MA: Author.

International Health, Racquet & Sportsclub Association (IHRSA). (2015). *The IHRSA health club employee compensation & benefits report* (p. 13). Boston, MA: Author.

YMCA of the Triangle. (2017). *Our mission.* www.ymcatriangle.org/about-y/our-mission

CHAPTER 3 Choosing to Be a Self-Employed Personal Trainer

Gerber, M.E. (2001). *The e-myth revisited: Why most small businesses don't work and what to do about it.* New York, NY: HarperCollins.

Hipple, S.F. (2010, September). Self-employment in the United States. Monthly Labor Review, 17-32. www.bls.gov/opub/mlr/2010/09/art2full.pdf

Internal Revenue Service. (2016, July 7). *Independent contractor defined.* www.irs.gov/Businesses/Small-Businesses-&-Self-Employed/Independent-Contractor-Defined

Internal Revenue Service. (2017, April 18). *Independent contractor (self-employed) or employee?* www.irs.gov/Businesses/Small-Businesses-&-Self-Employed/Independent-Contractor-Self-Employed-or-Employee

Schroeder, J. (2015, September). IDEA fitness industry compensation trends report. *IDEA Fitness Journal, 12*(9), 42-53.

CHAPTER 4   Choosing to Be a Personal Trainer and Facility Owner

Carter, B. (2014, May 1). The cost of building a new fitness facility. *Club Industry.* www.clubindustry.com/design/cost-building-new-fitness-facility

CrossFit. (2017). *How to affiliate.* www.crossfit.com/how-to-affiliate

Entrepreneur. (2017). *2017 Franchise 500 Ranking.* https://www.entrepreneur.com/franchises/500/2017?

Gerber, M.E. (2001). *The e-myth revisited: Why most small businesses don't work and what to do about it.* New York, NY: HarperCollins.

Goldberg, E. (n.d.). The benefits of the franchise model. *Franchise Update Media.* www.franchising.com/howtofranchiseguide/benefits_of_the_franchise_model.html

Herold, T.S. (2014, December 30). The 10 types of franchises to watch in 2015. *Entrepreneur.* www.entrepreneur.com/article/239709

Nisen, M. (2013, October 15). 16 free online business courses that are actually worth your time. *Business Insider.* www.businessinsider.com/best-free-online-business-courses-2013-10

Plummer, T. (2007). *Open a fitness business and make money doing it.* Monterey, CA: Healthy Learning.

Santa Rosa City Code. (2012). *20-36.040 Number of parking spaces required.* http://qcode.us/codes/santarosa/view.php?topic=20-3-20_36-20_36_040

Scudder, M.S. (2001, January 1). So you want to start a new club? *IDEA Fitness Manager, 13*(1). www.ideafit.com/fitness-library/so-you-want-to-start-a-new-club

U.S. Department of Justice. (2002, January 22). *ADA business brief: Restriping parking lots.* www.ada.gov/restribr.htm

CHAPTER 6   Determining Your Business Structure

Brodie, M.B. (1962). Henri Fayol: Administration industrielle et générale—A reinterpretation. *Public Administration, 40,* 311-317.

Internal Revenue Service. (n.d.) *Self-employed individuals tax center.* www.irs.gov/Individuals/Self-Employed

Nickels, B., McHugh, J., & McHugh, S. (2013). *Understanding business* (10th ed.). New York, NY: McGraw-Hill.

Peters, T.J., & Waterman, R.H., Jr. (1982). *In search of excellence: Lessons from America's best-run companies.* New York, NY: Harper & Row.

U.S. Small Business Administration. (n.d.-a). *Partnership.* www.sba.gov/content/partnership

U.S. Small Business Administration. (n.d.-b). *Register with state agencies.* www.sba.gov/starting-business/choose-register-your-business/register-state-agencies

U.S. Small Business Administration. (n.d.-c). *State licenses and permits.* www.sba.gov/starting-business/business-licenses-permits/state-licenses-permits

Wood, R.W. (2012, May 3). C or S corporation choice is critical for small business. *Forbes.* www.forbes.com/sites/robertwood/2012/05/03/c-or-s-corporation-choice-is-critical-for-small-business

CHAPTER 7   Screening and Hiring Your Staff

Conlan, C. (n.d.). How to answer the job interview question: "Tell me one thing about yourself you wouldn't want me to know." *Monster.* www.monster.com/career-advice/article/dont-want-interviewer-know

Grubbs-West, L. (2005). *Lessons in loyalty: How Southwest Airlines does it—An insider's view.* Dallas, TX: CornerStone Leadership Institute.

Peterson, T. (n.d.). 100 top job interview questions - Be prepared for the interview. *Monster.* http://career-advice.monster.com/job-interview/interview-questions/100-potential-interview-questions/article.aspx

U.S. Equal Employment Opportunity Commission. (n.d.). *Prohibited employment policies/practices.* www.eeoc.gov/laws/practices/index.cfm

CHAPTER 8   Obtaining the Right Insurance

Boniello, K. (2015, July 5). Woman hurt after risky exercises at military-style gym: Suit. *New York Post.* http://nypost.com/2015/07/05/woman-hurt-after-risky-exercises-at-military-style-gym-suit

Eickhoff-Shemek, J. (2013). U.S. negligence lawsuits. *Institute for Law, Government, and Policy.* https://lawgovpolicy.files.wordpress.com/2013/04/u-s-negligence-lawsuits.pdf

Heermance, B. (2013). Limit fitness facility liabilities. *Club Industry.* http://m.clubindustry.com/site-files/clubindustry.com/files/uploads/2013/10/CILegalSamplePages.pdf

Leve, J. (2015). AFS' guidelines to receiving custom insurance, plus 5 real life examples. *Association of Fitness Studios.* www.afsfitness.com/blog/475/afs-guidelines-to-receiving-custom-insurance-plus-5-real-life-examples.html

New York State, Department of State, Division of Licensing Services. (2016). *Licensing of health club services.* www.dos.ny.gov/licensing/lawbooks/HLTHCLUB.pdf

Ross, B., & Hutchinson, B. (2014, November 4). Woman sues Manhattan fitness club for $1M, claims exercise band snapped and blinded her. *New York Daily News.* www.nydailynews.com/new-york/woman-injured-manhattan-gym-sues-1m-article-1.1999480

Schoenfeld, S. (2015, March 22). 62-year-old awarded $750,000 in suit against Branford gym. *Fox61.* http://fox61.com/2015/03/20/62-year-old-awarded-750000-in-suit-against-branford-gym

Tucker, K. (n.d.). [Surety bond application package]. *Sports & Fitness Insurance Corporation.* www.sportsfitness.com/pdf/bondapplication.pdf

Turner, H. (2015, March 12). Health club to settle California employee lawsuit. *California Labor Law News.* https://calaborlawnews.com/legal-news/overtime-pay-laws-unpaid-111-20505.php

CHAPTER 9   Determining Your Offerings and Their Pricing

American Society of Composers, Authors and Publishers (ASCAP). (2016). *ASCAP music license agreements and reporting forms.* www.ascap.com/music-users/licensefinder.

Broadcast Music, Inc. (BMI). (2016). *Music licensing for fitness & health clubs.* www.bmi.com/licensing/entry/539487?q=Fitness+Clubs

International Health, Racquet & Sportsclub Association. (2015). *Profiles of success: The annual industry data survey of the health and fitness club industry.* Boston, MA: Author.

Pire, N. (2013). *ACSM's career and business guide for the fitness professional.* Baltimore, MD: Lippincott Williams & Wilkins.

Plummer, T. (2007). *Open a fitness business and make money doing it.* Monterey, CA: Healthy Learning.

Quinn, E. (2016, June 20). *How's your aerobic fitness? Try this 12 minute run to find out.* http://sportsmedicine.about.com/od/fitnessevalandassessment/a/12MinRun.htm

Schroeder, J. (2015). 2015 IDEA fitness industry compensation trends report. *IDEA Fitness Journal, 12*(10), 42-53.

U.S. Small Business Administration. (n.d.). *Apply for licenses and permits.* www.sba.gov/starting-business/business-licenses-permits/state-licenses-permits

CHAPTER 10   Developing Forms and Contracts

Bredin, S.S., Gledhill, N., Jamnik, V.K., & Warburton, D.E. (2013). PAR-Q+ and ePARmed-X+: New risk stratification and physical activity clearance strategy for physicians and patients alike. *Canadian Family Physician, 59*(3), 273-277.

Eickhoff-Shemek, J.M. (2005). The legal aspects: Legal liability associated with instruction. *ACSM's Health & Fitness Journal, 9*(5), 29-31.

Eickhoff-Shemek, J.M. (2007). The legal aspects: Using case law to understand the primary assumption of risk defense. *ACSM's Health & Fitness Journal, 11*(1), 35-37.

Internal Revenue Service. (2017, July 28). *Small business and self-employed tax center*. www.irs.gov/Businesses/Small-Businesses-&-Self-Employed

New York State, Department of State, Division of Licensing Services. (2016, June). *Licensing of health club services*. www.dos.ny.gov/licensing/lawbooks/HLTHCLUB.pdf

Nolan, N. (2015). Leasing gym equipment—Is leasing best for my business? *First Financial*. https://ffcash.net/leasing-gym-equipment

CHAPTER 11 Becoming Financially Profitable

Angeles, S. (2016a, November 2). Best accounting software for small business 2016. *Business News Daily*. www.businessnewsdaily.com/7543-best-accounting-software.html

Angeles, S. (2016b, November 2). Choosing the right accounting software. *Business News Daily*. www.businessnewsdaily.com/7542-choosing-accounting-software.html

Association of Fitness Studios. (2016). *2016 operating & financial benchmarking report*. http://mata-related.s3.amazonaws.com/afs-mata-market-research.pdf.

International Health, Racquet & Sportsclub Association (IHRSA). (2015). *The IHRSA health club employee compensation & benefits report, part 3: Hourly club-level employees*. Boston, MA: IHRSA.

Net Promoter Network. (2016). *The Net Promoter score: Leading growth indicator*. www.netpromoter.com/know

Retently. (2016). *What is a good Net Promoter score to have?* www.retently.com/blog/good-net-promoter-score

Rodriguez, M. (2014, November 7). Investing revenues back into your club. *International Health, Racquet & Sportsclub Association*. www.ihrsa.org/blog/2014/11/7/investing-revenues-back-into-your-club.html

CHAPTER 12 Marketing Your Services and Your Business

Aland, M. (2016, October 4). Radio advertising guide: How to get started today. *FitSmallBusiness*. http://fitsmallbusiness.com/radio-advertising

Duggan, M., Ellison, N. Lampe, C., Lenhart, A., & Madden, M. (2015). *Social media update 2014*. www.pewinternet.org/2015/01/09/social-media-update-2014

Godin, S. (2008, January 31). *Permission marketing* [Blog entry]. http://sethgodin.typepad.com/seths_blog/2008/01/permission-mark.html

Granovetter, M. (1973). The strength of weak ties. *American Journal of Sociology, 78*(6), 1360-1380.

Hoelzel, M. (2015, June 29). Update: A breakdown of the demographics for each of the different social networks. *Business Insider*. www.businessinsider.com/update-a-breakdown-of-the-demographics-for-each-of-the-different-social-networks-2015-6

James, G. (2010, November 10). How to write a press release, with examples. *CBS Money Watch*. www.cbsnews.com/news/how-to-write-a-press-release-with-examples

Kolowich, L. (2014, June 27). What is a whitepaper? [FAQs]. *HubSpot*. http://blog.hubspot.com/marketing/what-is-whitepaper-faqs

Lee, K. (2014, June 26). The art of self-promotion on social media. *Fast Company*. www.fastcompany.com/3032287/hit-the-ground-running/the-art-of-self-promotion-on-social-media

Lee, K. (2015, February 25). Infographic: How often should you post on social media? See the most popular research and tips. *Buffer*. https://blog.bufferapp.com/how-often-post-social-media

LinchpinSEO. (2017). Guide to buying and advertising on TV networks and cable. https://linchpinseo.com/guide-to-tv-advertising/

Marketing Charts. (2015, April 14). *Direct media response rate, CPA and ROI benchmarks*. www.marketingcharts.com/traditional/direct-media-response-rate-cpa-and-roi-benchmarks-53645

Rapaport, D. (2017, January 16). Super Bowl commercials: How much does a spot cost in 2017? *Sports Illustrated*. www.si.com/nfl/2017/01/26/super-bowl-commercial-cost-2017

Sugars, B. (n.d.). Learn to leverage the radio. *Entrepreneur*. www.entrepreneur.com/article/203246

Vaynerchuk, G. (2016, February 8). Why marketing for the year in which we actually live is a game changer: Your message must meet consumers on mobile with video. *Adweek*. www.adweek.com/news/advertising-branding/why-marketing-year-which-we-actually-live-game-changer-169459

CHAPTER 13   Learning the Art of Selling

Carmody, B. (2014, October 30). 3 little known sales secrets. *Inc*. www.inc.com/bill-carmody/the-know-like-amp-trust-growth-model.html

Carroll, M. (2015, January 27). Why people buy. *Sandler Training*. www.focusbusiness.sandler.com/blog_article/show/17277

Epictetus. (n.d.). [Quotation]. *BrainyQuote*. www.brainyquote.com/quotes/quotes/e/epictetus106298.html

Gitomer, J. (2004). *Little red book of selling: 12.5 principles of sales greatness*. Austin, TX: Bard Press.

Gladwell, M. (2007). *Blink: The power of thinking without thinking*. New York, NY: Little, Brown.

Maples, D. (2011, March 30). *How to spot a fake smile: It's all in the eyes*. www.nbcnews.com/health/body-odd/how-spot-fake-smile-its-all-eyes-f1C9386917

Pink, D. (2012). *To sell is human: The surprising truth about moving others*. New York, NY: Penguin.

Robbins, T. (2015, November 13). How to make a good first impression. *Business Insider*. www.businessinsider.com/how-make-good-first-impression-2015-11

Ziglar, Z. (n.d.). [Quotation]. *BrainyQuote*. www.brainyquote.com/quotes/quotes/z/zigziglar617767.html

CHAPTER 14   Communicating With Clients, Businesses, and the Community

Belchamber, J. (2013, July 16). *We hire people for their technical skills and fire them for their behaviour*. www.johnbelchamber.com/we-hire-people-for-their-technical-skills-and-fire-them-for-their-behaviour

DISC Insights. (n.d). *DISC: The history of DISC Personality Styles*. www.discinsights.com/disc-history#.VtNsjpMrKuW

Gardner, J. (2013, March 27). Tell, show, do, apply: The anatomy of good instruction. *eLearning Industry*. http://elearningindustry.com/tell-show-do-apply-the-anatomy-of-good-instruction

Goulston, M. (2010). *Just listen: Discover the secret to getting through to absolutely anyone*. New York, NY: American Management Association.

Hardman, E. (2012). *Active listening 101: How to turn down your volume to turn up your communication skills*. Seattle, WA: Amazon Digital Services.

Marston, W.M. (1928). *Emotions of normal people*. New York, NY: Harcourt, Brace.

Mueller, P.A., & Oppenheimer, D.M. (2014). The pen is mightier than the keyboard: Advantages of longhand over laptop note taking. *Psychological Science, 25*(4), 1159-1168.

VARK Learn Limited. (2016). *The VARK modalities*. http://vark-learn.com/introduction-to-vark/the-vark-modalities

CHAPTER 15   Identifying Options for Outsourcing Your Tasks

Brassfield, M. (2013). Delegation vs. outsourcing. *Ridiculously Efficient*. http://ridiculouslyefficient.com/delegation-vs-outsourcing

Ferriss, T. (2007). *The 4-hour workweek*. New York, NY: Crown.

Schleckser, J. (2014, August, 14). When to delegate? Try the 70 percent rule. *Inc*. www.inc.com/jim-schleckser/the-70-rule-when-to-delegate.html

Senger, M. (2012, July 18). The anatomy of an effective outsourcing plan. *IDEA*. www.ideafit.com/fitness-library/the-anatomy-of-an-effective-outsourcing-plan

CHAPTER 16   Growing Your Business

Association of Fitness Studios (AFS). (2016). *2016 fitness studio operating and financial benchmarking report*. https://member.afsfitness.com/content/2016-financial-and-operating-benchmarking-report

Ekstrom, R. (2004, May 25). Key characteristics of high retention clubs. *Retention Management*. www.retentionmanagement.com/key-characteristics-of-high-retention-clubs

Ferrazzi, K. (2014). *Never eat alone: And other secrets to success, one relationship at a time* (Expanded and updated ed.). New York, NY: Crown Business.

Godin, S. (2003, February). How to get your ideas to spread. *TED*. www.ted.com/talks/seth_godin_on_sliced_bread#t-434441

International Health, Racquet & Sportsclub Association (IHRSA). (2016a). *About IHRSA*. www.ihrsa.org/about

International Health, Racquet & Sportsclub Association (IHRSA). (2016b). *About the industry*. www.ihrsa.org/about-the-industry

McConnell, H. (2007). *Creating customer evangelists* (rev. ed.). Chicago, IL: Kaplan.

PTDirect. (n.d.). *Attendance, adherence, drop out and retention*. http://www.ptdirect.com/training-design/exercise-behaviour-and-adherence/attendance-adherence-drop-out-and-retention-patterns-of-gym-members

Statistic Brain. (2016, October 30). *Gym membership statistics*. www.statisticbrain.com/gym-membership-statistics

U.S. Copyright Office. (2012, May). *Copyright basics*. www.copyright.gov/circs/circ01.pdf

Index

Note: The italicized *f* and *t* following page numbers refer to figures and tables, respectively.

Mark A. Nutting, CSCS,*D, NSCA-CPT,*D, ACSM-HFD, ACSM-CEP, RCPT*E, is known for "training the personal trainer." He has more than 37 years of experience in personal training and health club management and over 10 years of intensive study about business practices and how to apply them to the fitness industry. Mark is an early adopter of the newest technologies and social media applications, and he is an eight-year veteran blogger to his large network of top professionals in general business and the fitness business. In 2017, Mark was designated as a Recognized Certified Personal Trainer Emeritus by the National Strength and Conditioning Association (NSCA). He was the recipient of the 2016 Personal Fitness Professional's Trainer of the Year Legacy Award and NSCA's 2009 Personal Trainer of the Year Award.

Photo: Francois Gagne

Find more outstanding resources at

www.HumanKinetics.com

In the **U.S.** call 1-800-747-4457
Canada 1-800-465-7301
U.K./Europe +44 (0) 113 255 5665
International 1-217-351-5076

eBook
available at
HumanKinetics.com

HUMAN KINETICS